Crunchy Cons

Crunchy Cons

How Birkenstocked Burkeans, gun-loving organic gardeners, evangelical free-range farmers, hip homeschooling mamas, right-wing nature lovers, and their diverse tribe of countercultural conservatives plan to save America (or at least the Republican Party)

ROD DREHER

CROWN
FORUM
NEW YORK

To Julie and Annik, paragons of patience and inspiration;
to Matthew and Lucas, who are the point, after all;
and to K-Lo, who, bless her heart, cracked wise at just the right time.

Copyright © 2006 by Rod Dreher

All rights reserved.
Published in the United States by Crown Forum, an imprint of the
Crown Publishing Group, a division of Random House, Inc., New York.
www.crownpublishing.com

CROWN FORUM and the Crown Forum colophon are
trademarks of Random House, Inc.

Library of Congress Cataloging-in-Publication Data

Dreher, Rod.
Crunchy cons : how Birkenstocked Burkeans, gun-loving organic gardeners,
evangelical free-range farmers, hip homeschooling mamas, right-wing nature
lovers, and their diverse tribe of countercultural conservatives plan to save
America (or at least the Republican Party) / Rod Dreher.
Includes index.
1. Social values — United States. 2. Conservatism — United States.
3. Popular culture — United States. I. Title.
HN90.M6+
320.52'0973 — dc22   2005017648

ISBN-13: 978-1-4000-5064-2
ISBN-10: 1-4000-5064-2

Printed in the United States of America

Design by Lauren Dong

10 9 8 7 6 5 4 3 2 1

First Edition

Hope is memory plus desire.

—Balzac

Contents

Preface

While I was writing *Crunchy Cons,* I hoped it would give voice to an overlooked segment of American conservatives—men and women who count themselves as part of the right but who don't quite fit in with the mainstream Republican Party. And I hoped my little book could show why the narrow and exhausted ideological nostrums that characterize the political debate today cannot adequately address the challenges facing America. It seemed clear that many Americans had become dissatisfied with the country's direction. *Crunchy Cons,* I believed, could spark some interesting conversations and perhaps even inspire a renewed focus on the practical virtues of faith, family, community, and domestic traditions.

What I didn't count on was how a series of events would bring into sharp focus the themes explored in *Crunchy Cons.* Consider:

• In late summer of 2005, Hurricane Katrina ravaged the Gulf Coast. As the people of New Orleans waited for help from a bumbling government bureaucracy incapable of handling mass catastrophe, the city descended into anarchy and chaos. Just weeks later, another hurricane, Rita, annihilated much of coastal southwestern Louisiana. There, however, the small-town and rural Cajun people of southwestern Louisiana instantly pulled together. The difference? In Cajun country, the ties of family and community were much stronger than in New Orleans. This point is central to *Crunchy Cons:* For the sake of communal self-sufficiency, we must recommit ourselves to building up family and social networks. Right now, joining the volunteer fire department or a local farmers' food co-op might be more authentically conservative than joining the Republican Party (not that there's anything wrong with that!).

• In the autumn of 2005, the President's Council on Bioethics reported that our aging society does not have the resources or the mechanisms to care for our elderly. The only way to cope with this problem, the report suggested, is to revive the bonds of family and community care. *New York Times* columnist David Brooks said the report "is a rebuke to the economic individualism of the right and to the moral individualism of the left." So is *Crunchy Cons.* To conserve the things we care most about, we must strengthen human relationships and move beyond the stale categories laid down by current political discourse.

• Even as the Democrats remained divided and bereft of ideas, the American public saw the GOP's idealism of yore compromised by scandals, out-of-control federal spending, politics-as-usual Beltway gamesmanship, questions about the war in Iraq, and more. With the Republican Party adrift and at war with itself, now is the time for a fresh conservative vision, and a new kind of conservative to step into the public square.

As you'll read, crunchy conservatism is not a political program but a practical sensibility based on what the wisdom of tradition teaches is best for families and communities. Its countercultural aims are modest but fundamental—and achievable by the "little platoons" of civil society that Edmund Burke, the founder of modern conservatism, taught are the real glue that holds society together.

When you meet the diverse conservatives in the pages of this book, you'll see that the kinds of things we crunchy cons talk about are ideas that offer a new and hopeful way to think about our lives together and new directions in our politics and our culture. I use the word "new" advisedly. True, much of this will sound peculiar in a conservative context to those for whom conservatism began in 1980, with the election of Ronald Reagan. Yet readers who know their conservative history will find that what follows comes straight out of the traditionalist school of Richard Weaver, Peter Viereck, Russell Kirk, and other seminal thinkers who helped spark the postwar renascence of intellectual conservatism. It's high time for a revival of their kind of conservatism, because today we are living out the fulfillment of Kirk's 1954 warning about naive libertarian optimism of the sort to which too many of us on the right have succumbed. Kirk wrote that "once supernatural and traditional sanctions are dissolved, economic self-interest is ridiculously inadequate to hold an economic system together, and even less adequate to preserve order."

Whether you are on the right, on the left, or in the middle, I hope you'll agree that crunchy conservatism is a fine old idea whose time has come again.

ROD DREHER
December 2005

A CRUNCHY-CON MANIFESTO

I. We are conservatives who stand outside the contemporary conservative mainstream. We like it here; the view is better, for we can see things that matter more clearly.

2. We believe that modern conservatism has become too focused on material conditions, and insufficiently concerned with the character of society. The point of life is not to become a more satisfied shopper.

3. We affirm the superiority of the free market as an economic organizing principle, but believe the economy must be made to serve humanity's best interests, not the other way around. Big business deserves as much skepticism as big government.

4. We believe that culture is more important than politics, and that neither America's wealth nor our liberties will long survive a culture that no longer lives by what Russell Kirk identified as "the Permanent Things"—those eternal moral norms necessary to civilized life, and which are taught by all the world's great wisdom traditions.

5. A conservatism that does not recognize the need for restraint, for limits, and for humility is neither helpful to individuals and society nor, ultimately, conservative. This is particularly true with respect to the natural world.

6. A good rule of thumb: Small and Local and Old and Particular are to be preferred over Big and Global and New and Abstract.

7. Appreciation of aesthetic quality—that is, beauty—is not a luxury, but key to the good life.

8. The cacophony of contemporary popular culture makes it hard to discern the call of truth and wisdom. There is no area in which practicing asceticism is more important.

9. We share Kirk's conviction that "the best way to rear up a new generation of friends of the Permanent Things is to beget children, and read to them o' evenings, and teach them what is worthy of praise: the wise parent is the conservator of ancient truths. . . . The institution most essential to conserve is the family."

10. Politics and economics will not save us. If we are to be saved at all, it will be through living faithfully by the Permanent Things, preserving these ancient truths in the choices we make in everyday life. In this sense, to conserve is to create anew.

CHAPTER ONE

What Are Crunchy Conservatives?

When we were young, the countercultural people had long hair, no socks, and didn't trust anyone over 30. Now, we are the countercultural people.

—JOHN BUCK, ARKANSAS PSYCHOLOGIST AND CRUNCHY CONSERVATIVE

A FEW SUMMERS AGO, in the *National Review* offices on the east side of Manhattan, I told my editor that I was leaving work early so I could pick up my family's weekly delivery of fruits and vegetables from the neighborhood organic food co-op to which we belonged.

"Ewww, that's so lefty," she said, and made the kind of face I'd have expected if I'd informed her I was headed off to hear Peter, Paul and Mary warble at a fund-raiser for cross-dressing El Salvadoran hemp farmers.

Lefty? *Moi?* But on the subway home to Brooklyn, I had to admit she was right.

A taste for organic vegetables is a left-wing cliché, and here I was, a writer for the premier conservative political magazine in the country, leaving my post on the front lines to consort with the liberals in my neighborhood as I filled my rucksack with the most beautiful and delicious broccoli, carrots, greens, and what-not in the city. What's up with *that*?

And come to think of it, what's up with those Birkenstock sandals on my feet? It just about killed me to buy them the summer before, given what Birkenstocks symbolize (you know, patchouli, pot, and ponytails on men). But New Yorkers walk a lot, and my sensible wife persuaded me that durable, comfortable Birks made sense for hot summer sidewalks. She was right. So that's how a pair of hippie shoes found their way onto my right-wing feet, which—alas!—had begun marching to a different beat than many of my conservative chums. Funny, I didn't *feel* any more liberal.

The summer before, I had been just like my editor, making fun of my wife's friends from her neighborhood moms' group for going once a week to a local church to pick up their vegetables driven in from farms in rural New York State. Just like liberals, I thought, having to have their politically correct eats. And then one day, one of Julie's friends told her that we could have her family's delivery that week, because they would be out of town. Julie and I were knocked flat by the freshness and intense flavors of the co-op's produce. Who knew cauliflower, the Sans-abelt slacks of vegetables, could taste so good? I had always thought of it chiefly as a delivery platform for ranch dip and cheese sauce.

We were no doubt responding to the just-picked freshness of the produce, not its organic status, but no matter. At some point, I started hearing more about the kind of lives the farmers who supplied us were living, and the values of simplicity, community, and self-reliance they honored. In all candor, these people were probably to the left of Ralph Nader, but they reminded me of the kind of older farmers and gardeners I grew up around in rural southern Louisiana—deeply conservative folks whose last Democratic presidential vote likely went to JFK.

As city people who nevertheless dislike factory farms, shopping malls, cookie-cutter chain stores, and all the pomps and works of mass consumerism, we admired what the scrappy New York farmers were trying to do. In my Louisiana hometown, some farmers spent the go-go nineties selling their pastures to developers, and the torrent of cash caused McMansions to pop up like toadstools after a summer rain. It's hard to blame folks for cashing in, I suppose, but the community in which I was raised was changing rapidly as economic growth caused it to become a bedroom suburb of Baton Rouge. In their own way, the New York farmers were doing what farmers in my Louisiana birthplace were not: conserving agrarian communal traditions by, to paraphrase William F. Buckley describing the founding mission of the *National Review,* "standing athwart history yelling Stop!"

Besides, their produce was vastly superior to what was available in the local supermarket. We didn't mind paying a little extra for food this good. The next summer, we joined the co-op, and Julie got a kick out of picking up our weekly deliveries in her *National Review* tote bag. When you get to our age, you have precious few opportunities to shock the middle class, so you take them where you find them.

Now, it had never occurred to me, except in a jokey way, that eating organic vegetables was a political act, but my editor's snarky remark got me to thinking about other ways my family's lifestyle was countercultural, and why, though we were thoroughly conservative in our morals and our politics, we weren't a good fit on either the mainstream left or right.

Three years earlier, Julie had left a fulfilling position as a magazine editorial assistant to stay at home and raise our young son, Matthew. As much as she loved her job, as useful as that extra paycheck was, and for all the grief she took from other New York women who disdained her for "wasting" her college degree, we both felt strongly that we had a responsibility to our son to put his needs first, as much as we were able.

Once, when Matthew was still an infant, a kind woman in late middle age stopped us to offer admiring comments about our son. She talked about what a disappointment her son was to her, how she and her husband had put him in an expensive private school, but he had become a pothead and a troublemaker. The poor woman lamented how she fought with her husband over disciplining their son, with the boy's father insisting that kids will be kids, and besides, dear, didn't you and I fool around with drugs back in the day? After all that, she asked Julie and me if we had made plans for Matthew's schooling yet—a perfectly rational question in New York City, where parents put their child's name on private-school waiting lists as soon as the blessed babe is conceived. We replied that we were strongly considering home-schooling. The woman recoiled.

"Isn't that what right-wing Christians do?" she spluttered.

The conversation went downhill from there, and we found a way to excuse ourselves as gracefully as we could. A few minutes later, walking home, I remarked to Julie that here was a woman whose heart was broken over what her child had become, and that all the money in the world spent at that posh private school couldn't make up for what permissive parenting and a lax educational environment had done to the boy. Here she was longing for the kind of self-disciplined, responsible son that religiously conservative families tend to produce—but she'd die a thousand deaths before actually making the kind of countercultural sacrifices many such families make for the sake of their children's character and future.

We didn't want to be like this sad woman. In fairness, there are conservative families who find themselves in the same despairing position, having thought that having the correct attitudes, the best of intentions, and enough income to pay for private school would be sufficient to raise good kids. We heard all the time—and still do—from fellow conservatives who are not shy about telling us that our kids are going to be socially maladroit freaks if we don't put them in school. "What about socialization?" they ask anxiously, to which we reply, "Well, look at youth culture today; do you really want your kids socialized into that?"

As he got older, Julie started making plans to homeschool little Matthew, and was delighted to discover that there was a small but vibrant homeschooling association in New York City. Unlike homeschooling parents in her native Texas, most of whom do so out of conservative religious conviction, these were primarily secular liberals who had nonetheless concluded that they could do a better job teaching their kids than the schools. In New York, at least, homeschooling was *not* what right-wing Christians did. Julie was startled to discover that she shared many of the same concerns about primary education with moms whose views on many political issues were diametrically opposed.

Because our faith is at the center of our lives, and because we believe proper Christian worship should honor both truth and beauty, we committed ourselves to an "ethnic" Catholic church in our neighborhood. The people of Our Lady of Lebanon Maronite Church are of Lebanese descent, and speak Arabic in the main. Going there the first few times was an eerie experience, because we naturally associated that language with Islam; it sounded to our untutored American ears like the PLO at prayer.

Yet these people's ancestors were worshipping Jesus Christ when our European ancestors were still praying to trees. Besides, where it really mattered, we all spoke the same language. It was an Eastern-rite parish, where the aesthetically rich, awe-filled fifth-century liturgy was celebrated partly in Aramaic, the language spoken by Jesus, and the priests were decidedly uninterested in trendiness. We couldn't take the smarmy, white-bread, middle-class American masses at the Roman-rite parishes around us, where the liturgies were washed out and banal, and the moral and theological grandeur of the historical Christian faith was discarded in favor of a piety that demanded no more of you than that you feel good about yourself. This was a form of Catholic Christianity that demanded more from us, and because of that, it was more rewarding. And it seemed so much more solid than Our Lady of What's Happening Now around the corner, where the priests embarrassed themselves trying to be hip and relevant.

The key thing is, we didn't become members of Our Lady of Lebanon parish because it sounded like a neat experiment in religious tourism. We did so because we are conservative Catholics, and we were hungry for worship in a parish where we could find the real deal, be it in English, Latin, or Aramaic.

We try hard not to be cafeteria Catholics, picking and choosing what suits our tastes from a supposed menu of options. Because of that orientation toward our faith, Julie and I do not use artificial contraception (besides, Julie said after seeing how the Pill affected some of her friends, she didn't want to jack up her body with prescribed hormones; "Better living through chemistry" is not a popular phrase in our house). We mastered a church-approved system of regulating fertility called Natural Family Planning, and were surprised to discover that even secular couples who shunned artificial contraception for health reasons used the same method.

NFP required us to monitor Julie's temperature and other bodily signs of fertility. This meant learning to pay attention to the rhythms and demands of both our bodies, and for Julie, acquiring a new awareness of how the food we ate affected her. When we chose to conceive Matthew, Julie paid even more attention to eating healthfully, and we cut out processed foods as much as we could. Once he was born, she breast-fed him exclusively, continuing to maintain her healthy diet for his sake, and when he began to eat solid food, she made his baby food at home, so she could be confident that he wasn't getting junk. If you had told us when we first married that within two years, we'd be acting like, well, hippies, we'd have thought you were nuts. But we had begun to realize that even though we were conservative Republicans, this stuff made sense, and it didn't conflict with our moral or religious beliefs; in fact, *it flowed naturally from them.*

Here's the thing: we didn't turn into droopy, pale-skinned dullards who washed down our nightly tofu with wheatgrass juice. My wife and I are still enthusiastic eaters of meat and drinkers of wine—maybe more so now than when we first met. We discovered early in our marriage that both of us had grown up in a time and place in which cooking was seen primarily as a chore, and food as ballast. Living as newlyweds in New York, one of the great food cities of the world, we were surrounded by opportunities for culinary adventure, and we took them all. We taught ourselves how to cook simple but delicious meals using fresh ingredients, and took great joy in the act of preparing meals.

When Matthew came along, we didn't often have the opportunity or the money to go to restaurants, so we spent many a weekend night cooking dinners for friends at home. Out of sheer curiosity and the pleasure of discovery, we learned about cheese and wine, and began spending some of the happiest evenings of our lives in the basement living room of our little apartment on the Brooklyn waterfront, laughing and talking politics, religion, books, movies, travel, and everything under the sun amid steaming platters of garlicky roasts, tureens of peppery rémoulade, crisp-crusted frittatas, tangy giambottas, napoleons of beefsteak tomatoes and basil from our own patio garden, and bottle after bottle of robust Italian and Spanish wine. For us, family, friends, and feasting was pretty much what the good life was all about. The food we prepared with such enjoyment and care was, at bottom, an expression of love for our companions, and our long suppers an occasion for communion.

Great, you say, but so what? Are there not liberals who like to cook good food and share it with their friends, just as there are liberals who disdain mass consumerism? Indeed there are, and we know liberal families who have decided television is by and large an unwelcome guest in their house, and for much the same reason as we conservatives.

But we are not liberals. For one thing, we don't share the liberal faith in the ultimate goodness and perfectibility of mankind. Because we believe in evil and the duty of good men and women to confront it with violence if necessary, we are not pacifists. We don't believe that morality is relative, and that each generation is free to find its own truths, and to adopt a moral code that suits its desires. We object to the idea that there's nothing wrong with our country that a new tax or a government program can't fix.

We don't believe it's the government's job to guarantee social equality, only equality before the law and, within reason, equality of opportunity. Guns don't bother us (unless they're in the hands of criminals), and neither, as a general rule, does capitalism (unless it, too, is in the hands of criminals). We prefer Fox News to CNN, think of Lucianne Goldberg as America's very own gimlet-eyed Auntie Mame, and count ourselves as members in good standing of the Vast Right-Wing Conspiracy. On the occasion that we watched the *CBS Evening News,* it was only to make sure we were there in case Dan Rather finally cracked up live on national television. Like Bocephus, we say grace, and we say ma'am (we know who Bocephus is, by the way). We honor the military, and are not embarrassed to say this is the best country in the world — and we don't qualify that with a "but . . ." We proudly fly the flag from our front porch.

And perhaps most crucially, we strongly dissent from the great liberal project of the last forty years, the sexual revolution. Smashing traditional sexual mores in the name of human liberation has led to chaos and misery, and turned what is the most intimate spiritual and physical communion possible between two people into a tawdry commodity. Worst of all, it has severely damaged the family, which Russell Kirk, one of the key figures in the renascence of twentieth-century American conservatism, taught was "the institution most essential to conserve." As goes the family, we believe, so goes a society.

But we are not mainstream conservatives either. Too many people who call themselves conservative share the same fundamental conviction of many liberals, namely, that individual fulfillment is the point of life. Conservative, perhaps, in their sexual views, they are, however, libertarian in their economic principles, and believe that the free market should be the guiding light of our lives together. Thus they believe that a merchant or a manufacturer owes no loyalty to his community, nor the community to that merchant or manufacturer. They feel no particular responsibility to be good stewards of communal life or the natural world; if something of real value has been lost because of economic decisions, hey, that's the free market. Cultivating an appreciation for art, architecture, and the world of beauty used to be considered by a previous generation of conservatives the mark of a civilized person; today, it is often disdained by many mainstream conservatives as an elitist pursuit. A college education is something you get solely as a ticket to a moneymaking career.

It is hard for conservative journalists and activists who live in Washington, New York, Los Angeles, and other large cities in Blue America to appreciate how difficult it can be for conservatives in the Red America heartland, where I was born and raised, to dissent from the Republican Party mainstream. A conservative who lives in a big coastal city will run across all kinds of political types in the course of his daily routine. He learns to appreciate the ideological diversity, both across the political spectrum and within the camps of the right. It's not like that everywhere.

A couple of years ago, Mike, a friend of mine who lives in a Southern city and who works in GOP politics, was named to his town's "smart-growth" committee. Mike quickly realized that most of his fellow committee members were either land developers or their attorneys, and that none of the smart-growth proposals they were to consider would put any restrictions on developers at all. My friend was not keen to see more land cleared and paved for the mindless construction of new subdivisions, strip malls, and parking lagoons, so he pointed out at the first meeting that the smart-growth plans were pretty much a sham. The head of the committee turned on him and accused him in front of a crowd of being a conservative in name only because he questioned whether or not it was in the public's interest to let land developers have their way.

Now, my friend has probably forgotten more conservative political theory than the Babbitt who dunned him ever learned, but in this very right-wing town, that kind of accusation can be enough to discredit someone. The true depth and breadth of historical conservative thinking is not widely known or shared in much of our country today. Ronald Reagan was a great man and a wonderful president, but he was neither the first nor the last word in conservatism. Conservatism was not born with Reagan's election in 1980, nor, believe it or not, did it come into being with the 1964 Goldwater campaign.

There is an older, less-ideological tradition, a sensibility that comes out in people I call *crunchy conservatives.* We are conservatives by conviction and temperament, and usually vote Republican (though to call us "liberal Republicans" is to fundamentally misunderstand us), but we're "crunchy"—as in the slang for "earthy"—because we stand alongside a number of lefties who don't buy in to the consumerist and individualist mainstream of American life. It seems to crunchy cons that most Americans are so busy bargain-shopping or bed-hopping, or talking about their shopping and screwing selves, that they're missing the point of life. Sex and commerce are fine things, but man cannot live by Viagra and the Dow Jones alone. A life led collecting things and experiences in pursuit of happiness is not necessarily a bad life, but it's not a good life either. Too often, the Democrats act like the Party of Lust, and the Republicans the Party of Greed. Both are deadly sins that eat at the soul, and crunchy cons believe that both must be resisted in our personal and communal lives. Mainstream liberalism and conservatism, as the agrarian essayist Wendell Berry said, are "perfectly useless" to combat the forces in contemporary American society that are pulling families and communities apart. Berry says most liberals won't take a stand against anything that limits sexual autonomy, and most conservatives won't oppose anything that limits economic freedom.

The mission of this book is to explore ways that we who espouse conservative values can live more true to them, despite living in a society in which the structure of the economy, the influence of mass media, and the prevailing cultural mentality serve to separate us from our values, our families, and our communities. This is not a book that means to change the world. This is a book that means to change individual lives and families, to help them live more truly and meaningfully conservative lives by proposing lessons from my family's life, and the lives of other crunchy conservatives around the country. It is impossible to be truly conservative nowadays without being consciously countercultural. This book will show you how lots of us are doing it and living it every single day.

I do not expect conventional liberals and conservatives to get crunchy conservatism, mostly because, it seems to me, they have confused means with ends. The liberty we enjoy in America today is certainly worth prizing and defending, but it is insufficient to produce virtue, stability, or happiness. The free market in ideas, commerce, sexuality, and so forth offers us various possibilities of how to live, but it tells us nothing of how we should behave to live as well as we ought. Both mainstream liberalism and conservatism are essentially materialist ideologies, and we should not be surprised that both shape a society dedicated to the multiplication of wants and the intensification of desire, not the improvement of character.

Crunchy conservatism is not, as you'll read here, a political program; it's a sensibility, an attitude, a fundamental stance toward reality, and a pretty good road map to a rich, responsible, fulfilling, charitable, and above all *joyful* life. It's about living a life mindful of and honoring the wisdom in tradition, and in so doing building a tradition to pass on to one's children, and to future generations. It doesn't aim to make folks wealthier, except where it counts: in their relationships to each other and to the natural world.

That fundamental stance toward reality is *sacramental*. In religious language, a sacrament is a physical thing — an object or an action — through which holiness is transmitted. Christians who celebrate Holy Communion are participating in a sacrament, because they believe that the consecrated bread and wine contain, actually or symbolically, the essence of Jesus Christ. On a mundane level, you can grasp sacramentality by considering good manners. You might practice good manners because life is more pleasant when people do, or you might practice good manners because you believe it's a matter of social obligation. A person thinking sacramentally may practice good manners because it's pleasant and socially correct, but she will do so primarily because treating others with that kind of formal respect conveys her fundamental conviction about human dignity. Someone living by a sacramental vision would therefore treat someone with the same good manners even if it were somehow unpleasant, or if there were no social expectations to do so. Being good is not something you do because it works; being good is something you do because it's the right thing to do, even if it costs you. At the risk of sounding pompously metaphysical, for people who adopt a sacramental way of being, everyday things, occurrences, and exchanges provide an opportunity to encounter ultimate reality — even, if you like, divinity.

To be perfectly honest, it didn't occur to me when I started writing how much the religious sense would inform the crunchy-con sensibility. But as I began interviewing people, over and over the discussion turned back to religious faith as the ground of both conservatism and crunchiness. In fact, critic James Howard Kunstler, who is a man of the left, told me that exactly one kind of conservative consistently came to his lectures about suburban alienation and the poverty of architectural imagination: religious intellectuals. Trying to figure this out, I thought about why crunchy liberals stand outside the mainstream, and I noticed that they also speak in quasi-religious terms about the sacredness of the earth and the importance of spirituality to a meaningful life. Their spirituality is not the spirituality of religious traditionalists, to be sure, but the common ground we share is a bedrock conviction that, in the words of Jesus, "Man cannot live by bread alone." That is, we are spiritual beings first and foremost, and it is impossible to thrive in a culture that does not honor and nurture things of the human spirit over and above material concerns.

You don't have to be a religious believer in the formal sense to be a crunchy conservative, but you do have to believe that accumulating wealth and power is not the point of life. Now, if you took a poll, ninety-nine out of a hundred conservatives would deny that they subscribed to that vulgar credo. But that's not how they live — even if they profess to be religious.

Though Julie and I didn't understand what was happening at the time, we were learning — by instinct, by the practice of our faith, and through raising our son — to see life sacramentally. That is, we were becoming the sort of people who viewed the physical aspects of our lives — the food that we ate, the place that we lived, and the world in which we moved — as being inseparable from spiritual reality. It sounds lofty and precious, but all this really means is that we began to take seriously the connection between the physical and the spiritual worlds, and how the good life depends on harmonizing the soul and the body. Conservatives are suspicious of that kind of talk because it sounds New Agey, but the basic idea is as old as Western civilization. Too many of us today, in our freedom and prosperity, have become alienated from the virtues that made that prosperity possible and sustainable over the generations. Crunchy conservatism draws on the religious, philosophical, and literary heritage of conservative thought and practice to cobble together a practical, commonsense, and fruitful way to live amid the empty consumerist prosperity of what Henry Miller called "the air-conditioned nightmare."

But we'll get to that later. I still haven't told you why I wrote this book.

After thinking for a few days about my editor's remark, I wrote a short essay for National Review Online, and titled it "Birkenstocked Burkeans," after Edmund Burke, the eighteenth-century founder of modern conservatism. In it, I shared some of the stories and ideas above, and ended it by saying that there's a lot more political and cultural diversity among Americans than most people think, and calling on readers to open their minds to it. As Russell Kirk taught, conservatism properly understood is not a rigid set of doctrines, but grows organically out of an examination of first principles, and a fair consideration of how we might live to realize those principles. There are many mansions in the American conservative house, and some of them are old and funky and smell like a pot of organic mustard greens cooking down on the stove.

Well, I had been a monger of opinions for nearly all of my professional life, and I have never received a favorable response to anything I've written like I did with the "Birkenstocked Burkeans" article. Folks wrote in from all over the country to say, "Me too!" I was startled not only by the number of e-mails I received, but also by their passion and diversity. There was the letter from the interracial couple, political conservatives and converts to Eastern Orthodoxy, who loved to shake up the preconceptions of liberal friends at their organic co-op. There was the pro-life vegetarian Buddhist Republican who just wanted to find somebody to discuss the virtues of George W. Bush with over a nice bowl of dal. A gay Republican wrote to say that he and his partner got fed up with city life, bought a B and B in rural Pennsylvania, and moved out to grow and can their own vegetables. Said a crunchy con from the Northeast, "When I talk to my lefty wife and friends, they are absolutely scathing about conservatives, mostly because they assume that all conservatives want to rape the environment, screw the poor, and keep women barefoot and pregnant. People are usually shocked to find out that I consider my pro-life position to be a feminist one, that I recycle faithfully, and that I give way more to charity than most of them do. This contradicts everything they've ever heard about conservatives."

There were urban crunchy cons from New York, Berkeley, and Ann Arbor. A number of naturalist-conservationist types wrote from out West, many complaining that their party—the GOP—doesn't understand the profoundly conservative reasons for preserving the natural environment. There were rural crunchy cons, like the woman who grew up a hippie red-diaper baby in California, but who now lives in rural Virginia and writes copy for the National Rifle Association—yet still lives the natural-foods lifestyle. "The difference between my husband and me and my siblings," she wrote, "is that for us, organic gardening and everything else we do is part of the good life. For my siblings, it is their entire life."

There were even conservatives crunching along as best they could in the heart of suburbia. One woman wrote from a small city in the heart of Red America to say, "Folks are 'perfect' in this 'conservative, Christian' town. As in many upper-middle-class areas, appearance is everything. The clothes, the makeup, the hair, the car, the country-club lifestyle, the house, the decorating, the vacations, the kids. Everything is expensive, name-brand and 'beautiful.' Ken and Barbie get boring after a while."

This Texas reader and her husband are both engineers, Republican Party activists, and busy in their Protestant church. She wrote me, "We have eight children, all of whom were breastfed for a year or so, most of whom were born at home, all of whom we home school. Our family makes its own bread (occasionally grinding the wheat ourselves), eats homemade meals, spends little money on clothing/makeup/jewelry and tries to live a simple, thoughtful life. Our favorite president is Teddy Roosevelt, we hate cookie-cutter subdivisions, we buy food from co-ops and natural food stores (NEVER go to the mall), we use our

TV only to watch videos, and we all read like crazy. When I'm in the mood, I even make granola! [And] we know tons of folks like us all over the United States."

She's lucky. About half the people who wrote said that they felt so alone until they read my essay, and were dying to meet people like them. Some even encouraged me to write a book to "start the movement."

Movement? I don't know about that. But I do know that something's going on out there. Hundreds of people from all over America wrote in to give their emphatic endorsement of the crunchy-con idea. And I still hear from them. Months after that piece appeared, I got a delightful e-mail that read simply, "Just wanted to let you know how surprised and delighted we were to read your article. We thought we were the only Evangelical Christians in the world with a copy of 'The Moosewood Cookbook.'"

I wanted to know how an evangelical Christian comes to think of purchasing a particular cookbook as a rebellious act. I want to understand how that couple, with their eight kids and no television, came to be so enthusiastically countercultural, living as they do in deepest Texas, where they stick out like sore thumbs amid all the big-haired Republican types. I wanted to talk to the right-wingers who wrote me from Wisconsin to say that they put up with all kinds of political grief from their fellow volunteers at their natural-foods co-op in Wisconsin, but keep going back because they love the food. And, they told me in an e-mail, they honestly love the fellowship with people who vehemently disagree with them politically, but with whom they share lots in common about what really matters in life. I wanted to get to know the Republican who wrote from California to say how much my essay resonated with him, and how it made him realize how stupid Republicans are to make Californians ("land of fruits and nuts") part of cornball right-wing stock humor rather than to seek to understand them and their concerns, particularly about the environment.

If my mail was any indication, there are thousands of people like this all over America. They want to know they are not alone. And they want to share their ideas with others on the right, the left, and in the middle. They — we — think we've found a great way to live, one that's underreported and overlooked because it doesn't fit into prefabricated ideas about conservatives and conservatism, clichés held by both the mainstream left and the mainstream right.

Boy, do some standard-issue Republicans resent this! The mail I got from my crunchy-right articles was overwhelmingly positive, but there were more than a few missives from right-wingers who were equally passionate in their rejection of crunchy conservatism. These folks took it personally. They believe crunchy cons are phonies, and to say anything critical about strip-malled America is to tip your hand as an elitist snob who hates the free market and the common man. Amusingly, they assumed that I, a Southerner with a middle-class background and state university education, living paycheck to paycheck on a writer's salary, was an Ivy-educated Rockefeller Republican. No doubt about it, some conservatives perceive this as a class conflict. They're wrong. I wrote this book in part to convince these good people that their unfounded prejudices and lack of critical thinking are helping undermine, even destroy, the kinds of things within their families and communities that they, as conservatives, profess to value.

Several years ago, I sat in an editorial board meeting at the *Dallas Morning News*, where I work as an editor and writer, listening to ambassadors from several Latin American nations, as well as U.S. business leaders, bid for our support for a new free-trade agreement. At some point, one of the Americans said that a coalition of small farmers was causing problems in Mexico for the treaty, because the farmers knew the treaty would effectively end their traditional way of life. The American official expressed confidence that the Mexican government would overcome the farmers' protest and pass the treaty. He spoke of the Mexican farmers with exquisite condescension, as if they were eccentric hicks who needed to be gently taken by the arm and shown the way to oblivion.

I posted something to a Catholic blog later, saying that I left that meeting thinking of these poor farmers, and an entire way of life that a rich and powerful American and his Latin American cohorts were willing to end for the sake of economic efficiency. This is a tragedy, I said, to displace these campesinos from their land, and their way of life. Another poster, a fellow conservative, sneered, "Yeah, Mexican farming, the wave of the future." The cult of efficiency wins again.

We have, over the past two generations, done the same thing to American farmers. Nearly all American agriculture today is carried out by agribusiness and its efficient factory-farming methods. Rural America is depopulating, and dying with it is an entire way of life and a traditional set of values derived from living close to the land. This is the cost of saving money on meat and vegetables at the supermarket. But few conservatives stop to think about that.

This should be a moment of triumph for organized conservatism in America. We have a Republican in the White House, Republicans are in control of both houses of Congress, and the forces of political liberalism are in disarray. As one woebegone Democratic strategist wrote in the *Wall Street Journal,* the leaders of his party in Congress don't look like they could fight a parking ticket, much less terrorists or Republicans. It's a good time to be a Republican, all right . . . so why do I feel so lousy as a conservative, and so uneasy about America's future?

For all our success at the ballot box, the trajectory the country is on does not inspire confidence. A few years ago, livestock scientist Temple Grandin discovered that many cattle being led to slaughter in a conventional straight-line chute would act up on their way to their demise, but that if you presented them with a bovine *via dolorosa* in the form of a long, gentle curve, they'd

move along without protest. The idea is that they couldn't see far in front of them, and thought they were progressing safely.

That, I think, is an apt metaphor for where we are in our country today. For most people, things seem solid, and there doesn't appear to be reason to worry; certainly not to protest or otherwise stand against the flow of contemporary American life. But can we go on like this forever? Can we really keep borrowing money against future generations to finance our consumerist lifestyle without the bill coming due in a brutal way? Could our economy, which depends on relatively cheap fuel to transport goods long distances, survive a serious oil shock? Has the loss of neighborliness and traditional familial and communal bonds that we've endured over the past two generations resulted in a society prepared to withstand the trauma and stress of a catastrophic terrorist attack of the sort that could destroy our national economy? Are we willing to sacrifice our individual desires for the greater good? Are we still the kind of people who can take care of ourselves and one another?

I don't think so. And I don't see that conservatives, in the main, are in much better shape than anybody else.

We conservatives say we value the traditional family, but don't act like it. Both parents work in many of our families, l[...]ing our kids to be raised by day care and the culture. Some have no choice for economic reasons, of course, but too ma[...]us have made our luxuries into our necessities, and work crazy hours to pay the mortgage on large houses that can'[...]be called homes, because little authentic family life [...]behind their walls.

We complain that the entertainment media are coars[...]children, but we let them devour television, pop m[...]games, and other junk culture as if resistance were fu[...]alism and selfishness are spoiling our kids, we say,[...]them whatever they ask for. We right-wingers grim[...]celebrated by mainstream culture, but we rarely

that greed is no less deadly a sin, no less destructive of human dignity. We look down on the liberal libertine who asserts the moral primacy of sexual free choice, but somehow miss that the free market we so uncritically accept exalts personal fulfillment through individual choice as the summit of human existence.

When we hear someone complaining about this or that aspect of the free market, we assume that they must be some kind of leftist, and therefore worth ignoring. Meanwhile, whole towns have been hollowed out economically, and community bonds weakened or severed, because of the market. We do not allow ourselves to ask why, or if it had to be that way. We talk about the value of thrift, but we run up Matterhorns of debt (as, by the way, have our Republican president and Republican Congress), and consume oil and other resources as if they were going to last forever.

We conservatives are big on bashing the public schools, which mostly deserve it, but please don't ask us to think about what education is for. For many of us, it's about no more than making sure our kids get into the right college, meet the right people, and go on to have a good (read "lucrative") career.

We poke fun at the sanctimony of environmentalists, and try hard to convince ourselves that the sprawling crapulence of big-box stores, strip malls, monotonous housing developments, and other degrading manifestations of our built environment some-how represents progress. We abandon or bulldoze old buildings and human-scaled neighborhoods, then create fake environ-ments (shopping malls) to re-create what we destroyed.

We want God back in the public square, but for too many of us, religion is a pious veneer over our own unconscious worship of materialism. We want a faith that makes us feel good about ourselves, not one that makes demands we'd rather not obey. We've turned religion into another consumer good. Our faith does not help us stand against the money-driven materialist cul-ture, but instead baptizes our participation in it.

Come on, y'all, can I get an amen?

I don't mean to be a scold. Look, I'm as guilty as the next guy of not living up to my ideals. But there comes a time when we conservatives have to ask ourselves just who we think we're fooling. We have to ask ourselves honestly how long we as individuals, as families, and as a society can continue down this path. Will unlimited economic growth, spectacular advances in science, and GOP presidents and Congresses stretched out into infinity deliver us from alienation and anxiety? And if the answer is no, then we should start thinking seriously about why we have become the richest and most free society ever to exist, yet our wealth and personal liberty have bought us so little happiness.

The answer is not to be found in a set of policy prescriptions, but in a considered critique of the assumptions on which mainstream American life is built, and a secession of sorts from the mainstream — all to conserve those things that give our lives real weight and meaning. Every one of us can refuse, at some level, to participate in the system that makes us materially rich but impoverishes us spiritually, morally, and aesthetically. We cannot change society, at least not overnight, but we can change ourselves and our families.

This is not to encourage a head-for-the-hills utopianism (though sometimes the hills do start to look pretty inviting), but rather a movement to change our own lifestyles so that they are more faithful to our convictions as conservatives, and over time rebuild the strength and stability of our communities, our schools, our churches, and all the "little platoons" that Edmund Burke identified as necessary to civil life. Most of all, crunchy conservatism is about shoring up the family, which, as I've said, is in Kirk's view "the institution most necessary to conserve."

We conservatives have got to clarify our thinking and return to our principles. We should ask ourselves what kind of society we want to live in, and want our descendants to live in, and ask whether the way we're living today is likely to get us there. Ideas have consequences, after all, and too many conservatives have unthinkingly accepted the mainstream Republican view that there is nothing wrong with the country that the free market cannot fix, at least over time. Unmoored from our philosophical grounding, we allow ourselves to be carried along on the swift currents of consumer culture, and end up in a place where "conservatism," practically speaking, ends up as general approval of whatever commercial interests want to do.

We have not been true to older conservative principles, particularly those found in all the great wisdom traditions of mankind, all of which warn against letting the love of material things become our master. We have unwittingly allowed a consumerist mentality to shape the way we think about nearly all aspects of our private and public lives. Too many of us have come to think of the "good life" in purely materialistic terms, and have allowed the means to acquiring material security, even wealth, to become ends. We no longer seek to organize our lives according to what's Good, True, and Beautiful, but by a kind of shopping-mall utilitarianism that allows us to call good whatever allows us to grow wealthier.

Conservatives are nothing if not realists, and we have to admit that there has been almost nothing that has done more practical good to improve the lot of humankind than the free market. But the market must be put into its proper place, for as Pope John Paul II taught, the economy is made to serve man, not the other way around. Economist and social reformer E. F. Schumacher identified the tragic flaw in our free-market liberalism when he wrote that "the modern economy is propelled by a frenzy of greed and indulges in an orgy of envy, and those are not accidental features *but the very cause of its expansionist success* [emphasis mine]. The question is whether such causes can be effective for long or whether they carry within themselves the seeds of destruction."

The essential point of crunchy conservatism is to ask that question, and to search for workable answers that will enable us to conserve those institutions and places worth holding on to, and not toss them aside for the sake of efficiency, pleasure, or fashion. The solution is surely not to be found in ideology but in a considered critique of the assumptions undergirding contemporary social and economic life, and a studied withdrawal, a secession of sorts, from the mainstream. We have the power within us to refuse to participate fully in the system that makes us materially rich but impoverishes so much else.

This is not a book of sociology, much less of political theory or any sort of maximum heaviosity. It is a collection of stories about my family and conservatives like us, exploring how we integrate our political and religious beliefs with a lifestyle that's doubly countercultural. To us, to be a committed conservative today is to go against the grain of the broader, lifestyle-libertarian culture. And to be devoted to things like preserving the environment, resisting television and the depredations of big business, and encouraging sustainable development is to pitch one's tent off the Republican reservation.

Crunchy cons tend to esteem agrarian values, but most of us don't live in rural America. I now live with my family — which has grown by one son, Lucas — in inner-city Dallas. If I won the lottery, we might buy a big farmhouse in the Shenandoah Valley and raise apples and a mess of children. But we'd probably stay right here in Dallas, fulfilling our vocations close to family and friends who share our outlook. We're doing fine here. You'll see in the pages ahead that anybody can live the crunchy-con way, no matter where they are. Here you'll learn something new about a distinct way of seeing the world, and make connections you might otherwise not have made with ideas that stand to improve your life and your family's. You might be like I was a few years ago, looking down on certain ideas and ways of living as hippie-dippy liberal, and therefore not worth taking seriously. Keep reading: the conservative folks you'll meet in the pages ahead will open your eyes, and in them you'll see a sensibility marked by what G. K. Chesterton praised as "sanity, humor and charity," but also a recognition that American life is in crisis.

Crunchy cons try to address this by putting truth and beauty first in their lives. They have something to teach not only their fellow conservatives, but also moderates and liberals who feel a closet affinity for some of the ideas associated with the political right, but who have resisted them because they may have thought admitting it would turn them into Tom DeLay. More and more middle-class Americans, burned out by the junkiness and ephemerality of mainstream culture, feel compelled to seek out the transformative wisdom in simpler, more traditional, more natural ways of living. Crunchy conservatism may be what they're looking for. One French reader wrote to say he found himself feeling increasingly at odds with what passed for liberalism, yet until he read about crunchy conservatism, he assumed that the only way to be conservative was to embrace a consumerist lifestyle and a set of attitudes that felt all wrong. Frédéric was more truly conservative than he realized.

NOT LONG BEFORE he died, Russell Kirk, whom I might as well claim as the patron saint of crunchy conservatives, addressed the following challenge to his readers: "What can you do, young men and women of the rising generation of the 1990s, to raise up the human condition to a level less unworthy of what Pico della Mirandola called 'the dignity of man'? Why, begin by brightening the corner where you are; by improving one human unit, yourself, and by helping your neighbor." That's the spirit in which this book is written, and the spirit I hope the stories convey to and inspire in readers.

CHAPTER TWO

Consumerism

[Modern man] struggles with the paradox that total immersion in matter unfits him to deal with the problems of matter.

—RICHARD WEAVER, *IDEAS HAVE CONSEQUENCES*

[T]o idealize markets and to call oneself a conservative is to distort reality.

—ALAN EHRENHALT

As SOMEONE WHO was standing on the Brooklyn Bridge and saw the south tower of the World Trade Center fall, I consider former New York City mayor Rudy Giuliani to be a hero. He kept the city sane and hopeful in those fearful days in the autumn of 2001, and that is no small thing. But he said one thing immediately after the attacks that was, frankly, appalling, though I know why he said it, and I believe it represents the crass spirit of the present age.

As the fires in the collapsed towers still raged, the mayor of New York had this advice for us: "Go shopping." President Bush said the same thing.

Now, to be fair, the point they were making is that the rest of us should live our lives as normal, because to change our routines would give the terrorists unearned victories. There's something to that, and it's undeniably true that if American consumers had quit spending out of fear in those dread days after the attacks, the economy would have suffered immense damage. "Go shopping" was a rational thing to say from a certain perspective.

But from another, it was pretty demoralizing. I think it's safe to say that 9/11 galvanized New Yorkers, and indeed most Americans, and readied us to do something heroic and self-sacrificing, like, say, embarking on a serious and determined national campaign to save energy so the nation wouldn't be so dependent on Middle Eastern oil. We were instead encouraged to think that the best thing we could do for our country in the moment of her peril was to buy stuff. This suggests that the essential statement of patriotism, the most elemental expression of American identity, is commercial.

And let's face it, there's more truth to that than not. We have become a society that gives the place of prime honor to material progress, placing the demands of the economy above the considerations of family, of community, of country, and even of religion. Consumerism has *become* our religion, and it is difficult to identify anything within the contemporary Republican Party that stands against the dogma of the Market Supreme. One crunchy-con homeschooling mother (and GOP activist) living in Midland, Texas, told me that she was living in perhaps the most explicitly Christian and Republican town in the United States, but when it came to the question of materialism, she couldn't see how her neighbors lived any differently from the secular liberals they disdained. They bought their kids all the latest fashions and gadgets, let them watch as much TV as everybody else, including the same programs, and so forth.

"It's amazing to me to see parents who have money, and who think they're conservative, abandon their children to the culture, and then turn around and express shock at what the culture does to their children," this mom told me.

The problem with too many of us conservatives is we think holding the politically correct (from a right-wing point of view) position, and faithfully voting Republican, is enough to guarantee our conservative bona fides. We talk the talk, but do we walk the walk? Not if we're consumerists first, and conservatives second. The two cannot be reconciled.

What do I mean by consumerism? It's an uncodified materialist philosophy that considers the acquisition of goods and services at the least expensive price to be a fundamental social value. Consumerism fetishizes individual choice, and sees its expansion as unambiguous progress. A culture guided by consumerist values is one that welcomes technology without question, and prizes efficiency. A consumerist culture also tends to cede authority to the secular priesthood of scientists and other professional experts. Its idea of liberty involves the steady increase of the individual's sovereignty (the choice thing again). A consumerist society encourages its members both to find and express their personal identity through the consumption of products. Its ultimate goal is the spread of happiness and well-being through the improvement of material conditions, and the creation and general increase of wealth.

And if moral and spiritual values get in the way of that, well, hey babe, you can't stop progress.

How can you be a traditional-values conservative in a society whose very economic structure is designed to separate you, your kids, and your community from those values, and each other? That is the question at the heart of this book.

This is not to demonize wealth, at least not wealth gained through hard work and fair play. There is nothing objectively wrong with material progress, and a great deal right with it. The modern American who complains about materialism runs the risk of being laughed out of the room; any fault-finding must begin with the acknowledgment that we have all benefited enormously from America's economic progress. Besides, there's something funny about a guy tapping out a philippic against materialism on a state-of-the-art laptop computer.

The problem is the way we relate to our material gains. Economist E. F. Schumacher noted that all the world's great religions and wisdom traditions have warned of the corrupting nature of wealth, and how it shackles us to our desires, preventing us from doing the right thing. In *Small Is Beautiful,* Schumacher said, "It is not wealth that stands in the way of liberation but the attachment to wealth; not the enjoyment of pleasurable things but the craving for them."

My parents like to say that one of the happiest times in their lives was the first few years of their marriage, when they lived in an old house trailer, and money was so tight that they had only $5 left over at the end of each month. They're merely observing what wisdom traditions the world over have always taught: There is often an inverse relationship between wealth and happiness. America today is the richest, most powerful, and most technologically advanced society the world has ever known. And yet only a blind optimist would argue that we are a spiritually sound, morally strong society of happy people.

Why is that, and what does one have to do with the other? This book is an attempt to answer that question for conservatives, most of whom recognize that our society is in trouble, but who have no real idea how to address the problem. We on the right are big ones for saying that people need to get back to family values, or make room for God in their lives, or elect more Republicans to office. But this rarely moves beyond the level of rhetoric and sentimentality, and the fragmentation and alienation that cause us so much concern continue unabated, because we have not dealt with the root causes of our unhappiness. Our confusion comes in part because we don't recognize the disjunction between the ideals we profess to believe in as conservatives and the consumerist way of life we uncritically embrace.

Conservatives love to lecture liberals about the destructive quality of an ethic that justifies indiscriminate indulging of the sexual appetite. And we're right about that. But "thou shalt not covet" is a nonnegotiable divine command, too, and few are the conservative pastors who pound the pulpit to denounce acquisitiveness. Come to think of it, I've bored scores of priests in the confessional over the years with my sheepish tales of ordinary lust, but I could probably count on one hand the number of times I've thought to confess incidents of envy or greed. We on the right tend to think if we've kept our minds clean and our pants up, we're paragons of righteousness. But that's not true— not from an authentically religious point of view, and not from a traditionally conservative point of view.

The fundamental difference between crunchy conservatives and mainstream conservatives has to do with the place of the free market in society. Crunchy cons believe in the free market as an imperfect but just and effective means to the good society. When the market harms the good society, it should be reined in. Because crunchy cons, as conservatives, do not believe in the perfectibility or essential goodness of human nature, we keep squarely in front of us the truth that absent the restraints of religion, community, law, or custom, the commercial man will tend to respect no boundaries in the pursuit of personal gain. Absolute power corrupts absolutely, whether it's in the hands of big government or big business.

Crunchy cons believe mainstream Republicans have forgotten this. My favorite example comes from my friend Mike, the guy I mentioned in the first chapter, who works in the home office of one of the most conservative Republican members of Congress. Because of his impeccable conservative credentials, Mike was appointed to the "smart-growth task force" of his city, whose putative task was to direct the city's residential and commercial development in a responsible way. At the first meeting, it wasn't long before Mike realized that the panel was merely a front for property developers.

"I made the observation that nowhere in the four-page [task force founding] document was there a mention of any possibility of any kind of restriction ever being placed upon development," Mike told me. "At which point the most vocal member of the task force, who also happens to be the most powerful developers' attorney in town and who represented a chain store's successful bid to steamroll a nearby community, cracked, 'This is a free-market conservative?'

"I pointed out that it wasn't my definition of a free market to see the highest-priced, best-connected attorney in town hired by a big corporation to make mincemeat of the simple neighborhood folk who resist their development; in fact, it seemed antidemocratic and anticonservative in its trampling of the individual and the community," Mike said.

It's telling that my friend wasn't merely opposed, but denounced as a fake conservative because he opposed business interests. That, I'm afraid, is what so much mainstream conservatism amounts to nowadays: whatever serves the interests of commerce is baptized as conservative. That's pathetic.

Bryan Greer, a crunchy con from Northfield, Minnesota, wrote me to say, "I don't think conservatives have much of an answer for people who feel a sense of loss when 'progress' destroys beauty and authenticity. Conservatives can only mumble about the necessity of economic progress. They don't seem to care that something of real value has been lost."

Bryan said he's a lifelong Republican, but he's afraid for Republicans to take over his town's government because he doesn't trust them to conserve the character of the town center. Which is another way of saying the Republicans in his town were capitalists first, conservatives second. Schumacher spoke to this point when he observed that in today's economy, "anything that is found to be an impediment to economic growth is a shameful thing, and if people cling to it they are thought of as either saboteurs or fools."

What drives this destructive materialism? Good old greed and envy, mostly, which are always and everywhere present, and which can be combated by moral exhortation and reform. But there is something else working to drive the materialist dynamo, something so basic to our way of life that few even think to question it, something so ever present that to propose resisting it is to present yourself as a latter-day King Canute, ordering the incoming tide to turn around and head back to sea.

I'm talking about technology.

Neil Postman, the late media critic, was a man of the left, but he is beloved by the crunchy right for his incisive analyses of how mass media and technology undermine cultural and social institutions that make for good societies. He delivered perhaps his most radical critique of contemporary culture in his 1992 book *Technopoly*, which depicts American society as having structurally surrendered its soul and its liberty to technology. The word "structurally" is important, because in Postman's view, we have constructed our economy, our society, and even our way of seeing reality to serve technology. Americans naively accept new technologies, thinking only of what these technologies can do, but never, said Postman, what they can *undo*.

Consider television, and the way it conditions us to interpret reality. Now, whenever conservatives get their dander up about TV, it's almost always to rant about salacious programming. *Run for your lives, it's Janet Jackson's unsheathed ta-ta!* Postman said this kind of thing is a pointless distraction, that those who complain about the content of programming "are like the house dog munching peacefully on the meat while the house is looted." He invited us to think more deeply into how the medium itself changes the way we think.

By its very nature, television technology teaches us to experience the world as a series of fragmentary images. It trains us to prize emotion and stimulation over logic and abstract thought. We are conditioned to expect quick resolution to problems, and to develop evanescently short attention spans. We expect the world to be entertaining if it is to hold our attention; eventually, we learn to judge the world by essentially aesthetic criteria. For the man who gets his metaphysics from television, boredom is the root of all evil. As media critic Read Mercer Schuchardt told me, "Morality today is very point-and-click; life is completely about image and surface texture now."

This is why if a law were passed tomorrow granting Michael Medved, William Bennett, and Pope Benedict XVI the power to control all television programming, our essential dilemma would change not one bit. It is extremely difficult to stay focused on the permanent things, much less to school children in them, when our minds are formatted in this way. The television medium is by its very nature a force against tradition, against continuity, against permanence and stability.

Schuchardt, a former student of Postman's who when I spoke with him taught media theory at Marymount Manhattan College, is raising his six children without television. His students find their crunchy-con professor's TV-less existence hard to accept.

"They'll say things like, 'What do you mean you don't have a TV?'—almost like they think it's illegal," he said. "Part of it is people feel almost embarrassed not to have a TV. When they ask, 'How will I stay informed?' I tell them you'll find that you can't turn off the television, even when you get out of your house. It's on everywhere you go. You can't escape it. You'll still know what's happening, but you'll have four more hours in your day to use creatively.

"The number one advice I give to my students is to be a culture creator, not a culture consumer," he continued. "You have to have time to create, and to create, you have to get rid of those things that steal your time. TV is the great time-stealer in American life."

I used to be a TV critic, actually, and finally got so bored with it that I quit my job and moved into a country house down South to put myself through media detox and figure out what to do with my life. I spent the fall and winter of 1993 living virtually alone there, with no television, no newspaper, and no Internet (I did have a radio, and got my news from NPR). All I had was books, silence, and solitude.

The withdrawal was difficult. I was jittery and easily distracted. The monastic quiet unnerved me. But gradually I reconciled myself to it, and came to love it. There was no buzzing in my head anymore. I found I could write long letters, and sit for lengthy stretches reading novels. Prayer became easier. I started living by the rhythm of the day, awakening at daylight, and going to sleep not long after the sun went down. I began to feel, well, normal. I discovered how to be alone with my thoughts, and in turn how to think in a sustained way. Had I ever known how to do that?

By the end of my four months at that house, I felt vastly less anxious, restored to myself, and I had learned to listen for life's quieter, deeper sounds drowned out by the daily media cacophony. That was a decade and a half ago, and many times since then I have wished I could pack up my family and move to a place like that, where we could live the tranquillity of a media-free existence.

Eric Brende is someone who took his technology fast much further. In 1996, the Yale graduate and his new wife, Mary, lit out for rural Missouri to live on a farm run by a community he calls the "Minimites." They are in truth a group of Anabaptists who live more strictly than the Amish and the Mennonites. For a year and a half, Eric and Mary voluntarily embraced a technology-free existence, which he recounted in his 2004 book *Better Off.*

A friend in New York tipped me off about Eric, saying that this guy sounded like a natural-born crunchy con. I figured Eric's journey into voluntary Amishness must have taught him something important about the surrender of American conservatives to consumerism. At first, though, Eric was reluctant to talk to me. He explained that he and his wife are practicing Catholics and cultural conservatives, but that he thought the label "conservative" was meaningless in contemporary America. Eric told me that most people who call themselves conservative today aren't really conservative in a deep sense, because in his view they don't stand for conserving the environment or worthwhile social institutions threatened by free-market capitalism. He pointed out that the philosophical developments that paved the way for the Industrial Revolution were advocated by English liberals, who are the true philosophical forefathers of most who claim the conservative mantle today.

"Industrialism destroyed a wonderfully integrated way of life," he said. "I'm sure it wasn't paradise, but it wasn't a bad way of life. The Industrial Revolution separated all those skilled workers from their children and threw them into factories, where they were exploited by the liberals of the day. Conservatives today who claim that heritage don't really understand where they come from."

When I told him about crunchy conservatism, Eric warmed to the idea, saying that he'd love to be part of something that popularizes an older strain of conservatism that he characterizes as "just plain common sense." Then he told me about how he went from being a theorizing academic to a farmer living without technology.

"My hunch was that we in modern society had gotten to the point where most of our labor, time, and energy was going to deal with problems that technology itself causes us," Eric said. "I figured that if we scaled back on the technology, we'd have more leisure time, and have fuller and richer lives. But I felt I needed more concrete data to support this hunch, hence this experiment."

The Brendes lived in a rental cottage in the community, and worked with the Minimite community. Eric went to the Minimite farm carrying *Monty Python*-ish images of stooped and miserable peasants digging turnips up with their bare hands. Farm life turned out to be a pleasant surprise.

"Of course, you just can't imagine what it's going to be like if you've been living in a technological environment your whole life," he told me. "This is living, breathing three-dimensional reality all the time. You don't get to turn on TV and watch any kind of pseudoreality. You don't talk on the telephone. Everything is face-to-face. The things that you get you get only because you've used your body, and performed some physical exertion. It was like shifting from two dimensions to three."

He cautioned that the simple life was not Eden. Some days were too hot, others too cold. There were boring stretches. The main thing, though, was "how much richer and fuller each moment was."

"Out there, it was completely different from what I call the voluntary quadriplegia of sitting all day in front of a computer terminal," he said. "You're using your body the whole time, interacting with your neighbors, enjoying the beauty of nature in all its seasonal variations. You're using your mind in various capacities. There are various skills involved. In fact, the hardest thing about it was the mental challenge, picking up new forms of knowledge and skills that we completely lack coming from the city."

We have forgotten those skills because technology, over time, obviated the need for them. But maybe we needed those skills for reasons we didn't anticipate; we no longer have to walk anywhere, for example, but our dependence on the automobile is one reason Americans are so fat and out of shape. Worse, said Eric, it's alienating us from reality by giving us the illusion that we're actually enhancing our native capabilities and real-life experiences, when in fact it requires that we give them up. Consider tonight's dinner: is microwaving a prepackaged frozen entrée really an improvement over a home-cooked version? It's quicker, certainly, but consider what using that technology for the sake of efficiency costs you in skill, quality, and aesthetic satisfaction.

(Reality check: a few days after talking to Eric, I pompously made this point to Julie. Thank heaven she didn't have her chef's knife in her hand when I did. She slid into that vinegary Florence–from–*The Jeffersons* voice she uses when she has to take one of the menfolk in our house down a notch and said, "Look, that sounds great, but there are lots of nights when I've had a hard day chasing Matthew and Lucas around, and I wish I could just pop dinner in the microwave and be done with it. I don't do that, because I believe in the value of home cooking. Anyway, you'll notice that I freeze a lot of the things I make, and warm them up for you when you get in from the office. I'm not saying you boys are wrong about the cost of convenience. I'm with you there. Just don't get on your high horse and diss technology too much, because if we didn't have that freezer and that microwave, I wouldn't have the time or the energy to do nearly as much home cooking as I do." *Ouch!* Yes ma'am, so noted.)

In any case, Eric thought the goal is not to get rid of technology, but to limit its use "to restore a more integrated life, where you have the physical, the social, the mental, and the aesthetic aspects of life blending as seamlessly as possible. When you make your technological selection, you have this one question in your head: does this enhance integration, or does it undercut it? The big three that tend to undercut it are television, computers, and automobiles. It's not so much that you want to get rid of those things as to limit their use so you can restore those things that the technology is taking away from you."

Consider the television. The great gift you give to yourself and your family when you turn off the television is time together. I can't make the point often enough that television is not the enemy of the family primarily because of its content; it is the enemy of the family because it devours precious time. Studies have shown that people who get a TiVo to record only the best programs end up watching significantly more television than they did before they welcomed the device into their homes. Look, I know that there are truly great television shows available now, and I concede that it is possible, with the help of TiVo, to watch lots of TV without ever having to waste time on crap. But does anybody lie on their deathbed wishing they had watched more television? How many couples drop their eighteen-year-old off at college for that first freshman semester and drive away reminiscing about all that great family time in front of the tube when she was growing up?

Now, here is where I confess my computer addiction. I love blogs, and Web sites, and e-mail. Julie rides me all the time about the time I spend at home on the computer. What can I say? She's right. I tell myself that being online is not like watching television, because it's not passive, it's active. I'm engaged in discussion and debate, which I find stimulating. *That's not the point*, Julie keeps saying. *You are spending time alone, communing with the computer and not with your family.* I have no defense. In this way, the computer is TV for intellectual snobs: a time-waster for eggheads who would never throw away an evening watching cable, but who tell themselves the evening was well spent jumping around blog comment boxes and conducting five debates simultaneously on e-mail.

I told Eric that some urban and suburban types have a romantic view of rural and small-town life, thinking of it as a haven from the corruption of the city. This is a fallacy, I said, thanks to technology. Before the electronic media age, small towns and the countryside may have been seen as bastions of traditionalism, but that's over. In my rural hometown thirty years ago, everybody was taking their moral and social cues from TV shows produced in Los Angeles. They still are.

My friend Terry Mattingly, a college professor who once taught in a small Appalachian school, used to seethe over the way television culture corrupted his students with envy. Terry said that the constant message these kids received from TV while growing up was twofold: "Life is supposed to be about nonstop excitement, and that's not happening where you live." Terry's a twelve-string folk guitar player and a fanatic for bluegrass, which is the native music of his part of Appalachia. The young people wanted nothing to do with the cultural traditions and natural beauty of their region, Terry said. All they wanted was a mall.

Eric and I agree that because of the socializing power of television, small towns and rural villages can be more difficult places for conservative families than bigger cities. "Though there's this veneer of orderliness there, those pressures of conformity in small towns now conform people to abide by the values of *Sex and the City*," he said.

Still, when they left farm life after their eighteen-month experiment was over, Eric and Mary decided to stay in a nearby small town, which they thought was just about perfect.

"This town was one of the last places in the state, and maybe in the whole Midwest, that had a well-preserved urban core. There simply wasn't any room to put a big-box store, because of an accident of geography. The town was full of historic buildings, most of which had been preserved, and had all kinds of local shops that were still being used by the local people. All kinds of little restaurants."

But in the eight years the Brendes lived there, they saw what was special about the little town die.

"Gradually, one by one, the stores closed, because people would drive to other towns thirty miles away to go to the big mega supermarkets and box stores. Even the president of the Chamber of Commerce did her grocery shopping in that town thirty miles away. Can you believe that? So all the little shops in this town folded one by one. What took the cake for me was when the city fathers decided to subsidize the moving of the one grocery store in the center of town to a strip mall two miles outside of town, which wasn't even on the way to anything."

The people of this town, following their consumerist instincts, did not conserve the small businesses, the commercial institutions that made the local economy work and made it a more human community to live in. When things got to the point that it was no longer possible to walk or bike to get the things they needed to run their household, the Brendes left in disgust. Now they live in an old, gentrifying neighborhood in St. Louis, where they can use their bikes or their legs to get around.

"People don't know what they have until they lose it," Eric said. "Where we live in St. Louis, everything was lost, and now they're starting to recover it. We're thirty or forty years ahead of that town. I feel like now I'm part of something that's moving in the right direction."

Eric saw with his own eyes how the free market, and the technological capabilities that help it advance, undermined the social stability and communal values of a town filled with people who'd think of themselves as rock-ribbed conservatives.

"Edmund Burke realized that society is more than the sum of the individuals that make it up," he said. "It has a kind of fabric, a kind of texture to it. There are bonds and relationships that develop that make the total greater than the sum of its parts. But if you live in a society in which technology is constantly advancing and changing the rules of the game, then there's no possibility for genuine social stability."

The undeniable fact is that free-market, technology-driven capitalism, for all its benefits, tends to pull families and communities apart by empowering individuals and encouraging—even mandating—individualism. Most Americans would say, "Hey, what's wrong with individualism?" not thinking about the social costs of strained and even broken familial and communal bonds.

And both the political left and the political right exploit that sentiment in their own ways; there is no easier way to sell a product, even if the product is a politician, than to position its acquisition as choosing "freedom." In the face of social breakdown caused by Americans' sellout to consumerist individualism, and frustrated by both the left's and the right's inability to offer a plausible alternative, a few academic thinkers from both ends of the political spectrum have come together to ponder new ways to rebuild civil society, the informal network of voluntary associations—families, churches, civic groups, and so forth—that teach people how to work together and trust each other.

Civil society has been routed over the past thirty years. Since 1975, sociologist Robert Putnam observed in his book *Bowling Alone*, 33 percent fewer Americans make time for regular family dinners, 45 percent fewer of us have friends over regularly, and an astonishing 58 percent fewer of us attend club meetings. The social bonds we need to hold us together, to teach us to be responsible citizens, and — this point is crucial for conservatives — to help us appreciate the threats to our necessary institutions and to band together to conserve them are straining mightily under modern pressures.

I don't know anybody who doesn't yearn for the more orderly, cohesive world that existed prior to the tumult of the 1960s. Nobody wants to go back to the bad old days of segregation, lack of career opportunities for women, and suchlike. But among my older friends, baby boomers now becoming grandparents, there's a real sense that despite valuable progress, something important was discarded along the way. Among younger parents like Julie and me, who were born in the 1960s and 1970s, there is a sense of nostalgia for a place we've never been. Lots of us would like to get the good old fifties back, this time without the social strictures, especially racial and gender discrimination, that made "the fifties" a byword for conformity and repression.

Alas, you can't have that kind of community cohesion without discarding the consumerist values that have become second nature to modern Americans. The movie *Pleasantville* took a beating from conservatives for its comedic depiction of the 1950s as a stultifying era in which social cohesion came at the price of stifling individual passions and fulfillment. Despite its cartoonish excesses — and to be fair, it was meant to be social satire — the film's message wasn't far off the mark in terms of the way it framed the limited choices people had back then.

As Alan Ehrenhalt, who wrote a book about Chicago in the 1950s, said, "The residents of [a 1950s] neighborhood weren't hard-nosed consumers in the current sense. They had a different view of what was important in life."

They saw their commercial relationships in terms of personal relationships with the merchants, not as an impersonal set of transactions. I am old enough to remember this kind of thing when it still existed in my hometown. We bought hardware from Mr. Joe Rinaudo, winter hats from Mr. Kenneth Woods, cars from Popcorn Bennett at the Ford place (because we were a Ford family; Chevrolet people went to the Wilcoxes up the street). The teller at the Bank of Commerce knew my mom, and always had. We bought groceries from Gerald Bates at the Red & White (he would later give me my first job, as a bag boy), and oil filters from John Fudge. Most of these merchants gave back to the community by doing things like sponsoring kids' summer sports leagues. I played shortstop for the John Fudge Auto Parts Angels. It was a good way to live.

But I remember when they opened a brand-new Piggly Wiggly across the street from the Red & White (or "Gerald's," as everybody called it). Suddenly folks had a choice, and many chose to shop at the bigger, shinier supermarket. Mama was mostly loyal to Gerald, but sometimes she had to go to the Pig, as it was known, because the Pig had things Gerald's didn't. Poor Mama; she'd be so wracked with guilt that she'd drive out of her way to approach the Piggly Wiggly parking lot from the back, to reduce the chance that Gerald would see our Ford LTD parked out front, while the Dreher family was inside engaged in treachery. I felt guilty, too. I bet we weren't the only ones.

In time, you quit thinking that way. None of us felt too bad when one particular store went under. A former clerk there disclosed the secret price coding the store used to indicate the wholesale price on tagged merchandise. Once you knew the code, you could see how outrageously the store was marking up the merch. When our parents would go by the store to pick up something, my sister and I would compete to see which of us could find the product with the most astronomical markup. You can do that when you have a monopoly, and can depend on the loyalty of local folks. Eventually, they couldn't pull it off any longer, and went out of business. Twenty years or so later, the old store sits empty in the heart of downtown.

On the other hand, the same consumerist principles that brought down that store also shuttered a number of other small local businesses. People don't think twice about driving twenty miles or more to the Super Wal-Mart in a nearby town. You can save lots of money there. And to be fair, I can't say that I would do anything differently if I lived in my hometown today. The produce at the Super Wal-Mart is usually fresher than what's on offer at the two local supermarkets. I don't even know who runs the old Gerald's anymore, or the erstwhile Pig (now called Grocery Depot). It's easy for me to ballyhoo shopping locally in Brooklyn, because you could buy top-quality meat from the butcher, and first-rate produce from the greengrocer. Would I stand by the little guy if doing so meant paying premium prices for second-rate products? Nope.

Even if it meant standing by John the Butcher, the guy who gave lollipops to my kids when I stopped in for a London broil? Umm . . . well, probably not. In the end, I'd keep my head down and take the back street and go shop somewhere else, as guilty as my mother was skulking around to buy groceries at the Piggly Wiggly in the 1970s.

And that's Ehrenhalt's point: none of us today thinks about shopping like people in the 1950s did. We also have lived through a cultural revolution that firmly established the principle that self-expression is a virtual human right. And there has been a simultaneous commercial revolution that taught us to think of shopping as a form of self-expression. So when the modern American finds that she has limited consumer choice, Ehrenhalt said, she thinks of that as an unacceptable form of oppression. This idea has consequences, and you can see some of them in boarded-up shops in formerly vibrant downtowns.

The consumerist ethic that champions choice as an absolute value has greatly influenced social attitudes. When people say we can't return to *Ozzie and Harriet* America, they're right on one level, but on another, Ehrenhalt warned, they're trying to shut down any discussion of how society might rein in the chaos from rampant individualism. Notice what happens whenever objections are raised to violent or erotic television programming. The usual suspects scream censorship, and tell those prudes complaining about it that if they don't like the program, they don't have to watch it.

The problem with this is that very many people won't turn it off, and that programming will inevitably have an effect on them. It's all well and good for you to keep your kid from watching some trashy TV show, but if all the other parents on the block are letting their kids watch it, your gesture loses its power to socialize your child according to your own mores. This becomes especially true as your child moves closer to his teenage years, a time, as sociologists have found, when his peers have more influence over his morals and behavior than his parents do. Hillary Clinton got a bum rap from the right: it really *does* take a village to raise a child. The consumerist ideology assumes that individuals have a near-absolute right to consume products of their choice, and merchants have a near-absolute right to sell them. And what of society's interests? What right does society have to tell people what to do? the argument goes. Civil society, the middleman between marketers and the marketed-to, is disfranchised.

And so, the difference between the 1950s and today, wrote Ehrenhalt, "is to a large extent the difference between a society in which market forces challenged traditional values and a society in which they have triumphed over them."

Here's the problem: if we give in to an ethic of unrestrained individualism and materialism, it will become increasingly impossible to maintain a cohesive society — as *Pleasantville* admitted. The film, which was written and directed by thoughtful Hollywood liberal Gary Ross, ended by affirming that the messy freedom we live with today is still better than social order obtained at the cost of fifties-style conformity. What Ross didn't account for, though, is how the vulnerable contemporary teenagers coming of age amid broken families and a vulgar, violent, and often degrading culture are supposed to learn how to govern themselves, and build stable families and social structures in the general absence of strong social norms.

Conservatives have to concede that the decline in family stability is linked to real social advances, like the removal of barriers that kept women out of the workplace. Few people would advocate returning to the era when women didn't have that choice, but few can deny that it has taken its toll on family stability. Now we've gotten to the point economically where going to work is not so much a choice for many women as it is a requirement. And conservatives — yes, the very same ones who bemoan the loss of the traditional family — are every bit as complicit as the feminists we love to criticize.

One day, I got a shock when I picked up my copy of the *Dallas Morning News*. There on the front page was a story about the Kimbers, a family we knew from our Catholic homeschool group. They're as conservative, hardworking, and traditional a family as you could hope to find. Greg Kimber ran the family's small moving business, and when Joan wasn't busy homeschooling their kids, she helped out. The recession in the early part of this decade hit north Texas hard, and the Kimbers' business began to suffer. They had to put their kids into the state's Children's Health Insurance Program (CHIP), which provided supplemental medical and dental insurance for the children of the working poor.

State cutbacks in CHIP, led by the Republican legislature, forced the Kimbers to choose between filling their children's teeth or their bellies. The *News* account told their story.

I was poleaxed by this news. The Kimbers are proud people, and hadn't let any of us know what they were going through. My wife called Joan and offered to help financially, but Joan kindly said no, that they were going to find ways to handle it themselves. She was going to go to work. The kids would be entering public school (given the rather modest neighborhood the Kimbers live in, the school was not, shall we say, an altogether pleasant place to send your kids). In the meantime, I wrote a scathing column in the *News,* ripping the GOP legislature for the CHIP cuts, which yanked the rug out from under this traditional Republican family. I got in touch with my inner Russell Kirk, and thundered that in case the Republicans didn't realize it, the family is the institution most necessary to conserve. Their willingness to see families like the Kimbers suffer rather than raise taxes even the tiniest bit (Texas has no state income tax) showed where their values really were.

Well. Little did I know that I was a socialist and the Kimbers were welfare layabouts, until some of my fellow Texas Republicans pointed that out in a fusillade of stinging e-mails. I expected people to disagree with me, but I was not prepared for the contempt, the unshirted spite, that conservatives rained down on my head. I felt like my friend Mike, the guy who had his very existence as a conservative questioned because he spoke from conservative principle against a developer's plan. It was appalling to me, but quite instructive, to learn that for quite a few of my fellow Republicans, almost nothing matters more than keeping taxes low. If the economic structure we live under threatens the traditional family, well, too dadgum bad. You get the idea that for lots of these folks, "traditional family values" means nothing more than "keep the queers from getting hitched."

I don't know how we can keep living with the consumerist-driven economy, and the consumerist-driven society, without experiencing a major crack-up. Something's got to give. The showdown might come over immigration, as ordinary Americans come to realize how much business's demand for cheap migrant labor, which in turn keeps consumer prices down, is costing this country socially. More likely, it will be a severe economic crisis in the next two decades caused when the cheap and plentiful supply of oil upon which our entire far-flung economy depends effectively runs out (more on that in the final chapter).

The vast pool of oil that covered, so to speak, American society in the twentieth century, and still does, is like an unnatural lake created by the construction of a dam. That lake has been sitting there for a very long time, and we have come to enjoy its benefits so much that we have forgotten what the landscape below looked like. We have built our entire national and global economy — and, indeed, our highly mobile way of life — on the reliable presence of that lake.

But what if the dam should burst, and the lake disappear? The oil-dam burst this century will probably come from a combination of depleted oilfields and cutthroat competition from the rising economies of China and India. When that lake dries up, we will be rudely, perhaps violently, returned to the world as we left it — but without the knowledge, social structures, or habits of the heart to know how to live.

But let's say that our scientist-sorcerers conjure an unforeseen technomiracle, we avoid a petroleum catastrophe, and our consumerist utopia continues on its way. Can we sustain it? I doubt it. We can't keep going like this. It doesn't seem to be in our genes.

Consumerism is built on the sovereignty of the individual and his or her material desires, and all of us in the West have been acculturated to this norm. Recently, I heard Wade Davis, the Harvard anthropologist, deliver a lecture at a university, in which he spoke movingly of vanishing indigenous cultures around the world. He talked about how culture, in anthropological terms, is the imaginative layer between individuals and the world. It is the buffer between us and reality: the thing that helps us interpret the world, understand our place in it, and make our way through it.

Now, whether by evolutionary processes or divine design, humankind is communal by nature, and religious. We cannot long survive alienated from one another, nor without some overarching ideal, a mythological narrative and a metaphysics we believe is literally true, to sustain and inspire us. As Davis talked to his audience about how the modernizing processes that come with globalization shatter the communal patterns and the myths by which native peoples live, I couldn't help thinking, are we modern Americans all that different from those primitive people? Don't we need community, too, and to believe in something greater than our own material craving?

Of course we do.

After the lecture, I talked briefly with Davis, and told him that I thought the way we lived today in our country impoverished our spirit in similar ways as the tribal people in his lecture. He smiled weakly.

"We say we believe in marriage, but half our marriages end in divorce," he began. "We say we love our children, but look how we let them live. We say we believe in the family, but you don't see it in the way we behave. You can say a lot of things about Americans, but 'they're happy' is not one of them."

A society built on consumerism must break down eventually for the same reason socialism did: because even though it is infinitely better than socialism at meeting our physical needs and gratifying our physical desires, consumerism also treats human beings as merely materialists, as ciphers on a spreadsheet. It cannot, over time, serve the deepest needs of the human person for stability, spirituality, and authentic community. We should not be surprised that it has led to social disintegration.

What kind of economy should we have, then? I don't know; I'm a writer, not an economist. I do know this: we can't build anything good unless we live by the belief that *man does not exist to serve the economy, but the economy exists to serve man.*

When our consumer-crazed capitalism burns itself out, E. F. Schumacher, the late crunchy-con economist and social thinker who is due for rediscovery, can show us the way back to sanity.

In his classic 1973 work *Small Is Beautiful,* subtitled *Economics As If People Mattered,* Schumacher argued that in the West, economics is built on philosophically materialist assumptions, but in the East, the whole person is taken into account. Schumacher concluded that economics undertaken without spiritual, human, and ecological values is like sex without love, writing that "the essence of civilization is not in a multiplication of wants but in the purification of human character."

Materialist economics judges only in material terms, and fails to see the hidden costs of improving efficiency and production. Take the effect of moving married women en masse into the labor force (which Schumacher thought a terrible idea, perhaps the only serious issue on which his left-wing admirers disagreed with him). An extra income seems like it would help the family, but the cost of day care for preschool children can take a significant bite out of that income (which I personally know to be true: putting Matthew in New York City day care would have consumed 90 percent of Julie's salary as an editorial assistant). Then there is the monetary cost of having to rely on fast or prepackaged food to feed one's family, to say nothing of the health costs of that diet.

And then there are the costs that are impossible to measure, and impossible to deny. Julie has told me many times that as frustrating as being a housewife caring for small children can be, she can't imagine what it would have been like to miss the precious moments of our boys' young lives, strung out like pearls across the plain days of her housewifely life. It is hard to convey the gratitude and satisfaction I feel when I come home after a long day at the office to a delicious home-cooked dinner, and the security the boys and I have in knowing that Julie's always there, making our house a home.

That is quite literally priceless. We simply couldn't live this way if Julie were working outside the home. We're fortunate enough to be able to make it on my income alone, though we have forgone some of the material benefits that come with a two-salary household. The thing is, you really can't have it all. A few years back, I interviewed the editor in chief of a top women's magazine, who mentioned that she doesn't get home most nights till nine or ten. I asked her when she ever saw her kids.

"We schedule quality time together," she said crisply. And I thought, Lady, who are you kidding?

To Schumacher, an economy that left mothers with no *choice* but to work was not a just economy at all—or a sane one: "In particular, to let mothers of young children work in factories while the children run wild would be as uneconomic in the eyes of a Buddhist economist as the employment of a skilled worker as a soldier in the eyes of a modern economist."

The tragic flaw of Western economics is that it is based on exploiting and encouraging greed and envy. Schumacher gave the devil his due, though, admitting that these "are not accidental features, but the very cause of its expansionist success." Why a tragic flaw? Because an economy grown from these poisonous seeds is bound to destroy the community of which it is a part.

Our liberty and prosperity have made us feeble, because the things we've forgotten to conserve in the rush to riches were the very virtues necessary to build a stable society. Does anybody really believe we can grow our way out of our problems? Is another tax cut, gimmicky educational scheme, or entitlement reform — or whatever glorious program the Republican Party promises will call down the New Jerusalem — going to save marriages, restore children to their parents, heal the land, renew the commonweal? Come on.

Restoration of a sane economy, one that respects human dignity, has to grow organically, from individual human beings freely choosing to reform, not having it forced on them. Schumacher suggested that each of us should think of ways we've let our luxuries become our necessities, and then simplify our lives. If we can't do that, he said, at least we can recognize that material progress has cost us plenty, and stop making fun of those folks who, in looking for a better way to live, "are unafraid of being denounced as cranks."

A word about cranks: sometimes, they're the first to ask the questions that don't occur to the rest of us until later, after it's too late to do anything. As we've seen, to be a conservative who questions the free-market liberalism of the GOP mainstream is to open oneself up to charges of crankdom, or worse. We're starting to hear from more so-called cranks in the debate over Mexican immigration, as ordinary people sense that they are losing control of their communities because of unrestricted illegal immigration, supported in part by the GOP and its business interests, which depend on the cheap labor.

Not long after moving to Dallas, I interviewed a man in a suburb who had just sold the old house he and his family loved and moved to a new neighborhood because poor migrant Mexicans were moving into the neighborhood in droves. Not being familiar with this area and its social problems, I assumed that the man was probably a racist. That was wrong of me. Spending time with the man let me see that he had genuinely agonized over the move, and particularly worried that he had made the decision from discreditable motives.

What clarified his choice and eased his mind, the man told me, was the simple realization that he was tired of the police showing up constantly on his street to deal with the rowdiness and the crime the new immigrants, mostly young males crammed into rental houses, brought to the neighborhood. He'd begun to fear for the safety of his kids. He saw that the authorities either did not intend to do anything permanent about the problem, or lacked the ability to do so (my interviews with officials told me that it was a bit of both). Finally, he decided to cut his losses and leave.

Now, the point of this anecdote isn't to put down Mexicans. It is to say, though, that economic policies that wink and nod at illegal immigration because it's good for business can have an enormous social cost on both sides of the border. Conservatives who can see the price ordinary Americans pay from lax immigration policies favored by business interests ought to stop and think about costs to communities from economic decisions taken by corporations — and, cumulatively, consumers like themselves.

Schumacher believed in small businesses, small-scale manufacturing, and local economies. He favored family farms that use ecologically sensible methods to till the land and care for livestock. He counseled consumers to support small businesses, family farms, and artisans. He believed that we should have an economy where work fulfilled "man's need for creativity" — that is, labor that is humanized, not reduced to a cog-in-the-machine daily grind. He argued that beauty was important, however economically inefficient, because it comforted and elevated something deep in human nature.

And he insisted that wisdom had to return to the study of economics, and by that he meant the spiritual and moral dimensions, including a sense of prudence. We cannot carry on indefinitely under an economic system that pillages our resources, divides our communities, weakens our families, and compromises our character. Either we figure out a way to live our economic lives according to traditional values, or we advance the cause of chaos and our own demise.

Is all this airy-fairy nonsense? Only if you believe in nothing greater than the bottom line, and that the phrase "standard of living" refers only to the size of your bank account and the square footage of your house.

The key thing to get straight is that the ideas we carry in our heads about the way life at its most basic level works — that is, our metaphysics — determines the way we interpret reality. A rational and fulfilling human existence is not possible without a fundamental conviction that all people, individually and collectively, have a purpose. We need to believe that life is *for* something, and that everything we do has intrinsic value, and is not to be judged worthy based solely on its usefulness.

You may by now have guessed that Schumacher advocated a sacramental view of life, which, as we've seen, means simply that actions and objects convey spiritual meaning. All the great religions teach a form of sacramentalism, but you do not have to be formally religious to grasp the concept. As Eric Brende explained, those who live according to consumerist metaphysics

. . . see reality only as a means to some other end. So it's not something they savor for its own sake. If that's how you think, then the world around you is something to be used for something else, whatever goal you have in mind. Not only does that mean you lose a sense of appreciation of your immediate environment, it also means you're never going to be satisfied because you're always in motion towards a destination, but never getting to it. Whereas if you view your immediate environment and the processes you're involved in as intrinsically worthwhile, as intrinsically satisfying, then you have arrived. You don't have this need to run off to the next thing, because the reward is always with you. That's the ultimate efficiency: the thing you're doing is its own reward. The thing you're savoring is there for its own sake.

If you want to see the consequences that flow from a consumerist metaphysics, look around. Is that working well for us? Think we can keep this up for much longer? Will it be possible to conserve anything under these conditions?

By contrast, crunchy conservatism is a sensibility based on a sacramental metaphysics. The consequences that flow from the sacramental worldview are profound, and touch every aspect of our lives. To see the world sacramentally is to regard it with unjaded eyes.

The West used to live by this vision. We forgot how. If we want to recover what we've lost, and conserve the good that remains, we have a lot of relearning to do. Once we reclaim what tradition tells us the world and we are *for*—and believe me, it's not to be a better consumer—the rest follows naturally. I asked at the beginning of this chapter if it was possible to live according to traditional conservative values in an economy and a society that fundamentally reject them. You better believe it—and the rest of these pages are a handbook of the resistance.

CHAPTER THREE

Food

Tell me what you eat, and I will tell you what you are.

—JEAN-ANTHELME BRILLAT-SAVARIN

I GREW UP in a town without a McDonald's. It's hard to express how humiliating this was, to watch fast-food commercials knowing we were condemned to settle for crap from our local hamburger joints (which were perfectly good, but *not advertised on TV*). Or worse, home cooking.

My friend Terry, the professor who used to live in Appalachia, said that for country kids, TV exists to tell them that the place they live in is not good enough. That was certainly true for me with regard to culinary tradition. I think back now to how my mom's kitchen counter during the summer would groan with fresh tomatoes, green beans, squash, cucumbers, and suchlike from our own garden — stuff that I wanted nothing to do with, because it didn't come from either a fast-food joint or from the supermarket. No kidding. For me, the height of home-prepared culinary delight was a Swanson TV Dinner. Just like I'd seen in the ads.

So I grew up with terrible food habits. The more processed and advertised it was, the more likely I was to eat it. Unsurprisingly, I was a fat kid. I didn't give my diet a second thought until I married at age thirty, and moved right away with Julie to New

York City. Suddenly, I felt the obligation to be a grown-up about things, and that meant getting serious about my diet.

There was a practical reason for this, too. Julie and I both worked, but we couldn't afford to eat every meal out in Manhattan. With the eye-popping bounty of the Union Square farmer's market available to us every Saturday, when farmers from all over the region bring their fruits and vegetables into the heart of the city, we got interested in cooking. Neither of us grew up in homes in which our mothers, who worked, were all that interested in cooking. Both of us had thought of food as fuel, as ballast, and nothing more. Suddenly, though, we found ourselves enjoying making our own meals. I'll never forget the pale green of the creamy sorrel soup Julie made for our first Easter dinner together in the spring of 1998, and the salty crunch of the crusty leg of lamb we prepared and ate together at the table by the window of our sunny little apartment on East Fifty-eighth Street. We've made that sorrel soup several times since then, and there lingers something of the Easter sunshine of our first year of marriage in its savory taste.

We laugh today, recalling that first year together, lying in bed at night reading, and me pulling my head out of *Martha Stewart Living* one night, leaning over to Julie and saying, "I had no idea butter was this interesting." It's irresistible to make fun of that kind of yuppie jackass talk, but after we finished laughing at our own pretension, the plain fact was that butter *is* a lot more interesting than we had ever imagined. Lots of little things about food are. Neither of us had been taught to cook, and we really don't blame our mothers. They were raised working class in the rural South, and were hit with a wave of 1950s better-living-through-chemistry propaganda, telling women that traditional cooking was drudge work, and that processed food was a status symbol. Look back through old fifties food ads, and you'll see why home cooking washed away in that relentless tide of messages denigrating tradition. The same advertising that made me doubt the worth of my town because we couldn't get Dolly Madison snack cakes there had worked its wicked enchantment on my mom's generation. Julie and I found ourselves wishing we could spend time with our grandmothers, to find out what they knew about cooking that our mothers did not.

As time went on, we got better at cooking, and came to experience it as the most fun thing we could hope to do together. (Well, okay, the second most fun thing.) When our firstborn, Matthew, arrived, we were living in a small, dark apartment near the Brooklyn waterfront, and we found that we were pretty much housebound (it's no fun to wrestle a baby in a restaurant). We cooked at home for our friends even more often. Even today, years removed from those magical Brooklyn nights, whenever we prepare some of those favorite recipes, I can't help recalling Peggy's laugh, Father Wilson's funny stories, Santo's pulling the cork out of a bottle of Italian red, and the manifold joys of good friends and rich feasts.

I'd go to Staubitz Market, the venerable butcher shop on Court Street. The succulent taste of that meat would convey in part the pleasure of walking into Staubitz, knowing our butcher, and the pleasantries that would pass between us as we talked about meat, the weather, kids, the neighborhood, whatever. The bread we'd eat with our steak came from Christophe, the young Frenchman who ran a deli on Clinton Street. If we were feeling flush, Julie and I would buy a piece of *chèvre* wrapped in a chestnut leaf to serve our guests. And if we were feeling really flush, we'd stop by Tuller, the neighborhood cheese shop, and buy a wedge of Humboldt Fog and a thin slab of Manchego. We'd think hard about what would make us and our friends happy, choose thoughtfully, and prepare it with as much affection as we could muster. All these things we would lay out for our guests and ourselves, and man, oh man, that was the good life. It still is.

The point is, we learned in this way that food, properly understood, is sacramental; it carries within it the care of the farmers who raised it and the merchant who sold it, the love and devotion of the hands that prepared it, and the happiness of the friends and family who share it.

True, not every dinner is a special occasion, but we so often forget to slow down and savor what we eat. We are all pressed for time, and it's the easiest thing in the world to eat the quickest and most convenient thing. Families these days don't even eat dinner together; everybody's too busy to slow down and smell the pot roast. The imperative to convenience, ease, and cheapness — in other words, efficiency above everything — has created an enormous, and enormously lucrative, American food industry. It's the way we live our culinary lives now: fast, cheap, and out of control.

What does this have to do with conservatism? It all goes back to first principles, and the question, what is life for? If it's merely about fulfilling our material needs, then you could eat a bowl of Cheerios or a PowerBar in front of the TV every night and let that be that. There is no utilitarian reason to devote hours to preparing a delicious meal when you can save time by popping some tinfoil-encased gob of processed junk into the oven. Food not only nourishes the body, but it, and the rituals surrounding its preparation, nourish something in the human soul. When Julie and I would pick up our vegetables at the community-supported agriculture (CSA) co-op, we urbanites were participating directly in a system that supported agrarian life, which we hold to be a moral good.

I suppose a bit of that is sentimentality, but mostly it's gratitude. When you learn to love cooking, you also learn to be both mindful of and thankful for the quality of your ingredients. And when you learn how much care goes into the preparation of something good to eat, you can't help reflecting on how very much more of the same went into raising it and growing it. As we got to know how those CSA farmers lived, raising their crops the old-fashioned way (as opposed to with efficient industrial methods), we came to respect them for honoring the agrarian farming tradition, defined by Wendell Berry as "the proper use and care of an immeasurable gift."

I don't want to put on airs here; I could no more grow a potato or a carrot than I could sprout a horn in my forehead. But then again, I couldn't paint a Cézanne either, but I know enough about art to know when I'm in the presence of something worthy of respect and admiration.

Anyway, when we bought our meat from the neighborhood butcher, whose shop had been in that same spot for over a hundred years, and who knew our names and faces, we were personalizing commercial transactions, and, at the risk of sounding like a goony theorist, we were nurturing the economy of Cobble Hill, Brooklyn, the little patch of the planet where we lived, and over which we had been given responsibility because of our having chosen to be there.

By "economy," I don't mean strictly commerce, but the inchoate and complex system of human relations that bound us together as a community, and made Cobble Hill the kind of place worth living in and caring about. The Dreher family was not anonymous to John the Butcher, or to Christophe the Baker, and they weren't anonymous to the Drehers. That counts for something. And by choosing to shop at those places, we chose to conserve that rare and precious thing: a sense of beloved community, a sense of beloved place, in a world where the quest for efficiency and the monetary bottom line served only to annihilate tradition and atomize families and communities. That's a moral issue, and inasmuch as politics ratifies the moral consensus of any community, a political one as well.

But there were also materialist reasons we chose to eat as we did; these, too, have a moral cast. As I've said, Julie and I changed our eating habits when we learned how good food can taste when you shop sensibly and cook it yourself with care. But we also began to eat better because we had to. As I've said, we are practicing Catholics, of the orthodox persuasion, and that means we obey the Church's prohibition on artificial birth control.

Natural Family Planning, the method of birth spacing we practice, works by paying attention to the woman's body, and determining her fertile and infertile times of the month. The success of
this method depends almost entirely on the regularity of the
woman's hormonal cycle, which in turn depends greatly on
proper nutrition. Julie came to understand that she just couldn't
eat as haphazardly and thoughtlessly as before, and because
NFP-practicing Catholics are taught to think of fertility as
"our" thing, that meant I had to change as well. Besides, we were
adults now, and had no business eating like teenagers. After
making some fairly simple changes to our diet, we were soon
amazed by how much better we felt, and how much more we
were enjoying eating.

Now, observant Jews and Muslims have strict laws governing
their diets, but Christians generally do not. Yet here we were,
discovering a hidden connection between fidelity to our religion's demands and the kind of food we ate. As we came to see in
time, the separation between our political and moral convictions
and the lifestyle choices we made was by and large an illusion.
Just as ideas have consequences, so do actions. While nothing is
more tiresome and spirit-killing than trying to ideologize everyday life, it can't be denied that we show what we believe not by
what we say, but by what we do.

At first, we got hooked into the CSA co-op in our Brooklyn
neighborhood because the vegetables tasted so much better than
what we could buy at the supermarket, but once we learned more
about how these vegetables were produced, we had the good feeling of knowing that we were supporting small farmers trying to
make a go of it on their own, not big, impersonal agribusiness.
Sometimes, when we'd buy vegetables at the Manhattan or
Brooklyn farmer's markets on Saturday, we'd get to talk to the
men and women whose hands had picked the fruits and vegetables we were purchasing. We knew our money was going to support what *these people* were creating, and that includes agrarian

families trying to hold their own in an economy that says, in the name of efficiency, that they shouldn't exist.

To be frank, becoming an amateur home cook is what taught me, as a conservative, to mistrust and at times to loathe American industrial farming. What you do when you go to a farmer's market, if you are at all observant, is pick up on the direct connection between what you eat, where it came from, and how it got to you. If you're curious, you talk to the farmers about how they grew or raised the stuff. It's a cliché, I guess, to call it a labor of love, but it's plain to see how much the identity of these men and women is tied to their labor in the fields. It is a rare thing for Americans these days even to think about where their food comes from, but when you've seen the face of the woman who planted it, and shaken the hand of the man who harvested it, you become aware of the intimate human connection between you, the farmer, and the earth. To do so is to become aware of the radical *giftedness* of our lives.

Look, I don't want to get all mystical over a bunch of carrots, but it's worthwhile to meditate on these things. Learning the names of the small farmers, and coming to appreciate what they do, is to reverse the sweeping process of alienation from the earth and from each other that the industrialized agriculture and mass production of foodstuff has wrought. To appreciate how your food got to your table, to know how much we depend on the labor of others for our sustenance, is to begin to reestablish community, and even a kind of humility in the face of our radical dependence on each other. And that's worth something you cannot quantify on a balance sheet.

At first I thought of this small-scale organic farming as a sort of boutique thing—pleasant to have, like artisanal microbrewed beers, but only that. Then I started looking into how the government regulates the meat industry. It was shocking to see how agribusiness has gamed the system to keep small meat producers marginalized. Our regulatory system is designed to favor industrialized meat production, with its factory farms, its cattle jacked up with antibiotics and growth hormones, and its chickens raised in cages filled with their own feces. As a conservative, I am angry about this, not only on behalf of the small businesspeople slapped around by the deep-pocketed agribusiness behemoths, but because of how industrialized agriculture has made a traditional agrarian way of life difficult if not impossible.

We are told that small-scale farming is inefficient — this is true — and that because our factory farms feed the masses, and do so cheaply, we should be satisfied. And that's a deal that makes sense to nearly all of us: just keep the stuff showing up in produce bins and under cellophane in the supermarket cooler, and keep it relatively cheap, and we'll ask no questions. But in striking that devil's bargain, we sign away our responsibility for what's in that food, how it got there, and what was done to human communities to close the deal. To participate in a system and a way of thinking in which the act of eating is merely a commercial transaction is to sell out our spiritual and cultural patrimony. I understand the free-market reasons why Americans do this. But I don't understand why it is called conservative.

You don't have to be conservative to appreciate the healthful and sensual value of good food, but when I learned about the Slow Food movement, I realized that there are profoundly conservative reasons for taking food and food culture seriously. When I heard about Slow Food I thought, Man, if this isn't the quintessential crunchy-con phenomenon, I don't know what is. It should be said up front that it was started by a bunch of Italian Communists, which just goes to show you that (a) not even the dour pieties of Communism can extinguish the sensuality in the Italian soul, and (b) the crunchy-con sensibility makes for some fairly exotic bedfellows.

Carlo Petrini, the father of Slow Food, is an idealistic Italian Marxist who got fed up with how his political comrades seemed to think that pleasure was impermissible to the morally and politically engaged. In the early 1980s, Petrini began to worry that the culinary traditions of his native Piedmont were in danger of disappearing in a rapidly industrializing world, in which the agrarian way of life was becoming ever more rare. In a way that's hard for contemporary Americans to understand, Petrini grasped that the particular culture of his people is inseparably bound to the food they grow and eat. Lose local dishes and local eating habits to McDonaldization, and you've lost something profound.

His chief insight was that saving this food and this culture was not, and could not be, an elitist pursuit. No, for Petrini and his friends, it had to be something everyone could participate in. As Corby Kummer told it in his essential *The Pleasures of Slow Food,* "Simple, good food of the land and bonhomie were values in themselves, the friends said. They distrusted 'moralistic revolutionaries' and, worse, 'anyone who doesn't laugh.'" As the Slow Food movement grew beyond the bounds of Italy, its proponents realized that they could never succeed by trying to stop McDonald's and its ilk. Rather, they had to show people why the Slow attitude toward life — esteeming tradition, celebrating particularity in the face of mass culture, and taking time to enjoy life — is more sensible, more fun, more human.

Petrini told Kummer that he didn't care if people went to McDonald's if that's what made them happy, but that if they were offered an alternative, they'd likely take it. "Taste is like an umbilical cord," he said. "We all return to our grandmothers no matter how many detours we take along the way."

Slow Food knows good intentions won't change the world. That's why it established the Ark of Taste, a collection of foods from around the world considered to be in risk of extinction. The food can be a plant or an animal, or a food product like cheese, but it has to be local, traditional, handmade, and of top quality. The idea is to first identify endangered foods and food traditions, then to get busy trying to save them. One way to do this is by raising public awareness by promoting these foods and the restaurants and shops that serve them. Another is by conferring the Slow Food Award on people who do extraordinary things to maintain biodiversity in food-related areas.

What could be more conservative than this? The second of Kirk's famed Six Canons of Conservative Thought is "Affection for the proliferating variety and mystery of traditional life, as distinguished from the narrowing uniformity and equalitarianism and utilitarian aims of most radical systems." The traditional conservative will want to take a stand for the mom-and-pop cheesemaker over the pasteurized processed cheese food disgorged by the factory and sold cheaply.

Another way Slow Food does this is by having its chapters worldwide work to help farmers and small producers navigate the regulatory maze that puts the little guy at a significant disadvantage to big agribusiness.

This is a big deal. Distrust of big government is in the DNA of contemporary conservatives, and to see how state and federal regulatory bureaucracies put the hurt on small farmers, all to the advantage of big business, should be enough to send grassroots right-wingers to the barricades.

Several years ago, in covering this story for *National Review,* I talked to Jenny Drake, a former state health inspector turned organic livestock farmer. Drake, a feisty conservative, wanted to raise her chickens and beef cattle without using hormones and antibiotics, which are ubiquitous in factory farming. Those healthy chickens of hers were a problem, though. The state of Tennessee, where she and her husband live and farm, refuses to let any chicken be sold there unless the USDA inspects the processing facilities. Alas, there are no custom-kill processing plants for chickens in the entire American Southeast. Drake told me that to build a small processing facility to meet federal guidelines would cost her about $150,000.

"The Americans with Disabilities Act, for example, means a small producer has to put in restrooms that are handicapped-accessible," she told me then. "I'd have to build an office for the inspector. That office has to have its own phone line. I'd have to put in a paved parking lot. We have to meet the same physical standards as a Tyson's" — the industrial chicken megaproducer — "and we just can't do it."

I also spoke at the time to Joel Salatin, an evangelical Christian crunchy con who runs Polyface Farm in Virginia's Blue Ridge Mountains. Salatin is well known on the international small-scale sustainable farming circuit. He's had similar problems battling idiotic regulations (e.g., the government wanted him to build changing-room lockers for his employees, even though he has no employees on his family-run farm).

"A lot of [this] is being done under the guise of protecting the general welfare and guaranteeing clean food," he told me. "But what it really does is protect big agribusiness from rural independent competition."

Put simply, it does this by writing health regulations that only relatively large companies can afford to abide by. Economist Edward Hudgins told me that it's often the case that big companies willingly absorb the cost of extra regulation because those rules "have the effect of killing off the competition."

Without official government approval, small producers like Drake and Salatin may not be able to sell to anyone at all, or in some states aren't able to sell directly to grocery stores, which would help these farmers realize a much greater profit margin than if they had to use standard processing plants as middlemen. Salatin told me that he's tried to reason with health officials to allow them to test his meats for contamination without his having to build the expensive facilities required by law. The bureaucratic mind-set wins more often than not.

With regulations and economic barriers that make it virtually impossible to raise meat the old-fashioned way, it's no wonder family farms are disappearing. That's too bad, you might say, but isn't that a small price to pay for keeping the nation's meat supply safe? Arguably, yes — if the factory-farming system actually did so. As Eric Schlosser documented so brilliantly (if nauseatingly) in his bestselling *Fast Food Nation,* America's factory-farming industry has caused the rates of food-borne illness to shoot up, and resulted in a host of ancillary environmental problems as well. True, the economy of scale makes for cheaper meat, but as every conservative knows, or ought to know, you can't get something for nothing. There is always a hidden price to pay. Unsurprisingly, Schlosser has praised the Slow Food movement as a "necessary and long overdue" antidote to the industrialized food system.

In Dallas, the fledgling Slow Food convivium (as local chapters are called) hooked up with Robert Hutchins, an organic livestock farmer who lives with his wife and twelve kids on a ranch near Greenville, about an hour east of the city. I met Robert the first summer we lived here, when Julie and I bought meat from the booth he runs with two other Greenville farmers at the Dallas Farmers Market. The chicken, beef, pork, and lamb sold here is free-range, pasture-raised, and chemical-free. And, I should say, they taste phenomenally delicious. When a European visitor came to dinner one night, Julie roasted one of these chickens simply salted and peppered, with a punctured lemon in its cavity—and our guest said it was the most delicious chicken she'd ever eaten. I would have thought she was merely being polite, but it *was* one of the most delicious chickens I'd ever eaten too, almost the Platonic ideal of chickenness.

The name of the Hutchins booth is Texas Supernatural Meats, which made me wonder on that first visit if maybe these folks were religious, which, this being Texas, probably meant they were conservatives. I said something to the woman behind the counter about crunchy conservatism, and she said, "Oh, if you'd come here yesterday, you'd have heard Rush Limbaugh on the radio."

Imagine that! Dittohead organic chicken farmers! I had to know more.

One December morning, I drove out to Greenville, and found my way to Rehoboth Ranch, overseen by Robert and his family. At the time of my visit, Rehoboth had about four hundred regular clients, who bought either directly from the farm or at the Dallas Farmers Market. The three-hundred-acre ranch produces beef, lamb, chickens, eggs, and goat milk. It's an enterprise run entirely by Robert and his kids, who range in age from their mid-twenties to six-year-old twins.

Robert and I sat down in an outbuilding and had a talk. There had been a mad cow disease scare nationwide that week, and local news media had been out to Robert's farm to talk about "clean" beef. He'd been doing some interviews, and was frustrated that the media didn't want to go deeper into the issue of how we grow and harvest our meat in the United States.

"Most people want to talk at a superficial level. I had a reporter down here yesterday, and I told him we raise our cattle the natural way, and feed them only what they were designed to eat. They were created only to eat certain things, with their ruminant stomachs: that's grass and forage. They weren't created to eat grain, so we let them eat what they're supposed to eat. But that's skirting the issue.

"The real philosophical issue behind why we do what we do, is because we're Christians," he continued. "We would be called evangelical Christians, and probably fundamentalists also. We try to align our lives with what we understand from Scripture would be a God-honoring lifestyle."

Here I encountered something I would constantly run into when talking to conservatives of the crunchy persuasion: a strong, personally definitive degree of religious engagement. Crunchy leftists tend to have a secular basis for their countercultural outlook, but for crunchy rightists, it usually (but not always) starts with religious conviction.

Robert, a middle-aged man whose manner is friendly and open, but also quite serious, spoke of becoming a farmer as if it were part of his religious conversion.

"For many years, I worked in other jobs. It was always in my heart that I wanted to have a home-based business," he said. "And this is what we all enjoy doing. We enjoy doing it, and we feel that it's a calling to provide clean, safe, nutritious meat for other families. We feel a sense of mission here, like we're doing something worthwhile. It's not like selling insurance, or something that leaves us with no sense of purpose."

He'd grown up in Greenville, and finished high school in 1971. He was subsequently graduated from the U.S. Naval Academy, and served a five-year stint in the Navy before moving back home. He started working for a local defense contractor, and made it to the director level after eight years. When a national defense firm bought the Texas concern, Robert's responsibilities rose tremendously.

"I traveled a lot, and had somewhat regular access to the CEO. But after a while, I thought, you know, this is not me; this is not God's best for my family. I was making a lot of money, a nice six-figure salary. I'll not deny that that allowed us to have this nice farm, debt-free, for the last four years I worked there," he said. "But God convinced me that this kind of life was not what he wanted for me."

In 2000, Robert left the company after twenty years of service, to commit himself full-time to farming and recover his life.

"In that job, I was making so much money, and I had it in my mind that I could get to a level and to a position where I could conquer the job in a comfortable amount of hours, and have adequate time for my family," he said.

"But that was a pipe dream, because in today's environment, once you get to that level where you're making a six-figure salary, the job owns you. I was not willing to sell my soul for the good of the company any longer. I wanted to have some purpose, some calling for my life."

He undertook small-scale "sustainable" agriculture — "sustainable," explained Robert, "because the methods we use are organic, they don't pollute the environment, and we look at it as honoring God's creation and restoring it to its fullest."

This includes restoring the soil on his farm to grow healthy grass for his animals, so they in turn can produce optimally nutritious meat. If you take livestock out of their natural environment, Robert explains, and feed them a diet they were not designed to eat, unwelcome things happen to the meat they produce.

"The nutrition of the meat is far, far less. You've heard of omega-3 essential fatty acid, a cancer-fighter and preventer? Well, after a hundred days in a feedlot, on a grain-based diet, the omega-3 content of the meat on that meat steer drops by a huge amount. When you eat feedlot or confinement-raised meat, you don't get it. The nutrition is simply not there, and we don't get it because we think we know better than God about how to raise these animals. That's simply not true."

I asked Robert how his use of electric fencing to keep his herds moving fit into his all-natural plan. Technology is not the enemy, he replied, but in fact an ally if put to use helping farmers raise clean, natural meat.

"In our three hundred acres here, we have thirty-two different grazing areas," he explained. "Conventional cattlemen think we're nuts, but we rotate our herd from grazing area to grazing area, and we find that works. They're not standing in their own manure, reingesting parasites, and they're not grazing beneficial plants down to the ground level. We make sure that they have clean water, that they're never grazing in their own manure, that they're moving rapidly. We break the parasite cycle, we improve the forage and the soil, and we restore things to their natural rhythm. Everything we do is from that perspective."

He also keeps up with his customers by using the Internet — to a point. "We don't ship our meat, and I doubt we ever will. I have a strong belief that people should buy from their local suppliers. My vision is that one day, this country will be crisscrossed with a network of local farms supplying food to people in their region. It'll never be totally that way, but we can make a lot of progress on that path, and it'll be an answer to this Wal-Martization of America."

The Hutchins kids all help out on the farm. There's no outside help working there. The entire operation of Rehoboth's Grade A dairy is in the hands of two teenage boys. "They interact with the state inspectors, and flat-out run the dairy," their father said. "You don't often find teenagers given that level of responsibility. That type of character development is why we live the way we do: to be able to train our children in the way they should go."

They couldn't pull this off if the Hutchins kids were doing ordinary schooling. They're all taught at home by Robert's wife, Nancy. This limits the work they're able to do on the farm—their studies come first—but Robert believes that education does not consist merely of the accumulation of facts to be regurgitated on state tests.

"We started homeschooling in 1985, before it was as popular or as accepted as it is today," he says. "We didn't take our kids out of the government schools because the academics were poor, although they are. We took them out because we wanted an opportunity to train their character, not have their character trained by their peers or their teachers."

Choosing to homeschool back then was a radically countercultural practice. Robert says if they hadn't done that, there's reason to doubt they would have become an organic farming family.

"My theory is once you begin challenging fundamental common practices in today's society, once you challenge one, it's easy to challenge them all. Once we started seeing things in our children that led us to choose to homeschool, we started wondering if our eating habits were really lined up with God's best, and whether or not my occupation was lined up with what God really wanted for us. We started to think that maybe having a family business, where we could all participate, would be best, partly because we'd have a tremendous number of character-building opportunities to work together as a family."

Though some mainstream conservatives look at the Hutchinses' way of life with skepticism, Robert finds understanding across the religious and philosophical divide within the organic farming community.

"You find out quickly if you do small-scale sustainable agriculture whether someone is doing it from a Christian basis or a pantheistic, kind of earth-worshiping basis. You'll find both views in this community, but a lot of acceptance too," he said.

"I'll go to meetings of the community of people doing this kind of farming, and when people find out we do this from a Christian philosophy, that's accepted. It's okay to be a Christian in our community. It's almost like there's more acceptance for diverse viewpoints from within this community than there is from people looking in from the outside."

Crunchy liberals don't need convincing about the problems with America's food-production system, but mainstream liberals and conservatives have a lot to learn, Robert said. He called the mad cow scare in that morning's headlines a "teachable moment."

"The things that have become common practice in the industrial livestock business need to be brought to public light," he said, his voice rising. "I think people would be shocked and appalled to know about the blood being fed to calves"—it's called "milk replacer" by the industry—"and about the laxness of putting downer cattle [cattle that are unable to walk by the time they are slaughtered] into the food supply. I think people would be shocked to know that they feed cows chicken feathers and chicken droppings. I think people would be shocked to know about the advanced meat recovery systems, how the government allows industry to use these innocent-sounding terms like 'mechanically separated beef,' which sounds kind of harmless, but if you describe what that was—taking a beef carcass that's had most of the cuts taken off of it, and using a blast of high-pressure steam to remove ligaments, tendons, cartilage, spinal cord, every bit of tissue left on the bones—people wouldn't want to eat it. That goes into hot dogs, luncheon meat, all kinds of processed meats."

(According to one study, 35 percent of the flesh recovered that way contains some central nervous system tissue, which is the suspected vector for mad cow disease into the human population.)

"To me, that's just a bad practice," he continues. "Now, I'm not down on packers and processors, because the American public demands cheap food, at the expense of quality. In a processing plant where four hundred carcasses an hour are zipping by an inspector, you're not going to get the scrutiny you need. Our beef is processed at a small plant that's USDA inspected, and does ten cows a day, all individually. No advanced meat recovery system. Everything is done by hand. None of the meat is mixed with other animals. No spinal column tissue or fluids, or lymph glands, or any of the other things. We don't have processed meat. We have *real* meat."

That you do, I said to him, but your real meat is also real expensive. How can buying meat the way you raise it ever be affordable for families like mine to eat on a regular basis?

"Easy," he chuckled. "All you have to do is completely change the industrial meat infrastructure of this country. That's all you have to do. There are models around the globe in Argentina, Brazil, and Australia, where they have created an infrastructure to raise healthy meat."

In America, however, we raise our meat in industrial feedlots, he said, and feed them "all kinds of cheap by-products, all sorts of nasty, nasty things you would never put into your mouth, and they're standing around knee-deep in manure, breathing contaminated air, eating the cheapest possible things we can feed them, and getting injected with growth hormones to make them get as big as they can as quickly as they can, and antibiotics to deal with the sickness they get from the way they're being raised. You get cheap meat this way, but think of the quality. It's sacrificed big-time."

My host was on a roll.

"They process hundreds of cattle an hour and thousands of chickens an hour, these processing plants, without proper regard for food safety, and without any regard for the natural God-honoring way of doing things, which was shoved aside long ago for the sake of efficiency and technology," Robert said. "Our beef and lamb are sent off the farm for processing, but we do our poultry here. A state inspector comes out here and says, 'If I was at a high-volume poultry processing plant instead of here today, I would be looking at fifteen thousand chickens instead of your two hundred.' Now, there's no way you can look at fifteen thousand chickens in eight hours of work and properly evaluate the quality of that meat."

It was getting close to noon, and Robert's wife, Nancy, came in to invite me to stay for a bowl of lunchtime chili. Knowing how good Rehoboth's beef is, I could hardly say no. But before we went into the house, I asked Robert how he felt about the Republican Party.

"I think that the leadership of the Republican Party believes that globalization is inevitable, and it's best for everyone in the world," he said, in a tone of voice that made it clear he does not. "I think we're mindlessly going down the road toward unrestricted free trade, as opposed to thoughtfully considered fair trade. George Bush, bless his heart, does a whole lot of good, but he's dead wrong on this, just like he's dead wrong on genetically modified food, just like he's dead wrong on a number of things. And I think he's a good representative of the elite leadership of the party."

So do you vote Republican? I asked.

"Oh yes," he said. "The alternative is so much worse."

I know what he means. The Democrats have been not much better than the GOP on fair trade and immigration, and they are absolutely dismal on abortion and human biotech issues, which are of central importance to religious and social conservatives. At the end of the day, it's extremely difficult for a man like Robert Hutchins, who turned his entire world upside down to live in a way that he believes honors God and gives life—human and animal—proper reverence, to cast his vote for a politician who supports the right to abortion. If the Democratic Party opened itself once again to pro-lifers, it could pull some conservative votes away from the GOP on the kind of quality-of-life issues that engage crunchy conservatives.

When I asked Robert what he has in common with liberal counterculturalists, he said that there's a lot of antiestablishment contrariness in all of us — echoing the quip of Juli Loesch Wiley, a Catholic pro-life pacifist friend who says she went all the way from the left wing to the right wing without ever once trusting the government.

"Both the left-wingers and the right-wingers who follow this path, we're all looking for something better than and different from everybody else," Robert mused. "I heard somebody say the other day that their biggest fear is leading an ordinary life. These people are not intellectually lazy. We're raising a whole generation of people in this country who are intellectually lazy, who want to conform, who don't want to learn, who want only to pursue comfort and their own pleasures."

Robert said living the life of homeschooling agrarians has not always been easy or remunerative, but the rewards are priceless.

"What do I gain? The hearts of my children, for one. I gain the ability to be the dominant influence in their life, because I'm home, working with them. I gain the satisfaction of doing something I know is good for people. I gain opportunities to minister to people. I have a number of customers that are recovering from cancer or other illnesses who are into nutritional therapy because they have seen the effect that good nutrition has had on their health. There's a great deal of satisfaction in that. You know, the satisfaction of feeling like I'm walking in God's will for our lives. I never felt like that when I was in the corporate rat race. It's like a guy once told me, the only things running in the rat race are rats."

Being with his children, working their farm, and having home-church on Sunday mornings fulfills this man, who saw his father break himself working a job he hated so he could retire early and enjoy the good life — only to have his heart give out just eight years after he retired.

"He thought if he could just get to retirement and be at leisure, that would be fulfillment. But it wasn't," Robert said. "I remember once reading an interview with a retiring executive of my old company, and he was asked if there was anything he regretted, looking back on his career. He said the only thing was that he wished he had spent more time with his family. That pierced my heart. I said, 'Please, God, don't let that be my testimony.' But for years it was. I was seeking the wrong thing: the prestige and the money that went with working at that level of the company. Today, I can say honestly that these are the best years of my life. If you can't say that about today, then you're doing the wrong thing."

After sharing a delicious kettle of Texas chili with most of the Hutchins clan, I drove off down the country roads outside Greenville in search of Mike and Connie Hale's place. The Hales home-church with the Hutchinses, and sell the organic free-range chickens they raise on their farm at the Texas Supernatural Meats booth at the Dallas Farmers Market. The Hales do most of their retailing, though, to high-end restaurants in Dallas.

When I drove up, Mike was out in the fields on an errand, so Connie invited me into her kitchen. She was soaking almonds in water for her kids. The process activates beneficial enzymes in the nuts that wouldn't otherwise be present, as Connie explained. She learned about this from the Weston A. Price Foundation, a Washington, D.C., think tank devoted to the ideas of a Cleveland dentist who, back in the 1930s, became concerned about the poor teeth and bone structure of his younger patients, and other serious health problems in his adult ones.

"He had this brilliant idea: instead of just sitting in your own area trying to figure out what was wrong, get out in the world and see what other people were doing about it," Connie said. "So for the next ten years, he visited isolated cultures around the world—now, we're not talking Stone Age, just isolated from the industrialized world and its diet of sugar and white flour. He'd find people with perfect teeth, great bone structure, very, very few cavities. He would document what they ate and how they fixed things. These native peoples were pretty much on a low-carbohydrate diet, and if they ate grains, they were usually cultured, fermented in some way."

According to his book *Nutrition and Physical Degeneration*, Dr. Price found that even though the people he studied—Eskimos, Pacific Islanders, Australian aborigines, Swiss living in remote Alpine villages—differed widely in genetic characteristics and diet, their healthy diets had eleven factors in common. Generally speaking, these people avoided refined flour, white sugar, and processed foods, consumed animal proteins, and stayed away from vegetable oil in favor of animal fats.

"That book changed the way I looked at things," Connie said. "And you know, once you start asking questions, it's a slippery slope. Those questions lead to these conclusions, which set up new questions that lead to these conclusions. Conservative, liberal, or whatever, I think people who are starting to change their lifestyles and the way they eat are people who realize that you shouldn't believe everything you're told now, that you really should investigate it on your own."

I asked her how she and Mike got into farming. She said Mike became so fascinated by what the Hutchinses were doing with their farm and their family that he decided to leave his job as a math teacher to give it a try. As Connie was recounting the story, Mike walked in with Chris Bullok, a neighbor and fellow home-schooling organic-livestock farmer. As it happens, Chris, a former Dallas suburbanite, got into this agrarian lifestyle because he and his wife saw how much good it was doing for the Hale family, and wanted that for themselves and their kids.

"It's been a real blessing to have the Hales here," he said. "They have a wealth of experience to tell us what happens next."

This is how it happens, I thought. This is how you build community. Not by reading it in a book, or buying it off the shelf, but by one family teaching another, and celebrating their shared experiences and beliefs.

Mike said that a few years earlier he and Connie got to thinking seriously about agriculture. The more they learned about industrial farming, the more they wanted to separate from it. They'd read a lot about organic farming, and finally realized the only thing separating themselves from this lifestyle was their own free will. Now that they'd been in it for a while, they found it had deepened their religious faith ("When there's no rain, you get real serious about prayer," Connie joked), as well as given them an opportunity to evangelize, so to speak, for the agrarian lifestyle with their customers.

"We invite our customers out to the farm. We like them to see what we're doing, to have an understanding of what we're trying to do, and what we're doing for their tables, and what we've learned by separating ourselves from the industrial way of doing things," said Mike. "It's been a blessing to have cheerleaders who say yep, this is exactly what we need."

The Hales told me that they hoped the mad cow disease issue would make Americans think more seriously about where their meat comes from. Connie said most folks have blind confidence that what they purchase in the supermarket is going to be safe and good for them. Mike agreed.

"I think it's because government has become our god," he said. "We trust it to inspect our food, we trust it to educate our children. I'm not saying that government doesn't have a place in that, but beyond that, we need to take responsibility individually for our lives."

"Well, the government stepped in because the producer and the consumer no longer know each other," Connie said. "If you're getting it from the store, and not from the farmer down the way, how do you know that it came from an honest person who did everything he was supposed to do, safety-wise?"

We talked about how odd it is that the idea of raising and consuming your own meat, which used to be commonplace within living memory, is now so exotic. When I was a small boy, I was so horrified by the thought that we would consume the chickens we raised in our yard that I refused to eat them. I thought they were contaminated — not like those pretty chickens we bought in the plastic sacks at the supermarket.

"There was a break in our parents' generation," Connie said. "I don't know when it came in, but convenience became a big thing. My mother would tell me that her mother would stand over a hot stove, stirring a pot of jam, sweating because there was no air-conditioning. My mother never taught me how to do that because why go to all that trouble when you can just go to the store and get it off the shelf?"

Connie grew up in a military family that got all its fruits and vegetables in cans from the commissary. When she married Mike, she had never eaten a fresh pear, and didn't know she was missing out. "There was so much lost to my generation," she said. "So now I'm almost frantic to learn as many of those traditional skills as I can so I can teach them to my children."

After spending a couple of hours listening to the Hales talk about how hard it is to explain their way of life to those who don't share their values, but how much pleasure they derive from it (not least of which is the satisfaction of knowing that they're being true to their religious, moral, and political values), I told Connie that her old-fashioned farm family were just about the most countercultural people I'd ever met.

"Countercultural? We haven't done anything the way anybody else does it for so long I just don't care," she said, with a hearty laugh.

Months later, a friend in New York e-mailed me to urge me to contact his friend Kathy O'Brien, whom he described as a Catholic conservative. "She's a nutritionist who works part-time for some crunchy-con group called the Weston A. Price Foundation," he said. Connie Hale's people! I had to call.

Kathy is a Montessori teacher by training, and still does that one day a week with homeschooled kids. She's also a nutritionist, and, when she's not tied up with Price Foundation duties, consults with individual clients. Her mission is to teach people how to incorporate Dr. Price's findings into their own diets, to eat the most nutrient-dense food they can.

"This is tradition. This is the wisdom that people from various cultures discerned over the years," Kathy explained. "We've left that behind with the introduction of modern processed foods, and because of that, this can sound pretty radical, so I go slowly, whatever steps they can take."

She said she's seeing a "tremendous turnaround" in clients who make even small dietary changes. For example, one woman who had had stomach pain while eating for twenty years was healed two weeks after introducing apple cider vinegar into her diet. The trick is to get people to slow down and *think* about food — and that's not such an easy thing these days.

"I have clients that tell me they just don't have time to eat, they're so busy. I'm shocked by that," Kathy says. "Our attitude toward food often reflects our attitude toward reality. If you're just watching TV shoving food in your mouth, that's more like an animal feeding than a human being eating. People need to realize that when they eat, there's more than just nourishing the body going on. When people go back to the traditional foods, their health and their outlook change dramatically."

I told her that if you talk like that around a lot of conservatives, you'll get dismissed out of hand as a politically correct food fetishist.

"I don't know why there's that reaction, but I do get it sometimes," she said. "It's one thing if you're talking about tofu burgers, but when people really start to understand what I'm talking about, they love it. They want to eat butter, they want to eat real eggs, they want to eat meat, and that's fine; that's what they're supposed to be eating. I use salt, but I use quality salt. I use sweetener, but I use maple syrup. But you know, I'm actually pleasantly surprised by how many conservatives I'm getting now."

I explained to Kathy how Julie and I had gotten into healthful organic eating by accident, because we are conservative Catholics, and that once we'd gotten over our pointless right-wing cultural prejudices, eating well and supporting small farms and the families who run them dovetailed perfectly with our conservatism. Yes, she said, if you think about it, it's hard to separate your cultural and religious conservatism from your grocery shopping list—though many people who consider themselves conservatives do that very thing all the time.

"These people say they're traditionalists, but they're not really acting on it. What does that mean in your day-to-day life? How are you implementing it?" Kathy said. "At one point, I thought maybe I was spending too much time thinking about food before I got into it as a career. But something struck me, a quote by Saint Francis de Sales, who said that we should treat everything we have as a gift from God, and that we are a gardener caring for the king's garden. That struck me so much, because what I'm talking about is the body as the temple of the Holy Spirit. I don't see how God could be pleased by the way so many of us eat. And that's what motivates me. It's stewardship of the body and of the earth. I just don't understand why people have a problem with that."

Oh, I do. Because it's difficult. Eric Brende spoke earlier about how technology is misused when it removes from us things that we'd be better off doing ourselves. That's what our agribusiness and processed-food industries do. It's hard to slow down and prepare food yourself. It's a chore to think about what you're eating, and where that food came from. Once you start pulling that thread, a whole lot of assumptions we use to conceal unpleasant realities begin to unravel. It's easier to let big business and the government do our thinking for us. Wendell Berry wrote, "The food industrialists have by now persuaded millions of consumers to prefer food that is already prepared. They will grow, deliver, and cook your food for you and (just like your mother) beg you to eat it. That they do not yet offer to insert it, prechewed, into your mouth is only because they have found no profitable way to do so. We may rest assured that they would be glad to find such a way. The ideal industrial food consumer would be strapped to a table with a tube running from the food factory directly into his or her stomach."

And when people object to this, right-wingers make fun of them as food faddists. I know, because I used to do it myself, as a self-defense mechanism, a technique for having to avoid doing the kind of thinking that might cause me to change my way of life.

Kathy sees the "superficiality" of American food culture, where cheap, quick, junky food dominates, a symbol of the American soul. "Our food is a sign of what we've lost in general. I think if we could start slowing down for food, and rebuilding the quality of our plates, we could start rebuilding what we've lost in our culture. As my boss says, culture starts in the kitchen, not in the opera house."

After talking to Kathy, I decided to check in with Joel Salatin, with whom I'd spoken a couple of years earlier, after he'd tangled with state regulators out at his successful Polyface Farm operation in Virginia's Shenandoah Mountains. Joel's been in the small-scale-sustainable farming vocation a long time. He's also a political and religious conservative. I asked him what he says to our fellow right-wingers who call what he and the Hales and the Hutchinses do "romantic," and who say it will never feed the world.

"The premise of that statement is based on false modeling," Joel told me. "One of the problems with conservatives is that we tend to be very Western in our thinking. Greco-Roman-linear-segmented-compartmentalized thinking. We in the conservative community love the scientific method, double-blind studies, that sort of thing, as opposed to the Eastern mind-set, which thinks more holistically, and more along the lines of 'we' than 'I.'"

You'll recall that that's what British economist E. F. Schumacher found when he went to the East to study Buddhism in 1950. He discovered that thinking of economic questions as distinct from human society, with all its variables, could result in greater material output, but at the cost of a greater harmony needed to sustain the happiness and well-being of the community.

Joel continued: "So what happens is the conservative mind, when it's looking for answers, does not have a method to plug in all the variables. You only find the answers to the questions you're asking, and when you're only asking questions of economics, or production, you're not going to find other answers."

Sounded pretty abstract to me. Could he explain?

"A good example of this is when I was on Pat Buchanan's radio talk show a few years ago," Joel said. "Clinton was in the White House, and he'd hired this new French chef. The conservative talk shows were all over this French chef because he'd said he was going to serve free-range chicken at the White House. So they looked around for a free-range chicken farmer, and found me, and Pat Buchanan put me on his radio show.

"He calls me up and says, Tell me about how you raise your chickens. I said, First thing, our chickens don't do drugs. He said, Well, why do they give them drugs in the industry? and I said, It's because it makes them grow faster. He cut me off and said, What could possibly be wrong with growing faster? I said, well, cancer is a growth, too."

I was starting to see Joel's point.

"Conservatives tend to ask how we can be more efficient, not how we can be more effective. You can be very efficient at the wrong thing," he told me. "The Eastern mind-set brings to the equation a whole individual, a whole-system approach, understanding that there's an equilibrium, a balance to be maintained. If you grow that chicken to four pounds in four weeks instead of eight weeks, there will be trade-offs. It's important to understand that when people have this notion that this kind of production model can't feed the world, they have this very myopic, unholistic, fragmented research that prejudices or jaundices their thinking. And so the question is asked at a prejudicial level."

Joel was telling me that looking only at crop yields and production numbers gives us a false picture of what's really happening. We're not seeing the hidden social and environmental costs of industrialized food production, which we're going to have to pay for down the line.

"People have got to understand the cost of the way we do things now," he said. "Look at the USDA subsidies. Look at the environmental cost of factory farming. A lot of the ecological cost of flooding is because all the chemical fertilizers have burned out the porosity of the soil, and the soil is not as spongy and resilient as before. One of the questions people like me ask is, Can this be done for five hundred more years? And the answer is no, it can't, and not only that, but we are beginning to do things that are completely outside the realm of any historical precedent, like genetic engineering. When you're a Christian like I am, it's very worrying."

As far as Joel is concerned, too many religious conservatives separate church from life. That is, they think all that's required to get to heaven is to hold correct doctrine. Joel says that religious truth should illuminate and inform every aspect of a believer's life. He brought up a well-known chicken magnate who has a reputation for being a conservative evangelical Christian.

"But his chicken-processing plants are consistently raided by immigration agents who find illegal aliens working there," Joel said. "The children of those illegals come in and clog the school systems. And so what happens is the taxpayers end up picking up the tab for the additional school buildings that have to be built because suddenly all the classroom space that was used for instruction is now used for English as a second language tutorials."

Joel listed several other serious social and moral problems resulting from the chicken tycoon's exploitation of illegal Mexican labor. "My point is that when I eat that brand of chicken, I am supporting all that. People don't see that. See, that's the disconnect. We wouldn't for a minute say, Let's go to the cheapest church in town; let's hire the cheapest preacher we can get. We wouldn't say, Let's go to the cheapest brain surgeon. But we're very happy to put on the lowest respect level and honor level the stewards of our food system and the stewards of our landscape."

We talked about the role of factory farming in the depopulation of rural America. Whole regions of the prairies and plains are emptying out of people whose ancestors farmed those fields from the pioneer days. Machines, in effect, have replaced them. Maybe you can look at this as mourning the loss of the carriage-making craft when the age of the automobile dawned: sad, perhaps, for the carriage maker and his family, but no big deal in the grand scheme of things. That's not the case with the loss of the agrarian way of life.

"You know what we're losing? Common sense," he says. "There is a wisdom that comes into a culture when many of its people have a direct connection to the land and to life, to the living cycles. I see many of the political agendas today as being a total failure to understand life, seasons, accountability, and the connections of life and people to our community. There's just no connection, and so there's no reason, there's no common sense. You can blame as many people on the right as on the left."

Now, look. I'm worried that you may feel admonished by all this talk of how greatly we have sinned and fallen short of the glory of a righteous T-bone and an immaculately conceived rutabaga. Enough with the long faces! Like Joel says about farming, if the crunchy-con attitude toward food is merely dutiful and not fun, nobody's going to want to do it. I am wholly persuaded by Corby Kummer's insight that the Slow Food movement is popular because of "its aim to celebrate and preserve rather than criticize and vanquish."

Time for a corrective. I hold in my hand a most extraordinary cookbook, a delirious 1967 tome called *The Supper of the Lamb*, much treasured by foodies and brought back into print a few years ago as part of the Modern Library's food series. Its author is an Episcopal priest, Robert Farrar Capon, an amateur chef whose cookery manual is an exuberant tribute to the sacramental vision at work and at play in the kitchen. Father Capon warns against the error of not taking the natural world, and specifically the food we eat, seriously enough—we've been talking about this here, and Father Capon's entire book stands as a rebuke to the plodding dullness of the materialist for whom an onion is just an onion—but also the error of taking it far too seriously.

"The world exists not for what it means, but for what it is," he wrote. ". . . It is a false piety that walks through creation looking only for lessons which can be applied somewhere else." For the person who sees the acts of growing and raising and cooking and eating *only* as moral acts, the simple pleasure of sopping the savory juices from a well-roasted chicken with a chunk of French bread becomes elusive; he has turned himself into a superstitious pagan fearful of raising the ire of the gods. In such a case, Father Capon warned, "religion devours life," and "creation becomes too meaningful to make love to."

In writing about wine, Father Capon chastised both snobs who value the thing as an end, and Puritans who would deny it on moral grounds. "We were made in the image of God. We were created to delight, as He does, in the resident goodness of creation. We were not made to sit around mumbling incantations and watching our insides to see what creation will do for us. . . . It was St. Thomas, again, who gave the most reasonable and relaxed of all the definitions of temperance. Wine, he said, could lawfully be drunk *utque ad hilaritatem*, to the point of cheerfulness. It is a happy example of the connection between sanctity and sanity."

These wise words from the good Father should serve as a guiding principle for conservative thought about the proper relation between our daily bread and our daily lives. We must follow what he calls "the thread of delight" along the narrow path between the spirit and the flesh. Few of us could stand to live in a world in which every bite of broccoli and every morsel of meat loaf bore the weight of humanity's fallenness. I am not fond of Puritanism, and that po-faced righteousness you so often find among employees of health-food stores that used to keep me from taking anything they had to say seriously. If taking the quality of one's food and its connection to the natural environment seriously turns one into this kind of tree-hugging teetotaler, then I want nothing to do with it. How marvelous it is to discover, then, that the "either/or" need not exist! The Slow Food mentality shows how one can be both deeply conservative with respect to life-giving traditions and fully alive to the sensual pleasure of good food.

In a perfect world, lawmakers would roll back the worst excesses of factory farming, change the agricultural regulatory scheme to give small farmers and producers a chance to compete fairly, and encourage through tax incentives the development of small-scale, locally based agriculture. But let's face facts: this is not likely to happen anytime soon. There is no real constituency (yet) for these proposals.

The good news is that we don't have to wait for the government to act to take responsibility ourselves for creating conditions for cleaner, healthier agriculture, simply by choosing to meditate on the way we eat — that is, considering the sacramentality of our food and food traditions — and choosing to spend our money and our efforts wisely. Let's embrace the Slow Food attitude, and emphasize what we conservatives are *for* rather than what we're against.

• We are *for* delighting in good food and culinary traditions, and because of that stand against the modern impulse to industrialize and blandify the production of our foodstuffs.

• We are *for* celebrating the pleasure of home cooking and the family table, and because of that, we reject the haste and efficiency represented by our processed, packaged, fast-food, eat-on-the-go society as destructive of the kinds of traditions that sustain a family culture worth preserving.

• We are *for* an ethic of stewardship toward our bodies and land given over to growing and raising the things that nourish them. Thus, we exercise prudence in choosing the things we eat and drink, and act with an awareness of how those choices affect the broader human economy.

• We are *for* agrarian life as a positive, and affirm those who stake their claims there and pursue the vocation of the farmer; therefore, we try to support that way of life and the families devoted to it with our friendship and our trade.

What does this mean in practical terms?

I'm not about to move out to the country and raise chickens, and neither are most of you. But urbanites and suburbanites like me and thee can make it possible for others to do so by buying their meat, eggs, vegetables, and dairy products either directly from the farm, through CSA co-ops, or at farmer's markets.

One benefit of doing so, and encouraging our friends to follow suit, is the renewal of the land and the lives of the people who live there. The Weston A. Price Foundation, through its Internet site (westonaprice.org) and local chapters, guides customers to small organic farms in their region (local Slow Food groups do this, too). Kathy O'Brien told me she knows a farmer whose land was so toxic from overuse of chemicals that his family was getting sick. "His soil was ruined, and his family's health was being ruined. That's what motivated him to get back to a natural farm. When he started farming that way, the Price Foundation made sure the word got out about him. In the end, he told us we saved his farm because we connected people to it."

We can also work to incorporate more organic produce and clean meat into our diets. To be sure, this costs more money. I wince when I have to pay almost twice the price for a roasting hen from Texas Supernatural Meats as I do for the same chicken from the supermarket. But that price difference is about the cost of a single venti latte from Starbucks. If you do an inventory of where the family's food budget goes, it's not hard to find ways you can save by cutting out unnecessary and even unhealthful food (chips and soda, for example), and apply that money toward buying ethically and nutritionally superior food. And there are ways to save money in other areas of the household economy — the entertainment budget, for example — to free up funds to purchase healthier food. It's all a matter of priorities.

"If anyone says that being crunchy is fine for those who can afford it, you have my guarantee that they have no idea what they are talking about," said Meredith Robbins, an expatriate crunchy-con American living in London and working in the financial sector. She e-mailed to say that she has been bulk-buying organic meat and produce for years, and keeping records of how much cash she spent on food before she went organic, and how much she's spent since.

"I also have checked statistics on how much the average person in the UK spends on food per year. I can assure you that even with organic meat (though not steaks every night), this style of buying, cooking, and eating is *much* less expensive than the typical UK diet," number-crunching Meredith wrote. "Current per person expenditure is about £18 per person per week, or just under £1000 per year (and most of the people I know spend far more — I see my coworkers spending £4–5 on lunch alone most days). On my plan, I consider £1000 a year *ample* for excellent organic food for *two adults,* and could probably still manage three good meals a day (though I'd cut out the meat) on £250 per person per year."

Generally, it takes about two American dollars to make one British pound, so you do the math. The point Meredith makes is that with careful planning that includes bulk co-op buying, a thrifty family can make this lifestyle work.

It's also the case that we could eat smaller portions. I told Julie that I lamented how much organically raised meat cost, and wondered how we could afford to eat it exclusively. Then I realized that at any given meal, I ate much more meat than was necessary. As has been documented, over the past twenty years, we Americans have gotten used to supersized portions in all our meals, and it's simply not necessary. If I ate within reason, an organic pot roast would last twice as long as the supermarket pot roast I eat now.

As for setting priorities, if we would make the family dinner the most important thing the family does all day, and cut out sports and other activities that interfere with it, we could return a sense of order and peace to our homes, and resacralize the family meal. Dinner at night would be an opportunity for communion, not merely a pit stop for refueling before family members speed off to do their own thing.

And if mothers and fathers would seek to learn the joy of cooking and pass it on to their children by involving them in the preparation of family meals, our whole attitude toward nutrition and culinary tradition would change. Parents should strictly limit the exposure their children have to advertising. Whenever I think that maybe I'm being too strict about this with my boys, I think about how my unrestricted diet of commercials pushing Dolly Madison snack cakes, McDonald's, Oreos, and other junk foods screwed up my young mind.

I'm not prepared to claim that what the Hales, the Hutchinses, and the Salatins are doing would be feasible if all livestock farmers did the same. That may in fact be the case, but I'd like to see more evidence. That said, there is absolutely no reason for anybody to withhold support for these worthwhile projects, which do so much good. We're never going to know how this model would work on a large scale if we don't encourage its growth by committing our consumer dollar to it.

We can also encourage legislators to change state and federal regulations to make it easier for businesses like this to prosper. As a libertarian, Joel Salatin doesn't want a handout from the government;

he just wants the regulatory climate to change to "free up the entrepreneurial spirit in the countryside." Some conservatives will grow weary of life in the city and suburbs, and will want to light out for the country to make a go of the farm life. Just as the Hutchinses helped the Hales get started, and the Hales helped the Bulloks, crunchy-con farmers stand ready to assist and encourage those twenty-first-century pioneers who want to repopulate America's rural regions, and pursue a simpler life, one closer to the timeless rhythms of nature and traditional wisdom.

How great it would be if state, local, and federal authorities would provide incentives to make possible this kind of useful pilgrimage to the past! As one rural-affairs expert told the *New York Times,* "We give a lot of tax breaks and direct payments to big agriculture companies that don't do much for the local economy, but rarely do we give anything to the little guy trying to start a business and stay in town."

Does this sound romantic and utopian? Maybe. But the romance is part of the allure of it, and besides, what's the alternative? How long do you think we can keep living as we do, destroying country life, rural traditions, and the countryside to produce mountains of processed food that makes us less healthy, and letting lay fallow the sacred trust we've been given by our forebears? Care for this trust obliges all of us, but conservatives, because we profess a particular commitment to upholding tradition, are especially responsible for stewardship of the land and its cultural legacy. If we live as if we have no duty to the land and the agrarian traditions of the people who live there, then we ought to be ashamed to call ourselves conservatives. We are no more than market-mad consumers who vote Republican, and whose commitment to conservative ideals ends the moment it costs us something.

What are food and agricultural and culinary traditions for, anyway? You can't answer that question properly without first asking, what are people for? Answer that one, and the first question answers itself.

Besides, the benefits of the crunchy-con lifestyle are not all abstract. Consider this striking e-mail testimony I received from Jeff Johnson, a third-year Princeton graduate student and religious conservative from the Lone Star State, who testified to how much his own life had changed by going crunchy at the behest of his left-liberal colleagues.

"I'm from dry, dusty west Texas, and interacting with so-called 'liberal' communities has made me realize that in so many ways, these liberals are conserving what's most important about life," Jeff wrote. He went on to explain how his travels had taught him that living in walkable green places, turning off the television, and "opting out of mass culture and making time for conversation and community" were superior lifestyle values.

"My wife and my son and I are better for all this, and I think that's fundamentally conservative, and yet all the things I've just mentioned (with the exception of perhaps opting out of TV culture) are viewed with highly raised eyebrows where I'm originally from. A stupid label immediately discounts what I have to say, which shuts down conversation and thought and progress."

Jeff went on: "All my life I struggled with weight and image and health, and was morbidly obese before moving to Princeton. Here, I've stopped eating processed foods, gone organic and natural, started using my feet (thanks to pedestrian planning), started taking walks by the canal, and lost over 130 pounds. I've added years to my life, I've simplified, and I've put at the center of my life the things that really are of greatest value both in this world and the world to come. I think that's fundamentally conservative, and yet the greatest allies in my struggle have been lefties. What I get from most of my 'conservative' friends is an emphasis on utility. The most common questions about my graduate studies in Classics: 'What can you do with that?' or 'What good is that?'

"A lot of people," Jeff concluded, "myself included, in ways I'm blind to I'm sure, need to reconsider the disconnect between what they say they value and the lives they actually lead. And to reconsider where the arguments of their philosophical and spiritual forefathers actually lead on a practical, day-to-day basis."

Hear, hear! Raise a glass of microbrewed lager to Jeff Johnson, a crunchy conservative who understands the connection between eating well and doing good.

CHAPTER FOUR

Home

. . . a house that I love; with a reasonable love I think: for though my words may give you no idea of any special charm about it, yet I assure you that the charm is there; so much has the old house grown up out of the soil and the lives of those that lived on it; . . . some thin thread of tradition, a half-anxious sense of the delight of meadow and acre and wood and river; a certain amount (not too much let us hope) of common sense, a liking for making materials serve one's turn, and perhaps at bottom some little grain of sentiment. This I think was what went to the making of the old house . . .

—WILLIAM MORRIS, "GOSSIP ABOUT AN
OLD HOUSE ON THE UPPER THAMES"

MY FAVORITE HOUSE in the world is called Weyanoke. A funky antebellum mansion on a plantation near my southern Louisiana hometown, it has been in my friend Nora's family since it was built. Weyanoke is not the stuff of which moonlight and magnolia fantasies are made, but rather a fairly plain two-story wooden structure with cracked-plaster walls, unpolished plank flooring, and an air of shabby grandeur that captivated me from the moment I first saw it as a teenager. Back in the day, Nora had wonderful parties there, in which an intimate carnival of food and wine, music and mirth would trail long into the contented Louisiana nights. I came to associate Weyanoke with my ideal of Home: a place of grace, joy, fellowship, and belonging that was also old, simple, comfortable, and charming to its foundations.

For many years, my idea of perfect happiness was the feeling I got when I rounded the bend in the long gravel driveway and saw Weyanoke at the far end of the oak alley. I knew that in moments those dear old timbers would embrace me and work their everyday magic, making me feel at home in the world and enchanted by goodness and harmony. Of course, I could never hope to own a place like Weyanoke, but I always hoped that when I bought my first house, there would be something of Weyanoke in it.

Why does Weyanoke make me feel that way? Why has every friend I've ever taken to visit the house shared those emotions, even though there are many plantation houses throughout southern Louisiana that are far more elegant, richly appointed, and structurally interesting? (Weyanoke will never appear in glossy antiques or architecture magazines.) Aside from the generosity of its mistress, what people respond to in Weyanoke is the deep feeling of homeyness it conveys. To be there, even as a stranger, is to know that this weary but big-shouldered country house under a canopy of live oaks is the kind of house we secretly long for: a shelter that harmonizes perfectly with its natural environment, and is as beautiful and therefore pleasing to be in as it is useful. Folks are so startled to encounter that kind of thing these days that to see it breaks upon one like an epiphany.

You're thinking, Well, sure, anyone would be dazzled by a plantation house, even a shabby-genteel one, so what's your point? The thing is, I've discerned this quality in much smaller and more modest older houses — houses that were built before the Second World War, that is. Drive through a historic district of any town or city of reasonable size, and even if the houses there are down-at-the-heels from neglect, you will pick out beauty and harmony there that you cannot find in newer subdivisions, with houses that cost vastly more. Even shotgun houses built for the working class have more charm and dignity than contemporary McMansions. Long after my late grandmother's drafty 1930s cabin has fallen to dust, I will remember that simple house more fondly than the much sturdier and roomier redbrick 1960s house in which I was raised. Why is that? If the Mississippi River rose in my hometown and washed away all the houses, aside from the human aspect of the loss, history would mourn only a small fraction of the structures lost in the disaster — and nothing built after 1945. How come?

De gustibus non disputandum — you can't argue taste. Whenever I clash with conservatives about home architecture, and complain about the ugliness of sprawl, I often get called an "elitist" (which is a funny epithet for a conservative to deploy, but never mind), and told that these are merely questions of taste. Yet I doubt these folks would say there is no important difference between hearing Bach sung in a Baroque jewel box church in Germany, and some happy-clappy 1970s hymn burbled in one of those crapped-out Our Lady of Pizza Hut churches slapped together in suburbia during the Nixon presidency. Aesthetics matter, and anyone who has been to the beautiful cities and towns of Europe, and has seen how older buildings of greatly differing styles and ambitions exist harmoniously with each other and their surroundings, knows it.

Jonathan Hale knows what ails us architecturally, and that the cure lies in returning to the wisdom of the past, and submitting to its laws — not in indulging the libertarian homebuilding fantasies of Republican suburbanites. In his 1994 book *The Old Way of Seeing* — which, along with James Howard Kunstler's 1993 jeremiad *The Geography of Nowhere*, deserves a prominent place in the crunchy-con library — architect Hale argued that the rampant charmlessness of our built environment is a function of America's loss of historical memory:

Everywhere in the buildings of the past is relationship among parts: contrast, tension, balance. Compare the buildings of today and we see no such patterns. We see fragmentation, mismatched systems, uncertainty. This disintegration tends to produce not ugliness so much as dullness, and an impression of unreality.

The principles that underlie harmonious design are found everywhere and in every time before our own; they are the historical norm. They are the same in the eighteenth-century houses of Newburyport, Massachusetts, in the buildings of old Japan, in Italian villages, in the cathedrals of France, in the ruins of the Yucatan. The same kinds of patterns organize Frank Lloyd Wright's Robie House and Michelangelo's Capitol.

If a building makes us light up, it is not because we see order; any row of file cabinets is ordered. What we recognize and love is the same kind of pattern we see in every face, the patterns of our own life form. The same principles apply to buildings that apply to mollusks, birds, or trees. Architecture is the play of patterns derived from nature and ourselves.

As Hale shows, successful buildings from various historical eras and widely divergent cultures appeal to us for the same reasons we find certain trees, animals, and faces pleasing to look at: their forms all speak the same "pattern language"—a term coined by Christopher Alexander—of scale, line, and proportion. You don't have to understand what's being said with the pattern language to appreciate its effect. What Alexander was referring to with the term "pattern language" is the way certain combinations and repetitions of particular aesthetic forms cohere to form a harmonious and meaningful whole, in the same way a certain combination and repetition of spoken syllables creates poetry, while another amounts to gibberish. Why certain patterns strike humans as beautiful is a mystery, but Alexander observes that it seems to be embedded in our nature, and anyway, it's no less true for being mysterious. As Hale demonstrates, you can build any number of aesthetically pleasing structures using that pattern language, from humble cottages to grand manor houses, from the Chartres cathedral to a Frank Lloyd Wright prairie house. But if you ignore the secret language of patterns known even to the ancients, what results is ugliness, boredom, and dispiritedness—even if the layman lacks the words and the understanding to explain why.

Unless conservatives are willing to say that the childish scrawls of a Jean-Michel Basquiat are no more or no less significant than the works of a Titian or a Vermeer, then they have to admit that there is a reason why we idealize older, white-picket-fence neighborhoods, even as we live today in houses and apartments that are significantly larger, in some cases, and incomparably more comfortable. Have we given up on the idea that we could live in beautiful houses, too, no matter how limited our means? Yes, says Hale. "Around 1830," he writes, "people began to believe, as both John Stuart Mill and Tocqueville wrote, that magic was not to be expected in everyday life, that dullness was the price of comfort, or of social equality. I do not see it that way."

Nor do I, though in my case it's an act of Romantic defiance, not an informed judgment. Maybe I'm just acutely sensitive to my surroundings, but the most depressed I've ever been was when I lived in the bland bourgeois sprawlsville of Fort Lauderdale, and the most joyful was the three years I lived with my wife, Julie, and son Matthew among the nineteenth-century brownstones in Cobble Hill, Brooklyn. Yet unless we won the lottery, there was no way we were ever going to be able to afford a place of our own in our beloved Brooklyn, or in any other pleasant neighborhood in New York City.

That didn't bother us when we first moved to the city after returning from our honeymoon, and living paycheck to paycheck paying exorbitant rent for a tiny Manhattan third-floor walk-up. When we had Matthew, we moved to a slightly bigger place in Brooklyn, but a year or two later, when Matthew became mobile, our cozy Cobble Hill apartment seemed awfully crowded. Thus did the dream of home ownership take deeper hold of our imaginations.

(I know, I sound like a commercial for a mortgage broker, but if you're like me, you'll find as you grow older a strange new respect for the middle-class clichés you spent your smart-ass youth making fun of. Knife. Fork. Crow.)

For us, the longing for a home of our own was more than a yen for more space. We discovered a growing desire to be rooted to the ground, to quit living as if anything might happen to blow us here or there. What seemed like freedom when we first married — the idea that as renters we could pick up and leave whenever we wanted, as fate or whimsy dictated — came to feel like a burden, and the notion of being fixed to a place by commitment struck us as liberating. We didn't see the paradox sneaking up on us, but when it did, we had no real choice but to leave New York for a place where we could afford to buy a house.

This was one of the reasons we moved to Dallas in the spring of 2003. We chose to rent for a year, and to spend that time thinking about what kind of house, and what kind of neighborhood, we wanted to live in. Our rental was a small, modest redbrick job in a late-1950s neighborhood on the east side of town. This was not the kind of place we wanted to end up in. The house was comfortable but charm-free, a nothing-special midcentury cottage which I am appalled to tell you would sell for over $200,000 if it were to go on the market. Most of the houses on the street were nicer, but essentially the same thing. Our new neighbors were wonderful, friendly, interesting folks, but you'd only really see them if you were out mowing grass at the same time, or going to and from your cars parked on the street. Going from the liveliness, color, and variety of sidewalk neighborhood life in Brooklyn to the aridity and bareness of our new street, with its parallel rows of nondescript houses, was hard to get used to. Where did all the people go? Why isn't there anything worth looking at here?

And yet that neighborhood is not so different from the kind of suburban and exurban neighborhoods most Americans live in. Even if the houses are newer and bigger — the fabled McMansion in the newer exurbs — there is a certain sameness, an inhuman quality that makes them seem like houses, but not homes. You walk around a place like Cobble Hill, Brooklyn, and the nineteenth-century town houses remind you of convivial folks standing around a pleasant Saturday afternoon garden party. You walk down our old street and you think about expressionless salarymen queuing up to catch the bus on Monday morning.

Why is that? For one, there are no front porches on those houses, and therefore nothing to encourage neighbors to open themselves to street life. Those houses turn their backs to their neighbors. For another, the utilitarian sameness in row after row speaks a pattern language of monotony. There are no parks, no playgrounds, no common areas. These stolid brick houses don't aspire to be more than shelter. There is no ornamentation, none of the human touches that endear us to older, traditional architecture, no matter what the style. To drive down our old street, or almost any residential street built in Dallas after the Second World War, is to encounter a monosyllabic pattern language that says the same word, over and over: *efficiency.*

To understand why our modern residential landscape leaves so many of us with a vacant feeling, it's useful to see our houses and neighborhoods in the way I've come to think of as sacramental. What ideals do they convey in their physical reality? How do these habitats make those who live in them feel? What kind of life is possible here? What does living in such places teach its residents? How does it shape their character and outlook?

These aren't silly questions, or the kinds of things that only the well-off can afford to think about. Your typical conservative will scoff at them defensively, but he can only dismiss these questions if he is determined to ignore human nature, and the way the built environment both expresses humanity's deepest longings and aspirations, and the way it shapes them.

Thought experiment: You are standing at mass in the great Gothic cathedral at Chartres, beneath the vast symphonic complexity of the building's soaring arches; now you are standing at the same ceremony inside an equally vast modern American suburban megachurch, which looks like an expensively built gymnasium or theater. Theologically, the ceremony has precisely the same meaning. But in which place do you feel closer to God, more aware of the holiness of existence? From which of these churches are you likely to emerge with a glow of exaltation? If a terrorist with a truck bomb forced you to choose which of these structures you'd rather see destroyed, would it make a difference to you? Why?

Granted, this is an extreme example, but the same principle applies to our houses. The way they look, and the way we build them, matters. We have been trained to think that beauty is a luxury; consequently, most Americans now live in places that they find hard to love, and that make ordinary human community difficult. I'm thinking of a story my friend David, who lives in Washington, D.C., once told me about a conversation he overheard one day at work, between two older African-American women who were surprised to run into each other. The women had been neighbors in a supposedly run-down neighborhood in the District, one that had been marked in the 1960s for expensive "urban renewal." The government bought the residents out, bulldozed their houses, and built—ta-daah!—housing projects. You can imagine how well that turned out.

David said that listening to those women talk about what they had known in their old neighborhood, for all its faults, was to understand what spiritual violence had been done to those people in the name of progress. A complex web of human relations that had been spun by generations of neighbors was brushed away by the benevolent hand of the state. Those folks who remained were warehoused in giant concrete boxes that they did not care for because, well, who in their right mind would care for something so dehumanizing? The community collapsed.

Now, the government is not forcing suburbanites and exurbanites to choose to live in sterile houses and neighborhoods, but the fact that we beggar and do violence to ourselves by the places in which we choose to live hardly makes it right, or healthy.

Our old street is an example of what the prophetic crank James Howard Kunstler meant by "the geography of nowhere." Kunstler is a ferocious critic of the man-made environment in contemporary America, which he believes "has ceased to be a credible human habitat." He contended that since about 1945, we've been building neighborhoods not to suit authentic human needs for beauty and community, but to move product as cheaply and quickly as possible. For reasons of expedience and efficiency, Kunstler argued, Americans cut themselves off from architectural tradition, a tradition rooted in the same ancient wisdom about pattern language and its effects on the human psyche that Jonathan Hale cites. We began to build houses and neighborhoods and cities that have no connection to the past or the future, and that ultimately are not worth caring about. Our built landscape, Kunstler has written, "ends up diminishing us spiritually, impoverishing us socially, and degrading the aggregate set of cultural patterns that we call civilization."

"This is the price that we pay for ignoring our own psychology and millenniums of tradition that proceeded from it in the form of practical wisdom," he wrote. "I daresay many Americans don't care what their own houses or their neighbors' houses look like. We chalk this off to good old American pragmatism, or patriotic individualism, but the consequences are rather serious: a world outside the confining walls of the home that nobody cares about, a country made up of places that are not worth caring about, and a nation that is not worth defending."

That's harsher than I would have put it, but his point is

essentially sound. It is supremely ironic that the chief defenders of a status quo that violates tradition so radically are . . . conservatives.

Julie and I knew that the thing that we had to keep at the front of our minds when choosing to buy a house, no matter what the style, was that it had to be a place for which we wouldn't begrudge writing thirty years' worth of mortgage checks, if it came to that. The kind of house I'd be comforted to walk into after getting out of my car after a hard day of work. A house we didn't just tolerate as a necessary evil, but cared for, even loved, as a blessing. A house that, however modest, felt like Weyanoke.

But in a city where most everywhere is like our old street, more or less, what choice did we have? We couldn't even have afforded to buy the vanilla rental house we were living in! By spring of 2004, we'd had our second child, our lease was almost up, and it was time to find our dream house. I prepared myself to reconcile with stark reality, assuming we would have to move to one of the newer suburbs simply to afford a reasonably decent place.

All those snotty things I'd once said about the suburbs came back to me, but now, as a father of two young boys trying to raise a family on one salary, I understood why people chose to live there. I thought we were headed there, too, and among other gloom-inducers, I dreaded the long commute to my downtown office. And I had come to despair that for the sake of comfort and affordability, we would have to make our peace with suburbia.

We had one advantage, though, that might keep us in the city proper: as homeschooling parents, we weren't going to have to use the city's dreary public schools. That gave us the freedom to consider options that many middle-class families cannot. We were able to think about living in gentrifying neighborhoods overlooked by families like ours because of the poor school situation.

Which is how Julie found herself one day standing next to a FOR SALE sign outside a little wooden cottage on a small street in Junius Heights, an old neighborhood dating back to the first two decades of the twentieth century. In 1914, when the bungalow was built, Junius Heights was a suburb at the end of the streetcar line. But the area fell into decrepitude as the century wore on, until adventurous middle-class folks who loved the mature trees and the architecture began moving in and gentrifying it. It's no longer what they call a "transitional" neighborhood, but Junius Heights is still pretty funky.

Julie called me at work about an hour before I knocked off. "You've got to come see this place," she said. "I think I've found our house." When I walked in later that evening after a short twelve-minute drive from the newspaper, I knew my wife had found our hip-pocket Weyanoke.

The beauty of the little wooden house is its elegant simplicity. It is not much bigger than the redbrick rental house, but the effect is startlingly different. This is a house with dignity and humanity. It starts from the sidewalk, looking at the facade, at the low-pitched roof, the wide-eyed eaves, the brick chimney, and the square-columned porch. A porch to sit on! Even if porch-sitting isn't one's idea of a good time, the presence of a porch softens the appearance of a house, offering a transition between the street and the living room. Rather than having its back turned to its neighbors, the house with a porch welcomes them. The comforting psychological effect is palpable. Drive down a street of houses that have porches, and you get the sense that sociable people live here.

This only occurred to me later, when I was analyzing why I'd fallen in love with the little bungalow, and why it made me think that it was the kind of place a hobbit would be tickled to call his own. I'm sure Jonathan Hale could explain in thirty seconds why this house enchanted me at first sight. You see a small front porch, large vertical windows, two smaller windows looking out from an upstairs bedroom above the front eaves. There is nothing special about this plainspoken house, yet because of its arrangement of architectural patterns, there is music in the movement of its lines.

As I walked through the front door directly into the living room, a small hearth on the far wall caught my eye. I grew up in a house with a fireplace, and cherish memories of late nights as a kid with my sock feet up on the hearth, watching the cherry-red glow of the embers fade away, and feeling sheltered and serene. Daddy would get up in the morning before us kids, and have a blaze roaring when we padded up the hall to have our hot-buttered honeybuns for breakfast. There is something about a fireplace that to me bespeaks fatherly providence and contented domesticity. And here was a hearth at the center of this house's living room! This place had promise.

The living room opened into a dining room, and both rooms were lined with large windows opening onto leafy vistas. I noticed that this street was significantly narrower than the one we lived on at the time; you could call out from your front porch to the neighbors across the way sitting on their front porches without raising your voice much. You can't do that on most suburban streets: the houses don't have front porches in the first place, and if they did, they're set too far back from the street. Peering through the living-room windows taking measure of the neighborhood, I noticed that people actually used the sidewalks here. Hmm.

The bedrooms were sunny, thanks to the large windows, and the rear bedroom looked out onto a lovely backyard in which a handsome wooden fence enclosed a fig tree, a peach tree, a slipper magnolia, a redbud, a dogwood, a mulberry tree, rosebushes, and wisteria vines in blossom. There was a potential office for me, and a spare bedroom upstairs that the previous owner had built out of the attic.

"What do you think?" Julie asked.

What could I say? I loved it. The house was small, to be sure, but big enough for our needs. It seemed sturdy. Besides, we had been looking at more spacious, modern houses, but none of them had the character this old house did. And the price was right: more than $20,000 less than the least expensive modern house we'd seen (in a dispiriting subdivision), and with no major repairs needed, either. I didn't want to betray my excitement to my wife, who was clearly swooning over the place, so I simply said, "This might work. We'll see."

Our real-estate agent, Julie's mom, said the house was listed as a "Craftsman bungalow," as most of the houses in the neighborhood were. This meant nothing to me, but I was curious as to why a house as simple as that one struck me as the kind of place I'd love to call home. So, one night, I Googled "Craftsman bungalow," and discovered what I've come to think of as the ideal architectural and design expression of crunchy-con principles: the Arts and Crafts Movement.

I should probably tell you now that the founder of the movement, William Morris, was a revolutionary socialist. Do not panic. As you'll see, this fact only goes to show how confining contemporary labels are in discussing ideas.

Morris was born in 1834 to a comfortable middle-class family in Victorian England. He grew up in a time of rapid industrialization, globalization of trade, and the unmatched prosperity they brought. London's Great Exhibition of 1851 showcased the imperial power and commercial splendor that made Great Britain the most powerful nation on earth. Morris biographer Stephen Coote showed the confidence of the nation's leaders when he quoted from a speech Prince Albert, husband of Queen Victoria, gave to a group of merchants and bankers at the time.

Nobody who has paid any attention to the peculiar features of the present era will doubt for a moment that we are living at a period of most wonderful transition, which tends rapidly to accomplish that great end to which, indeed, all history points — the realization of the unity of mankind. . . . The distances which separate the different nations and parts of the globe are rapidly vanishing before the achievements of modern invention, and we can traverse them with incredible ease. . . . Thought is communicated with the rapidity and even the power of lightning. . . . The products of all quarters of the globe are placed at our disposal, and we have only to choose which is the best and the cheapest for our purposes, and the powers of production are entrusted to the stimulus of competition and capital. So man is approaching a more complete fulfillment of that great and sacred mission he has to perform in this world.

Better living—indeed, morally improved living—through technology and consumerism. This principle is what Morris's life's work was a reaction against. If the prince's words sound similar to a speech given by one of our recent American presidents, you begin to see where the radical socialist and the crunchy conservative have surprisingly similar interests at heart.

The influential critic John Ruskin helped lead the intellectual and artistic resistance to the Industrial Revolution. He claimed that the economic and technological innovations making England rich came at the cost of her soul. Industrial capitalism was turning workers into cogs, and debasing the soul of man by treating people as mere consumers. The price paid for this machine-based progress was a loss of the human in everyday life. Ruskin and those Romantics who followed in his footsteps were to idealize the Middle Ages, with its guilds and artisans and Gothic churches soaring with spiritual grandeur, as a golden age of human happiness, and to exalt the natural world in counterpoint to the smoke-and-grime-filled cities.

In 1856, Morris moved to London to take up the study of painting under Dante Gabriel Rossetti. He couldn't find decent furniture for his flat, because the economy of mass production turned out wagonloads of cheap, gaudy crap. A disgusted Morris decided he could do a better job himself, and built a "settle," a kind of medieval sofa, and a heavy, handcrafted table and chairs.

Well, Morris had a knack for this sort of thing, and started a successful design studio in which he put into action his belief that furnishings and interiors should avoid vulgar ostentation, and be simple, handmade, and in accord with nature. As a committed socialist, Morris believed that the lives of ordinary people could and should be made more beautiful and dignified through a revival of traditional handicrafts and decorative arts. For Morris and those who followed him, their designs reflected a moral vision, one that they hoped their houses and furnishings would instill in those who lived in and among them. Their vision was that a society whose humanity had been deformed and degraded by industrialism and mass capitalism could be reformed starting in the home, where sturdy virtues that sustain families and communities against the forces of fragmentation and alienation could be lived and taught. As C. F. A. Voysey, a prominent late-nineteenth-century English architect, put it, "Simplicity, sincerity, repose, directness and frankness are moral qualities as essential to good architecture as to good men."

The problem was, all this robust, back-to-basics simplicity cost a lot of money because of the intense and time-consuming labor required to honor the handmade purity of the Arts and Crafts vision. If the goal of the movement to bring good design to the masses was to be realized, it would have to be by adapting it to modern methods of production. Fortunately, the practical Americans who took up Arts and Crafts in the late nineteenth century didn't adapt the "handmade" dogma. Gustav Stickley, a furniture maker who became one of the leading lights of American Arts and Crafts, published a magazine called the *Craftsman* to publicize his ideas, and called the houses he designed "Craftsman homes." Though there were other bungalow designers of note, particularly California's famous Greene brothers, Stickley's description of the moral foundations of bungalow houses speaks for them all: "We have planned houses from the first that are based on the big fundamental principles of honesty, simplicity, and usefulness — the kind of houses that children will rejoice all their lives to remember as 'home,' and that give a sense of peace and comfort to the tired men who go back to them when the day's work is done. Because we believe that the healthiest and happiest life is that which maintains the closest relationship with out-of-doors, we have planned our houses with outdoor living rooms, dining rooms, and sleeping rooms and many windows to let in plenty of air and sunlight."

The classic expression of the Arts and Crafts house was the bungalow, an inexpensive one-story house that became a suburban standard for many middle-class families from around 1905 through 1930. You could even mail-order them from Sears, Roebuck and other companies. Though there was considerable regional variation in the bungalow style, the typical bungalow featured porches and large windows to give the homeowners a greater connection with nature, a fireplace as the metaphorical center of the house, rooms that flowed comfortably together, and a garden out back.

It turns out that the Junius Heights bungalow neighborhood had been built in the early twentieth century for the clerks in nearby factories. The managers lived a few blocks over, in houses four and five times larger, and the owners lived a bit farther away, in grand mansions. What's compelling about this is to learn that the little house we'd fallen for was standard lower-middle-class housing a century ago. It stood as a plainspoken rebuke to the idea I had growing up that loveliness and grace are architectural qualities only well-off homeowners can aspire to. Why is it that men a century ago knew how to design and build inexpensive but attractive housing like this for the working and middle classes, but today, despite all our advances, this knowledge has evaporated? Why is it that nobody seems to care?

I was beginning to understand now why the humble wooden bungalow in Junius Heights struck me as so beautiful and charming, far more so than much larger modern houses that we had considered. I could see raising a family there, and being proud and happy to live in that house. Moreover, I had taken to driving through the neighborhood, and I was delighted to discover that this entire gentrified district was filled with rehabbed bungalows in a variety of styles. No wonder residents walked around a lot here; the neighborhood was cheerful and inspiring. These were houses worth caring about. This was a neighborhood worth coming home to, and worth fighting for.

Houston lawyer Bill Davidson, one of a gaggle of Arts and Crafts–loving crunchy cons, understands. He lives in a bungalow in an area of town called the Heights, which was the first suburb to be annexed by the city, back in 1920. "We've got a whole lot of the Birkenstock crowd living here, liberal Democrat-type people," Bill says. "But we've also got a lot of conservatives who like the small-town atmosphere that you get with sidewalks and houses close together. You don't get that in the suburbs."

Bill and his then-wife bought their three-bedroom, one-bath brick bungalow in 1990, after driving through the neighborhood and falling in love with its front porches, mature trees, and foot traffic on the sidewalks. They bought the place for $90,000 from a retired schoolteacher who had been there for fifty years, and who had last renovated it after the Second World War.

"I like the high ceilings, the wood floors, and the airiness. It's like the house is made for moving around in, instead of having little corners, like suburban houses," Bill said. "My parents couldn't understand why we didn't get a house twice that size with more bathrooms. As a matter of fact, we looked at those kinds of houses in suburbs with good schools. We liked the feeling of this neighborhood better. The fact that the houses had porches meant people were outside, even in Texas in the summer. The funny thing at the time was that I was working in the suburbs, so I was commuting against traffic.

"The other thing that I liked was that my kids were going to school with people who were different from them," he added. "My little blond son had friends named Juan and Carlos whose parents might not speak English. I liked the fact that getting to the cultural stuff downtown—plays, the symphony—was easy. When you're in the suburbs, getting into that is a hassle."

Bill said that the quality of his bungalow's construction makes it stand out by comparison to many more expensive suburban houses. "Where we were living before was a center for McMansions and teardowns. We were watching them being built, and my then-father-in-law, a retired chief engineer with NASA, would walk over there with me to look at them. He'd point out how the contractors were using substandard materials behind the walls, and expensive materials on the outside."

A developer of some of these houses ended up as a legal client of Bill's. "He was laughing about how people who bought $80,000 houses were pickier than the people who bought the McMansions. The people who bought the less-expensive houses were going to live there forever, and the McMansion people weren't. A lot of them were planning to move out before there were problems."

This disregard for craftsmanship and ethic of disposability rubbed Bill the wrong way. "It seems to me the essence of being a conservative is appreciating what's there, what you have. Conservatives seem to be not so willing to cast aside what they have just because something new and superficially more interesting has come along. They ought to have the same views about their homes and communities."

David Holme has been in his 1930s Grosse Pointe, Michigan, bungalow for ten years. He draws a strong distinction between the way he and his family have chosen to live and the lifestyle choices made by his brother. David believes the luxury suburbs are bad for family life—which, as far as he's concerned, is the point of living in the first place.

"My brother has a McMansion, the thirty-five-hundred-to-four-thousand-square-foot thing, with a nice balcony looking out over their two-and-a-half-story great room," said David. "I didn't even think about a place like that, because I didn't want an hour commute to work. I'm about twelve minutes from the office here.

"And there's no character in a house like that," he continued. "I don't know whether it's just a difference in our personal styles, but I didn't like what that neighborhood brought. My wife, who has an MBA, is the one staying home. The perception I have of that [McMansion] neighborhood is that typically both parents work, they drop their kids off at seven in the morning and pick them up at seven at night, and they might spend two and a half hours in the day with them. Each kid has a television and a computer in their room. There's a six-foot TV in the living room. People just tend to sit in front of them and go to mush. The houses are so large that people go off in their own little area, and they don't interact. You never run into anybody, so you never have to play a game with anybody. People get to be like strangers living at the same address."

David says his son Jack can ride his bike to the library, to school, and to his friends' houses, but his brother's suburban kids have to be driven everywhere. "It's a fifteen-minute drive to the library out there," he says. "Consequently, you stop using those resources.

"Look, my brother is by all lights very successful. But he doesn't interact with his kids, and they don't interact with him. I think I have it better. I know Jack comes home from visiting his cousins and says, 'Boy, they have a big house,' and yeah, they do. We have the smallest house on the block. But I tell him we love each other. I mean, where's the quality of life in spending an hour and a half on the road each way to work? If you live close in, like we do, you can spend more time at home with your family.

"If family is so important to us conservatives, why do so many of us bring into our daily lives so many things that take away from family life?"

In talking to crunchy cons about why they chose to live in old houses in overlooked neighborhoods, the conversations usually centered around the family. Rachel Balducci and her husband, Paul, are in their thirties, with four small children and an old Augusta, Georgia, house that sounds like Arts and Crafts enthusiast Charles Keeler's ideal of home as "the family temple." Rachel, a stay-at-home mom, said that she wants visitors to their home "to come in and feel a sense of peace, because the people who live here really love each other, and love God, and invite him into their house.

"I'm a political conservative, but I see myself as so much more than that. I don't know that what draws us to live here in this house would resonate with a strictly political conservative," she said, meaning a right-winger whose conservatism consisted mainly of voting Republican for the usual reasons (lower taxes, limited government, smite the Democrats, etc.). "I would say to that sort of conservative that family is the most important thing, and that you need to be living in a place that can make your family stronger. That is at the heart of what Paul and I are doing."

What the Balduccis are doing is unusual. They're living in the same neighborhood in which Rachel grew up as part of a charismatic Christian community, mostly Catholic, started thirty years ago. Community members believed that they were called to live out the Gospel in community, so they pooled their money, bought a number of worn-out duplexes in a crime-ridden part of Augusta, and began their experiment in communal living.

Notice how countercultural this is. In a period of American history when communities were coming undone in large part because of the relentless stampede to the suburbs, where the Holy Grail of individual fulfillment beckoned, these conservative religious people made the conscious choice to stand against the outrushing tide, and to stay together as a community, *even though individual families had to pay a cost.* They believed first of all that this was what God was calling them to do. And they believed the good that living together as a community would do for them collectively, sharing their lives and their values in common, was more important than whatever gains individual families could achieve living atomized lives in the suburbs. They gambled that it would be easier to raise children who lived out their own conservative values, and kept the faith, if they did so with the mutual friendship and support of a community of like-minded folks.

For the most part, it worked.

"Over time, this neighborhood has drawn back a lot of people who grew up here," Rachel said. "The older I've gotten, the less it's been 'this is what I know' and more of 'this is how I want to be.' For me, I'm choosing to live in a neighborhood that's very authentic. The people here are not all about how their houses look. My brother and sister-in-law live in one of the nicest country-club homes in the area. It's very nice. But I feel like my personality is sucked out when I go through the gates. I like that our neighborhood doesn't have gates. I like being in a *real* place."

The Balduccis do not live in a small house, but it is old and they did get it cheap from Paul's dad, a widower who wanted a smaller place. Paul's grandfather did the renovation on the place when he lived there many years before, which means that Paul and Rachel's boys are the fourth generation of Balduccis to live under that roof. "I love the history of this home," Rachel said. "That's what I love about older homes: the history of people who lived there. Paul's mom died thirteen years ago. She had a heart attack in this house, and the house kind of died with her, because Paul's dad had such a hard time. This became the house that time forgot. We had to update it when we bought it. It feels like a home again."

For Paul and Rachel, their house is not simply a place to live, but a family legacy, a trust to be cared for and passed on. Yet they have faced a great deal of disbelief from friends and Paul's professional colleagues ("Not too many lawyers live in a neighborhood like this," Rachel joked) who don't understand their choices.

"We even get it from friends who grew up in this community and left, and don't want to come back — though now that they're starting to have kids, they're starting to see the beauty in what their parents did, living around people you know and trust," she said. "In Paul's profession, most people are trying to get the biggest and best house they can, and, well, here, you can go one or two streets over and there's abject poverty. Our friends think the suburbs are the answer to protect yourself from crime, but I think it's silly to think that just because you move to the suburbs, you're going to avoid bad things. I'm getting to the point where I don't care what people think of us. It's just blessing our family to live this way."

Because my wife and I were thinking about buying an old house, I asked Rachel if there are any creature comforts she thinks her family is missing out on by choosing to live as they do. "A huge bathtub," she said, but couldn't come up with anything else. And then she mused about how she and Paul feel fortunate to have escaped the preoccupation with materialism that many of their friends who live elsewhere seem to have fallen into.

"With my friends who live in these bigger, newly built suburban homes, there's this drive to have the latest gadgets and appliances," she said. "I just don't want to fill my home with the biggest and the best televisions. Maybe they're more in tune with the cutting edge. I just see this desire to have access to stuff. I also find, too, that when I talk with these people, those are the things that excited them: which neighbor has the plasma TV, which neighbor is buying the most DVDs. These are smart, good people, but their priorities are so — I don't know, boring. They talk about *things*.

"I find that our friends' weekends are filled with going to birthday parties and doing things to be entertained," she continued. "It's funny, but they build these huge homes, and they're never home. They're always out, staying busy. You could spend all your family time out doing that kind of stuff, but it doesn't *build* anything."

As someone who had never owned a home, I was having a blast talking to folks who had taken the leap of faith that Julie and I were considering, and who passionately loved their houses because those houses allowed them to live in a way more true to their traditional values. The more conversations I had with them, the more I understood that their choosing old houses in old neighborhoods had to do with far more than aesthetic taste.

Theirs was a conscious rejection of suburbanism, which, however comfortable and prosperous those neighborhoods are, they associate with alienation and a loss of community.

In 2003, Brenda Resch and her husband, Matt, graduates of Michigan's conservative Hillsdale College, bought a two-story 1908 bungalow just south of downtown Lansing. Their conservative friends who live in the suburbs can't figure out why they choose to live as they do.

"You know how we conservatives have the whole free-market thing piled into us, and we get into that mind-set: *new is good, expansion is good, growth is good.* I think it's really easy to get caught up in that, and I think that must play a role in the decisions people make," Brenda explained.

She says that she and Matt wanted a place with character, one that was also attractive—and they don't find those qualities in newer houses, no matter what the modern amenities. People these days think that beauty is either a luxury or an affectation, but the Arts and Crafts Movement taught that not only is simple, elemental beauty possible for ordinary people to achieve in their houses, it's a humanizing and necessary thing.

"Beauty is important. It feeds my soul. It's so important to me what I choose to surround myself with. I don't choose to live in the desert because I don't think it's beautiful. Same thing with my house. Every night I say to my husband, 'I love our house.' The way the light comes through the windows. The shape of the rooms. The proportion to them is so graceful. Just walking through them makes me happy. It's as simple as that. And beyond that, it's thinking of the people who lived there before us, the person who took the time to craft a particular detail of the house. That's so uplifting to me. And it's important to me, too, to surround myself with things that are uplifting, because so much of the world isn't."

Lansing is not a beautiful city, in Brenda's view, so they see their house as an oasis in the middle of industrial squalor. This made sense to me as a relatively new Dallasite. There are a lot of good things to be said for this flat, hot, modernist city on the plain, but "it's a beautiful place to live" isn't one of them. Brenda and I agreed that when you don't live in an attractive or interesting urban environment, a place that feeds your soul, making your house into a retreat is all the more important.

As we talk, the word "authentic" keeps popping up, used by Brenda to describe what she and her husband were striving to be. What, I asked, is inauthentic about living in a suburban McMansion?

The answer, she explained, has to do with accepting a prepackaged, off-the-rack lifestyle instead of working to make something your own. She and Matt bought the bungalow in part because they didn't want to be like the herd, and they wanted to put their own labor into fixing it up and tailoring it into a reflection of themselves.

"I'm always watching these makeover shows when they redo a house or a room, and they completely design it for the people who live there," Brenda said. "Even when it looks nice, I wonder, What's the point of that? A total stranger coming in and picking out a place for you to live in? That's so emblematic to me of the mass mentality out there: make it look nice, and don't worry about there being anything personal to it, or anything meaningful to me."

She tells a story about going to a housewarming party at a friend's newly constructed suburban manor. "This was the nicest, most aesthetically pleasing McMansion I've seen in this area, but the things that made it so were the attempts to duplicate things in old houses where they still exist, but are of a much higher quality. But these people don't want to go where these things actually are! I thought, You spent so much money to re-create what we have in our house. If I had been you, I'd have taken that money and made our house so much nicer."

The instinct to rehabilitate what already exists instead of building something new is a deeply conservative one, though not necessarily, it must be said, in the political sense (which is why the most conservation-minded homeowners and neighborhood defenders these days are liberals). While their political brethren confine their conservatism to the voting booth and their stock portfolios, many crunchy cons see historical preservation as almost a spiritual calling.

Tim McNabb, thirty-eight, lives with his wife, Gemey, as well as a single mother and her child whom they've taken in, in a two-story Arts and Crafts–style dowager in a St. Louis suburb. The McNabbs bought the house five years ago for less than $100,000, and Tim finds great satisfaction in caring for his place.

"To me, a house is a house; the relationships among people are the important thing. But there is something warmer about this house," he said. "I'm an evangelical Christian, so I don't want to sound like a New Age fruit loop. But look, there's inch-and-a-half molding in the arch between the living room and dining room. I'm a carpenter, and I know how hard this was to put in. The idea that Günther and Hans, my mythical immigrants, came over here from Germany and spent all day putting this crown molding in, and the care and craftsmanship that went into it—well, it's something else. It had to be hand-fit with hand tools, and that took a lot of skill. This is a place full of skill. It's been taken care of. There's something permanent about this place.

"And I go into a McMansion, having worked in the trade, and I'm sorry, but hanging Sheetrock is not the same thing. There's a hollowness to them."

When I called, cheerful Tim said he was having problems with the plumbing. Low water pressure. "That's going to be a big thing to fix. But so what? This is my home. I'll learn how to do it. Unless God has other plans, they'll have to carry me out of here on a stretcher. I look at this home and think, This house has lasted eighty years. What do I need to do to make it last another eighty years?"

The McNabbs' neighborhood is called Holly Hills. Their house was built in the mid-1920s, but there are homes there that have been around since the turn of the twentieth century. The streets are relatively narrow (snowplows can't come down them in the winter), the yards are twenty to thirty feet deep, and the houses, all of which are brick, are fifteen feet apart. Many of the houses have front porches; the McNabbs' is ten feet deep, and runs the entire length of their facade. It's a cozy neighborhood, which Tim finds invigorating.

"I'm standing in my living room talking to you," he said at the other end of the phone line, "and I can read the numbers on the house across the street. We're close. The on-street parking. People want to have their garages, but if you have that, you pull in and never have to see your neighbors. That's so isolating. I think the detached garage has led as much to the collapse of civilization as Janet Jackson baring her breast."

We laughed, but his point was a serious one. "Living here requires you to develop certain habits that make you more social. When we lived in the suburbs, we had a lot more friends from church than from the neighborhood. Here we know our neighbors, because we're all visible to each other. When we first moved in here, we had some Bosnian refugee kids in the neighborhood, and before you knew it, I was like their uncle. Soon, I had them around here every afternoon. I'd tutor them and put them to work around here. That's how the neighborhood is. There are some people who would be put off by a pack of six refugee kids piling onto their front porch and wanting to play with chalk. But those people will move out to the suburbs."

Tim thought that his suburbanite McMansion-dwelling friends, conservatives who are up to their eyeballs in debt, might learn something from what he and Gemey have discovered by moving into the city, into a fine old house they bought for a song, just to see what would happen.

"Our neighborhood seems very conducive to the sort of rich family life a conservative would like," Tim mused. "When I lived in the burbs, I seldom talked to neighbors. Here, the porches and proximity make visiting almost effortless, and I feel much less isolated than when living there. I'll have my house paid off before McMansion owners start making principal payments, and I have lots of resources for better things, like taking the grandkids out for Bohemian Weekend. Last year, we spent a weekend at the art museum, checking out the graffiti wall and eating weird food. You can't blow a hundred bucks on Indian food, lattes, and authentic Thai if you're worrying about making a $2,400 mortgage payment.

"See, McMansions, with their vaulted ceilings and fashionable kitchens, are glamorous, but our house is beautiful," Tim boasted. "They are like the hot prom queen you luck out and marry, only to learn she has a drinking problem and is terrible with the kids. She dumps you while her looks are still going for her, sticks you with alimony, and shacks up with a guy who owns a Porsche. My house is the solid girl next door who is pretty and loyal and makes you want to be worthy of her love."

You will not be surprised to learn that Julie and I bought the Craftsman bungalow. We had work to do on the place to get it ready to live in. Granmom and Grandad, Julie's parents, got busy helping us clean and fix things. Granmom and I painted the peach (ugh) walls rich Arts and Crafts colors—a mustardy gold for the living room, a velvety chianti for the dining room, slate blues for the bedrooms, and a mossy-hued green for my office. Julie's grandmother drove in from East Texas and sewed curtains for the windows. Granmom sealed the wood floors, and we moved in. For the first week or two, I would wake up with the sunrise, and stand at the kitchen window looking out at the glistening green backyard, wondering what the peaches and the figs would taste like later that summer. I would stand at the sink on those mornings saying silent prayers of thanksgiving.

Some mornings, we'd walk down the street and around the corner—just like in Brooklyn—to the Garden Café to have breakfast. It's a neighborhood hangout where, in growing season, the cooks plan the day's lunches based on what's fresh from the plantings out back. In the afternoon, the *paleta* man comes by pushing his cart, selling frozen Mexican treats. One warm Saturday afternoon after we first moved in, Matthew and I bought ice cream from him, then sat on the front steps eating our goodies and taking in the neighborhood. Across the street, Laura the librarian's cats played on the sidewalk. In the backyard next door, a parrot named Tortilla squawked, and the breeze shook loose a soft fragrance from the pink powder-puff mimosa blossoms on the branches hanging low over our front yard. We were at home.

"Dad, I just love our house," Matthew said to me about once a week for the first few months we lived here. He'd never said that before. I don't think I know too many people of my generation who could say that about the house they grew up in, even though many of us were raised in houses that dwarf our relatively inexpensive little bungalow. My pal Terry Mattingly's thirteen-year-old son, Frye, captured the appeal of living in an old house when he described their 1930s bungalow in a blue-collar Baltimore suburb as "like visiting grandmother's house, only we live here."

One Sunday afternoon, I turned on the stereo to listen to a rebroadcast of *A Prairie Home Companion,* a radio program I learned to love while visiting Nora at Weyanoke on many a Saturday evening, sitting at her kitchen table drinking a cold beer and finding the whole world hopelessly agreeable. Standing in the cool of our bedroom in this dear old house, listening to Garrison Keillor's comforting baritone rolling warmly across the wooden floors, I turned to Julie and said, "You know, I think I've found my Weyanoke."

"Really?" she said to me.

Really.

So, yay for the Drehers, but truth be told, we really lucked out. My friend Chris lives in an Arts and Crafts bungalow in suburban Los Angeles that's about the same size as ours; it's worth four times as much. We happen to live in a city where most people haven't yet discovered the pleasures of bungalow life, and strongly prefer Big and New to Small and Old. So when these houses come available, they're relatively inexpensive. Besides, as I mentioned, we had a prior commitment to home-schooling, which made it possible for us to consider a less-expensive house in a lousy school district. I think it's pretty safe to say that most crunchy cons don't have the opportunity to own the kind of house Julie and I do. So what is the artsy-craftsy crunchy con to do?

There are lessons from the Arts and Crafts ideal that can be applied almost anywhere.

Make the interior of your house a refuge from the outside world. The Arts and Crafts Movement arose as a reaction to the Industrial Revolution, and was in part an attempt to restore a sense of humanity to the lives of men who had been working hard in factories and mills all day. Our working lives aren't remotely as brutalizing as what those workers had to go through, but most of us do put in long, demanding hours on the job all the same. Many kids live in a loud, jangly, intense environment at school and among their friends, as well. Home should be a place of peace, quiet, and domestic tranquillity.

We should therefore strive to decorate and arrange our houses with care and thoughtfulness, to make them places where it is easy to rest and rejuvenate, and be aware of the sacramental principle teaching that the physical environment conveys certain ideals. There is no formula, because people's tastes vary. Let yourself be guided by Gustav Stickley's rule: a good house will be a place that "children will rejoice all their lives to remember as 'home,' and that gives a sense of peace and comfort to the tired men who go back to them when the day's work is done." No matter what the outside of your house looks like, you have a lot of control over the interior. Make it fit your family's ideal.

Simplify, simplify, simplify. The Victorian era was a period marked by a great deal of decorative lavishness and frippery, as befit the rising prosperity of industrial England. The Arts and Crafts Movement said good-bye to all that, advocating a more ascetic ideal. Today, many of us live in houses jam-packed with stuff we don't need. Even if one can afford these things, it's better not to buy them, as an act of spiritual discipline for oneself and one's family.

Choose quality over size. Americans have completely unrealistic ideas about how much space they need for their families. Living in New York City, where nobody but the extremely wealthy has a lot of space, taught us that a family can live happily in relatively close quarters. In fact, as David Holme said, big houses can be positively harmful to family life if one's home is so big that it's easy for family members to stay away from each other, or if the parents have to work so hard to afford the place that they don't get to spend as much time as they should with the family. Crunchy cons believe that the Arts and Craftsman Charles Keeler was right when he said the home should be the "family temple."

Bill Davidson and Tim McNabb both testified to the enduring value of choosing a house built with quality workmanship, as opposed to a shoddily and hastily constructed house in one of the new developments growing like kudzu in America's exurbs. If you are thinking of building your own house, consult Sarah Susanka's Not So Big House books, which are treasuries of great home architectural ideas constructed around the principle that it's wiser to spend your money constructing a top-quality, intelligently and beautifully designed small house than an ordinary big one.

Be smart about choosing your neighborhood. Most of us don't have a lot of flexibility in this regard. The most important thing for most families is to be in a safe area close to a good school. To achieve that, lots of parents condemn themselves to lengthy commutes. Hey, we all do what we have to do for our kids' sake, but it pays to consider all the hidden costs of living in this or that neighborhood. For example, it might be worth living in a less-than-ideal house to cut down on the commute, in order to spend more time with the family.

If possible, look into New Urbanist housing developments in your area. New Urbanism is the ultimate crunchy-con residential design dream. Led by Miami architects Andres Duany and Elizabeth Plater-Zyberk, the New Urbanists are part of a back-to-the-future movement that envisions residential areas with the features that made older, pre-suburban neighborhoods such pleasantly diverse, humane, spiritually uplifting places to live: functional porches, sidewalks, narrow streets, small stores located amid housing, and various incentives to create a lively street life. New Urbanism believes that the way a house and a neighborhood look matters to the public character of the place. The book to read on New Urbanism is James Howard Kunstler's *Home from Nowhere*, a prescriptive sequel to his diagnostic classic *The Geography of Nowhere*.

Follow the Way of the Balduccis. To do as Paul and Rachel Balducci have done, and commit to living in a neighborhood built around an intentional community, is obviously unrealistic for most people. But shouldn't we at least think seriously about it? Their parents' generation, chiefly for religious reasons, came together as a community and purchased property to establish a real neighborhood of like-minded families. It has held together because enough of the children who grew up there saw the priceless value of living in a neighborhood where folks shared the same values, and looked out for each other and the community's children. It took real vision and faith in each other to pull this off, but these Catholics did it, and live so much more richly for their efforts.

They have something that the rest of us only dream of: a real community, knit together not only by neighborliness, but also by common bonds of faith, friendship, and shared ideals. Unlike most of us, they aren't merely a group of random people who happen to share the same few square blocks, but who have little more than that in common. I've only seen that before in some of the older ethnic neighborhoods in New York City, and it's fast disappearing.

Can you and your friends do the same? Isn't it worth considering? Five or six like-minded families committed to buying or building houses on the same block or two, or pooling their resources and buying a small apartment building in the city, would be the seed of community renewal. In the Balduccis' case, the community went into a neighborhood that had been discarded by the middle class, bought old houses inexpensively, and helped each other renovate them. That's a radical step to be sure, but talking to Rachel Balducci about the return on the investment their families made is thrilling—and it might just inspire some idealistic crunchy cons to take the leap of faith.

Wherever we choose to live, and however we order our homes, we crunchy cons have to be mindful of the sacramentality of domestic life. The environment in which we live, and in which we raise our children, says something about the kind of people we are, and the kind of people we aspire to be. When our children are grown and gone, we want them to remember not that we provided them with a big, fancy McMansion or just an indifferent place to sleep, eat, and get out of the rain. We want them to carry with them sense memories reminding them that they grew up in a nurturing place, one with charm and character and family closeness. Not just a house, but a home.

CHAPTER FIVE

Education

Education cannot help us as long as it accords no place to metaphysics.

—E. F. SCHUMACHER

BEFORE I HAD kids of my own, I thought homeschoolers were pretty much religious conservatives who didn't want their kids exposed to evolution and sex education. It's easy to hold such shallow prejudices if you don't know any home-schoolers, or if you think the word "values" used in the context of discussing schooling is code for No Sex and No Darwin.

In fact, the values question goes much deeper than Darwinism or condoms in the classroom. It's why homeschooling—though not possible for everybody—is the ideal crunchy-con way to educate your children.

When Schumacher said that education is useless unless it teaches metaphysics, he was saying that it cannot be separated from teaching not only morals, but more deeply, the nature and purpose of reality. When people say they want prayer returned to the public schools, I think what they're grasping to articulate is not a wish for sectarian piety, but an anxious desire for public schooling to provide their children with a basic metaphysical framework to help them live meaningful lives with a sense of purpose. Those days are over, and they're not coming back anytime soon. But the official neutrality of public schools is not neutrality at all, nor can it be. As one homeschooling mother in Manhattan told me, "The fact is, all education is directed to *some* end, and if parents don't make conscious decisions on what that end is, they are simply abdicating their role in setting the direction" of their children's lives.

Put another way, if you don't educate your children for metaphysical truth and moral virtue, mainstream culture will do it for you. Absent shared commitment to these spiritual and moral verities, it is hard to see how we renew our families, our communities, and our country with an ethic of duty, self-restraint, stewardship, and putting the needs of people, not the state or corporations, first. The ultimate point of all education is not to accumulate facts and technique, but to become virtuous — that is, to discover how the knowledge we acquire ought to be applied. This is the difference between knowledge and wisdom. We are called to be wise.

Donna Steichen is a former schoolteacher and a writer friend of mine who lives in Southern California, near many of her twenty homeschooled grandchildren. Her daughter, writer Laura Berquist, is a leading national authority on homeschooling. Donna has been warning me for years, even before I had children of my own, that it is simply not possible for a conscientious parent these days to outsource his or her child's education. You can do it two ways: by engaging the system (public, private, or parochial), which often means fighting teachers, administrators, and school boards at every step; or by teaching your kids at home. Either way demands enormous expenditures of time, energy, patience, and dedication. There is no escape.

"Back when I was raising my own children, homeschooling was considered an exotic necessity for diplomatic families on jungle postings. So I took the first route: I met teachers, baked brownies, judged speech contests, served as a classroom, lunchroom, playground, and library volunteer, held offices in home and school associations, et cetera, et cetera, et cetera," she told me.

"Later, as difficulties arose, I argued with teachers, confronted pastors, principals, and department heads—especially but not exclusively Religion Department heads—served on advisory committees, and eventually, more than once, engaged school boards in public combat. It was a strenuous and emotionally exhausting way of life. It was also futile."

So she decided to put the same energy into teaching her children herself. Now she's got second-generation homeschooled kids in the family, and believes devoutly in the superiority of this method. Though Julie and I have only been homeschooling for about two years—and to be clear, we're not pure homeschoolers—everything I've learned from personal experience and from talking to other homeschooling families has borne out Donna's wisdom.

"The time is past when parents could sort of hand their children over to a school system and expect that the system could form their children to be part of the same community that the children live in. We've gotten more splintered than that," said Frederica Mathewes-Green, a Baltimore writer, activist, and old friend who homeschooled her three children for part of their young lives. "The parent has to take on the primary responsibility for forming the child into an adult—and not just education about geography, math, and so forth, but their sense of right and wrong, their sense of justice, and how they should relate to other people."

You can't automatically trust religious schools, either, as both Donna and Frederica discovered. When Frederica and her husband, who is an Eastern Orthodox priest, went to visit a Catholic high school in suburban Baltimore, hoping it would be good for their oldest son, David, the teacher giving them the tour told them that the school didn't introduce the concept that other religions are equally valid ways to reach God until the students were seniors, because younger students might not be mature enough to handle it.

"I remember looking at a crucifix in a classroom and thinking, 'If it doesn't matter, and all religions are equally true, then what did Jesus do that for?'" mused Frederica. "I thought if you can't even trust a Catholic high school to teach and affirm basic Christian orthodoxy, where is there to go? That's when we decided to homeschool."

For the Mathewes-Greens, who had had their children in good public schools before they moved to the Baltimore area, the spiritual integrity of their children and their family was at risk from the public and parochial schools. That's why they took the leap of faith into home educating. If Russell Kirk is right, and the family is the institution most necessary to conserve, there is almost nothing we crunchy conservatives can do that's more important than homeschooling our kids.

Homeschooling tests a husband and wife's commitment to the idea of *family as mission.* That is, do you think of your family as something that exists for no discernible purpose, or do you conceive of it as serving a larger mission? Sociologist Brigitte Berger has written about how the modern nuclear family came to exist to serve the mission of educating children to be self-sufficient adults in industrial society. Other researchers, as journalist Kay S. Hymowitz has reported, show that the most important difference between kids who fail in school and those who succeed is not race or poverty, but the extent to which the child's parents have a missionary level of commitment to child raising.

The question is not whether or not you love your child, but what that love demands of you. Before thinking seriously about homeschooling, you have to think seriously about marriage and family — that is, what they really mean to you, and what you're prepared to sacrifice for their sake. Homeschooling is not a neat thing you try, like a new diet or exercise routine; it is a demanding way of life, and it soon becomes the focus of a family's life. It begins by facing an unavoidable fact: that choosing to homeschool is choosing to have one parent — almost always the mother—give up a conventional career, and dedicate herself to full-time homemaking and home educating.

I got to thinking the other night about when Julie and I made this choice about her career. We had married as soon as she graduated from college with a journalism degree, and moved to Manhattan. Julie got a job working for *Commentary*, the opinion magazine that she used to read admiringly in the University of Texas library, never imagining that she would one day land a gig there. Hers was quite literally a dream job. She loved it, really loved it, and because she was good at it, they seemed to love her, too.

But one Sunday afternoon, after about a glorious year of living as newlyweds in the city, we were ambling along Third Avenue on the Upper East Side, and got into one of those crazy young-married arguments that aren't really about what they're about, if you follow me. As we stood on the corner of Sixty-third and Third, a frustrated Julie started slapping the back of her right hand against the palm of her left, struggling to make a point. "I just think that we ought to be—what? what?—living in an apartment over our bakery in Brooklyn or something, and building something. We need to be struggling to produce something. We're just marking time!"

It finally hit me: "You want to make a baby."

"No!" she blurted. "I mean, maybe. Yes. Okay, maybe yes."

A baby, now? I warmed to the idea quickly, and bada-bing, we were suddenly having a kid. In her seventh month of pregnancy, Julie left *Commentary* and we moved to Brooklyn and waited for the baby to come. Thinking about it recently, I couldn't recall that we had a moment's difficulty making the decision for Julie to be a full-time mom, with an eye toward eventually homeschooling. It was entirely hand in glove for us.

The other night, with the two boys asleep, and me lying in bed working on my laptop, I asked Julie if she thought it was weird that she hadn't had the slightest doubt about leaving the professional world to be a housewife—especially given that she had been driven hard in college by her dream of being a journalist.

She looked up from her book. "Actually, I had no doubts at all.

"My mom was home with us till I was fifteen, and then she went back to work because she had to. She was really involved with everything we did in school. Once she went back to work, I saw the massive difference, all the stress she was under trying to work and do the same things for us kids," she said. "As a mother myself, I can look back and see how often my brother and I asked way more of her than we should have. As the child, I experienced the stress it placed on us, and was old enough to see the stress it placed on her as a mother, and I didn't want any part of either one."

She explained that she learned intuitively, from an early age, that a woman can have a fulfilling career or a fulfilling family life, but will likely burn herself out if she tries to have both.

"Women don't like to hear that, but that's how it is," Julie said. "I mean, maybe you can, but you work yourself to death, and you never feel like you're doing enough, either at the office or at home. You ought to read the women's magazines sometime. Women drive themselves crazy worrying about this. A lot of women aren't in the financial position to make the choice, but I was, and I'm glad I didn't try to do it all. We haven't had a lot of the things we could have had if I was working, but I think we made the right choice. Don't you?"

Yes, sure, I said. But I told her that her status as a modern, college-educated young woman who has no problem becoming a stay-at-home mom is unusual.

She nodded. "Well, I guess. Faith has everything to do with it. Faith was the only thing that separated me living in New York and pregnant with my first child, quitting my job, from every other young woman in our income level and background pregnant and *not* quitting their job. The kind of books that I read, the kind of magazines that I read, the kind of women that I looked up to — those women modeled for me the ideal that I should be home with my children. When I looked around and saw women who made me think that's the kind of person I want to be, that's what they did."

I reminded her that of the four or five close stay-at-home-mom friends she had when we lived in Brooklyn, most were not religious, and all of them as far as we could tell were liberals. Julie agreed, but said that they were all united in the belief that there was something supremely important about caring for their children.

"All of us wanted more than anything to be a real part of our baby's life. A baby, that's a human being. That's a soul. That's a life. The baby is not an accessory. He's not part of life. He's everything," Julie said. "The kind of women I look up to and think are real heroes tend to have a gravity, a real earthiness about them. They tend to have a sense of mission and calling without taking themselves too seriously, but they also tend not to rule things out because they're outside of the norm that you see on TV."

(Notice: *"outside of the norm that you see on TV."* The mark of the twenty-first-century nonconformist — the ability to imagine a life outside of the boundaries set for us by media culture.)

"These are women who are willing to sacrifice themselves for something else," Julie said. "A lot of times that comes with faith, but plenty of times it just comes out of motherly love. You meet women in La Leche League who aren't necessarily religious, but they want to do what they believe is best for their children, no matter what it costs them, and no matter if it seems odd to someone else."

I told her I couldn't believe that none of this had ever occurred to her in college. No, she said, it's true: she never stopped to think about it.

"I assumed I'd have this brilliant career, and I'd figure out the family stuff if and when it came up," she told me. "I think that might be one reason why so many women have such trouble with this. They never think about it, and they end up just trying to make it work.

"I was lucky that I met the man I was meant to marry early on, and I always had total confidence that our marriage was going to work," she continued. "I wonder sometimes if a lot of women who work are doing it because they worry that their husbands won't be there for them. This is where faith comes in. I have faith in you because we share the same vision of what life is all about."

Julie told me she has confidence that because we share the same deep religious faith, one that teaches that marriage is forever, she feels totally secure that I will honor my vows. It was humbling for me to hear this. But she's right: my marriage vow was not only to my wife, but also to my God; because of this, our marriage is an objective reality, a fact as real as the roof over my head and the ground under my feet. Knowing that Julie shares the same bedrock conviction also gives me deep peace. Because our view of marriage is the traditional "till death do us part" one, we don't believe we are free to define our marriage to meet our own desires. Rather, we conform our desires to the spiritual reality of the vows we made.

Yet for a woman to have the confidence to put her own career aspirations on hold for two decades or more to raise and educate children requires a heroic leap of faith in her husband — particularly in a society that offers so little support for marriage.

"Look," she said, "on paper, I did something really, really stupid, dropping out of the workforce at a young age to be a full-time mom. On paper, I am not qualified for a whole hell of a lot. If you left me, things would be very, very bad. And that affects a woman's decision making. If you're a woman who really wants to stay at home and take care of your kids, there is this voice saying, 'What are you going to do if something bad happens, and your husband leaves you? What are you going to fall back on? If you're in a shaky marriage, it's going to be hard for you.'"

But come on, I said, doing the laundry, the cleaning, the grocery shopping — all of that can be an incredible drudge. I kind of feel sorry for you, I told her, when I come home at the end of the day, and I've been writing and editing all day, talking on the phone and with people at the paper about news and ideas, and you've been doing housework and hovering over Matthew getting him to practice his handwriting or do his math lessons. That's true, she said, but reading helps one keep one's mind on the significance of the everyday.

"Little things that all of us do matter more than most people think," she said. "If you read Dickens, and you see Mrs. Jellyby" — the woolly-headed idealist in *Bleak House* — "and the profound implications of her neglect of her children, you do have that little thing inside your head during the day where you say, 'Yeah, I could be off saving the world like Mrs. Jellyby, but I've got to have what's right in front of me squared away first.'"

It seems to me that what Julie was talking about here is, again, the role of a sacramental vision in household life. The mundane daily rituals of the housewife and stay-at-home mom actually symbolize and mediate deep spiritual truths about the home and its place in human experience. When I was a child, my own father told me on a number of occasions how much it meant to him as a little boy to get off the school bus and run up the hill to the little cottage where his family lived, and to know he could count on Mama being there with a piece of pie for him. It was a little thing, but it meant the world to him, and conveyed to a child growing up in the Depression, whose father was usually on the road trying to make money to support his family, that he was loved, that he would be provided for, that there was a shelter for him from the storm. The power of that simple yet iconic gesture — Mama with the pie at the back door after school — was felt throughout my father's life.

As we talked, I reminded Julie about our Third Avenue argument, and what it revealed to us both about our secret desire for children, despite the fun we were having as newlyweds in Manhattan.

"Well, what can I say?" she mused. "It sounds goofy, but we were married people, and this instinct welled up in me: *we should be bearing fruit.* It was total instinct; that was not the kind of girl I ever was. It caught me by surprise."

Instinct! Well, yes, in the scope of human history, it's *normal* to be young married people who want to have children. Isn't the desire to extend the going-out, cocktails-at-1-a.m. lifestyle indefinitely in some way a refusal to grow up? Don't get me wrong; I loved it when I had it, and there are nights when it would be blissful to get dressed up and go steppin' out with my baby instead of stepping into the bedroom to change the baby's diaper. But the self-indulgent pleasures of the childless life can get old. You start to think, Is this all there is? It starts to feel like a distraction from the real business of life.

If we had had any idea how our lives would change when we had kids, I told Julie, I don't know that we would have been so quick to jump into it. But I wouldn't change a thing. It makes no sense to do what we did, given how much freedom we had without kids, and how much fun we were having. But by the time we wanted to have a baby, we were happy to give back that freedom, because having children gives your life a weight, and a seriousness, that can feel paradoxically liberating.

"Well, we knew that this idea that you should have everything, and that life should be easy, was bogus," Julie mused. "I will say, though, that knowing someone like Frederica [Mathewes-Green], which is not something most young women have the chance to do, was very helpful to me. When I look at her, I see someone who married young, had children young, and who has had a fruitful career after that. There was a sequencing there. I think a lot of people my age don't, quite frankly, have the attention span to stop and realize that you don't have to do everything at once, and that you simply can't do it all. You have to choose."

That's the thing nobody wants to hear, I suggested.

"Well, the problem with a lot of women my age is that we were raised in a total self-esteem culture," Julie said. "We were brought up to think it was all about us, and that we should be happy and content, and that we should do whatever we need to do to be happy and content. For some women, having children is something they do thinking it's going to fulfill them, and when raising kids turns out to be difficult, it's a terrible disappointment. If you stay home with your kids because it's the right thing to do, you'd be surprised by how much strength you find to get through the hard parts, and to find real satisfaction, even joy, in them. It's all about your attitude.

"I mean, look, if I were still evaluating my life now by the criteria I used when I was twenty years old, I would probably be very unhappy. When I was a junior in college, if you had told me I would consider it a really good day if the boys and I had packed you a nice lunch and put love notes in it for you and driven it to you at the office, that would have seemed like the most mundane thing, a horrible waste of intelligence. But not now.

"There's freedom in putting your family first, and knowing that's what counts," Julie continued. "I've gotten to a place where I don't really care what other people think. I'm going to do what's right for my family."

And that, ultimately, is why we chose to homeschool. If you can't say the same thing, if you can't say you're going to do what's right for your kids no matter what, *you'll never make it as a homeschooler.* As Connie Hale, the homeschooling farm wife from Greenville, Texas, told me, "My husband and I constantly take digs for doing this, and it's only our strong convictions that sustain us."

Julie again: "When you've lived with your children through their infancy and their toddler years, and you've been with them all day, and you've taught them all the things you teach toddlers, from how to eat with a spoon to how to use the potty, things like that—well, you see yourself as their primary teacher. It didn't seem like there was some hard and fast point at which I said okay, my job stops, now we pass you kids off to somebody else. It just felt like a natural progression from all the things I'd been teaching them."

I asked Julie why she thought it was important for conservatives to give homeschooling serious consideration. She went back to the whole "bakery in Brooklyn" thing.

"Homeschooling forces you to see your home as a place where more than just consumption takes place. It leads you back to the traditional view of the home as a place where something was produced. It keeps you from seeing home as just a place where you sleep and eat before you go out into the rest of the world to do the really important things. It keeps you from feeling dependent on experts to do the serious teaching of your children.

"There's nothing more important we can do than raising our children," Julie said, growing more emphatic. "Teaching them, shaping their intellects and their character. Of course it's hard, but 'easy' is not the point. Doing the right thing is the point. Homeschooling is not right for every family, but I believe that for ours, it's worth the sacrifice."

Reading the history of public education in America through the eyes of a father who believes society should be organized primarily to support the family is a disillusioning experience. The earliest proponents of public schooling in America explicitly sought to undermine the family. In 1838, the famous pedagogue and educational activist Horace Mann and his circle founded the *Common School Journal* to advocate for public schooling in the new republic. Sociologist Allan Carlson noted that "strong criticism of family life" was a regular theme of the magazine, which urged the state to use public schooling to usurp the formative role of parents in their children's lives.

For example, "there are many worthless parents," the magazine observed, and public schooling succeeds because these mothers and fathers, "although the most sunken in depravity themselves, welcome the proposals and receive with gratitude the services of ... moral philanthropy in behalf of their families." Mann even denounced "monster families," and argued that public schooling was the best antidote to their parochial influence.

Over and over, one is startled, alarmed, and indeed insulted to encounter this unfettered elitism and hostility toward traditional life, including the role of the family as the primary shaper of the next generation's character, and the incubator of civilization's values. "[T]he child should be taught to consider his instructor ... superior to the parent in point of authority," said California school superintendent John Swett, in his 1864 report to the state legislature. "The vulgar impression that parents have a legal right to dictate to teachers is entirely erroneous. ... Parents have no remedy as against the teachers."

Public schools by their very nature serve to separate children from the influence of their families. Princeton sociologist Norman Ryder, echoing the statist, utopian views of nineteenth-century educational revolutionaries, extolled public education as "a subversive influence." In the struggle between the state and the family for the minds of the young, said Ryder, the public school is "the chief instrument for teaching [a new] citizenship, in a direct appeal to the children over the heads of their parents."

Mind you, Ryder is not a conspiracy theorist. He is a distinguished and influential mainstream scholar who thinks it's a very good thing indeed that public schooling displaces the traditional family as the chief authority in a child's formation.

Commenting on this, fellow sociologist Carlson said that Ryder understood that the specific functions of the family are what makes it strong — or not. "For example," Carlson wrote, "when families educate their own children, serve as the focus of religious life, and raise the largest share of their own food, the persons in these families are more likely to fix their first loyalties on the home. When these functions pass over to rival institutions, families lose these claims and diminish as institutions."

Strong, healthy individuals and strong, healthy societies cannot be made without strong, healthy families. Homeschooling puts the family first, and involves all its members sacrificially in helping its youngest learn and grow. Those families with the means and the will to embrace homeschooling strike the single most effective blow against the marginalization of family life in contemporary American culture.

"We are people of quiet faith who want our children to know what we believe, and why," said Julia Attaway, a Manhattan Catholic homeschooler of five children, the oldest a ten-year-old daughter. "Kids learn by example, and the examples they are shown in [public] school often aren't what we want taught. We want our children to be thoughtful and perceptive, to be able to weigh information and make wise, well-grounded decisions. We want faith to be an integral part of their lives, not a separate subject. If someone's going to put spin on a topic, it's going to be my husband, Andrew, and me, and it's going to be in the direction of what we believe to be right and true."

"Most important," she adds, "our children know that we have made a conscious decision to structure our lives around what we think is best for the family. My kids know I could be earning a salary and thus providing them with more material goods, but that I have chosen to spend time with them instead."

Homeschooling builds up the family not only by reinforcing the mission, and the family's core spiritual and moral convictions, but through more practical means. Julia says that homeschooling gives her a better sense of where each of her kids is emotionally, and helps her attend to their needs early. Ellen Vandevort Wolf and her husband, Karl, crunchy cons homeschooling their five children (the oldest, Max, is twelve) in Long Island City, Queens, find the same advantages. She says that while she's not entirely convinced that all that togetherness 24-7 is a great plan, she notices that when they're away from the house, the kids show a strong awareness of one another, especially the older ones for the younger ones.

"When Max was in school, he would come home angry and silent and take it out on his siblings," Ellen said. "It would often take two or three days before the event that caused the problem surfaced in conversation. I realized that things were happening during the day that he had few skills to handle. My ability to help him through it was severely hampered after two days had passed."

Now, however, when something troubling happens to Max, either with other children or within the family, she's aware of it at once, and can work it out before it gets to be a problem. As a father who didn't have an easy time of it socially in school, and who chose to internalize a lot of my problems and anxieties rather than share them with my parents, I appreciate this aspect of homeschooling.

Academic excellence isn't an ideal particular to crunchy cons, but a willingness to take on the sacrifices required by home-schooling in part for the academic quality of your child's educa-tion is. There are always exceptions, of course, but the general record of America's state schools in imparting useful and important knowledge to students is not impressive. Is it the fault of poorly trained or incompetent teachers? Bad pedagogy? Bullheaded teachers' unions? Poor school administration? Undisciplined stu-dents? Apathetic parents? Insufficient funding? Overcrowded classrooms?

In a word, yes. Whatever might be said about the effect of lousy public schools on a kid's character, consider that if Amer-ica is to compete effectively against India and China this century, radical public school reform is imperative. But I'm not holding my breath. I want my kids to learn as much and as fast as they are capable, which is a big reason we homeschool.

"Homeschooling allows each child to progress at his or her own pace," said Julia Attaway. "It's relatively easy to tailor what you're teaching to the child's learning style, too, which makes school more efficient."

Julia explained that her oldest is a reader; if she wants the child to learn about something, she hands her a book. Her second child learns better through hearing, so they have lots of discussions about academic topics. Julia's third child is an extrovert who learns best in a mini-classroom setting along with her siblings.

"It's also possible to have a much richer education than is possible in a large group," Julia added. "We can go into much greater depth when the kids get interested in something. We did medieval history this year, and my ten-year-old's favorite things were *Beowulf*, *El Cid*, and *Ivanhoe*. She's working on Algebra II, takes an online class in symbolic logic, and reads about quantum mechanics in her spare time. My eight-year-old boy takes Chinese and goes to a rigorous ballet school. His particular interest is history."

Frederica said that the structural artificiality of formal schooling can be an impediment to learning. Being confined to the same age group, having to sit quietly at a desk and focus on the same subject for fifty minutes, then moving to the next one, and so forth, is often a poor way to learn.

"Every parent knows what an individual each of our children is. If you put them on that school bus every day, you send them to an education factory, where they are treated like a cog in a machine," she said. "If you homeschool, you can tailor the education to your child's strengths and weaknesses; a teacher in a normal classroom is too busy to focus on your child's specific needs, understandably."

Her son David was a fast learner, and finished his daily schoolwork by noon. This freed him to spend the second half of the school day composing music at his keyboard, which was his passion. He didn't have to endure the boredom most children do at school.

No parent can be equally competent to teach every subject. Homeschoolers typically find outside help to teach higher-level math and science, as well as foreign languages. Some seek out individual instruction, and others do it cooperatively. For example, our son Matthew takes private Spanish and music lessons weekly with a handful of homeschoolers. Frederica found a parishioner in their church who had a master's degree in physics to teach their daughter a high-school science course. The oldest Wolf child is part of a terrific math club run by a fellow Ellen described as a "math guru who doesn't believe the standard curricula need to be so plodding, that kids can learn very complex mathematics at an early age." As homeschooling grows more mainstream, some enlightened public-school districts are beginning to open their classes to homeschooled kids on a pick-and-choose basis.

The biggest question—and it's usually in the form of a complaint—homeschooling parents are most frequently hit with is "How will your kids be socialized?" What the person asking that usually means is "Aren't you going to turn them into antisocial nerds?"

To which the screamingly obvious response is, *look at the values predominating in youth culture today; is that really working for us?*

Julie and I don't have much use for many of the moral values of the mainstream, and don't want our boys to be socialized by them. It's not just about sex. We recoil from the moneyed, media-savvy, techno-driven, status-mad cult of cool that reigns today. We don't want our kids to be in a school where they'll pay a price for being a nonconformist. We want them to learn in an atmosphere informed by our religious, moral, and philosophical values.

Research has shown that by the time a kid hits his early teen years, his peers exert far more influence on his choices than do his parents. What does that mean? For one, it means that kids in today's schools are surrounded by a materialistic and hypercompetitive value system that exalts money, looks, and athletic achievement above all. School has no doubt always been that way, but as our society has become more affluent and increasingly unmoored from traditional values, the stakes for kids have grown higher. We have athletes in some of the best suburban schools around Dallas getting juiced on steroids to improve their performance, to say nothing of the cutthroat status culture that comes with the money flowing through town, through the fingers of parents who are afraid to say no to their kids.

And then there are drugs and alcohol. There is no way to protect your kids entirely from these temptations, but you can better their odds. When I was in my hometown high school in the early 1980s, alcohol was the drug of choice, and the pressure to get sloshed on the weekends was immense. How quaint those sloe gin and 7-Up days seem now that kids back home in my sleepy small town are overdosing on Ecstasy — and dying.

But the thing that worries me the most is the progressive eroticization of young people. This is something about which some of my liberal friends with kids and I totally agree. Kids today marinate in a sexually aggressive popular culture that teaches them that life is supposed to be an erotic free-for-all. A sixth-grade teacher friend who is close to my age told me that as the mother of a daughter who will soon be in her class, it shakes her up to think about how much those twelve-year-olds know about sex — and how much pressure the boys put on girls to service them.

"We want to allow our children to grow up at their own pace, instead of having pop culture, not to mention liberal values, stuffed into them by outsiders at a tender age," said Julia Attaway. "One particular concern to us is the hypersexualization of American culture. In homeschooling our kids, we're not looking to create an artificial environment, but a *natural* one where our kids can be kids for as long as they need to be.

"It's hard enough for an adult, mature in faith and with a coherent moral and political philosophy, to withstand the barrage of sexuality and materialism she encounters every day. How can we begin to hope that our children can sift through that on their own and come out unscathed?"

Donna Steichen bristled over this issue. "The common agonies we call 'socialization'—playground cruelties, intimidating classroom snickers at mistakes, disabilities, or differences—more often serve to harden than to heighten the child's sensitivity to other people's pain. Homeschooled children for the most part don't have to deal with that, and are more likely to retain their natural compassion.

"Real socialization—that is, learning to get along with other people—doesn't have to happen in a herd of peers," she continued. "Parents are other people, too, and so are brothers and sisters, cousins, grandparents, aunts and uncles, neighbors, the mailman, the doctor, the dentist, the librarian, and all the many others a child meets in the normal course of life. Learning to get along with them, peacefully and courteously, is the best kind of socialization, the kind kids will need for the rest of their lives."

When nonhomeschoolers express concern over socialization, Ellen Vandevort Wolf wonders if those people have as much concern about the way kids in standard schools are socialized.

"There's nothing civilized about exclusion and ridicule, which are the two most frequently used socialization tools in middle school, along with deflecting ridicule and exclusion," she said. "Schools have our children for the most productive part of the day, and simply drop the ball on character-building, all the while espousing tolerance and the 'everybody plays' mantra."

By way of contrast, homeschooled kids, who socialize with siblings and with other homeschooled kids, don't feel pressured to form cliques, and frequently spend time with people from a wide variety of age groups. One thing you notice about homeschooled kids, especially teenagers, is how they can converse naturally and easily with adults, rather than lapsing into that tight-lipped, sullen silence that many teenagers do when confronted with grown-ups.

And they know how to behave in public. Going to events with parents and their kids from the New York City Homeschool Educators Association was an eye-opener for Julie. Very early in our homeschooling career, she came home from a theater event at which classes from traditional schools had been present, along with the homeschoolers. She reported that the classroom kids acted like loud, abusive boors, and that their teachers struggled to keep basic order. But the homeschooled kids treated each other and the occasion with polite respect. It was a real teaching moment for my wife.

Besides, in a country where more than a million kids are in homeschool, unless homeschooled kids live in a rural setting, they can easily meet other kids like them. Additionally, there are hybrid programs, like the small church school we have Matthew in, in which kids, many of them homeschooled too, get classroom instruction for half a day, and have the opportunity to make friends with kids whose parents share the same countercultural values.

This speaks to another crunchy-con advantage to homeschooling: it helps build authentic community. People these days go on and on about the need to build strong communities, but it's hard to see how that's possible without shared basic values. Frederica remembers going to parents' night at her son David's school when he was in second grade, and noticing that on the wall next to her son's drawing of an apple tree and a meadow was a classmate's drawing of the *Nightmare on Elm Street* slasher, Freddy Krueger.

"These kids were seven years old," Frederica recalled. "You have to ask yourself if you really want your child to be socialized into a community where a parent lets his or her seven-year-old watch slasher movies. No matter how hard you try to shield your kids from the worst of pop culture, they are going to be exposed to people who are open to all of that." After the Mathewes-Greens opted for homeschooling, their kids found themselves spending almost all of their time in a community of diverse people who were nevertheless committed to the same basic moral values.

Homeschoolers have to pull together to help each other out — it is very, very difficult to homeschool solo — and in so doing, they form natural communities. You want your kids to play with kids raised according to the same values, and your kids will need a peer group, especially as they grow toward their teenage years. So you make a point to get to know the parents from the local homeschooling association. Everyone there will be as committed as you are to the mission of raising good kids. These are the kinds of people you want to know.

Julia Attaway, the Catholic in Manhattan, said that even if she wanted her family to spend all its time with people who shared its conservative religious, moral, and political convictions — and she doesn't — it would be quite difficult to pull that off in New York City. She talks about how twenty-five of her neighbors, almost none of whom share the Attaways' beliefs, once got together and bought, then installed, a new dishwasher for her family when she was pregnant with her fifth child. That's real community, too, and it's important not to denigrate or dismiss it.

The thing to do, Julia said, is to relish the things you have in common with the people who live in the place you've been given, and make the best of it. She's right about that. As my wife, Julie, learned from spending the first three years of Matthew's life in Brooklyn, the women in her moms' group, though they shared few if any of our conservative moral and religious values, were invaluable friends, if only because they were as mission-minded as we were about raising their kids.

Nevertheless, there is something about choosing to home-school that provokes people, and would-be homeschoolers should be prepared for that. Connie Hale told me, "When you tell someone that you homeschool, and they send their kids to a public school or even a Christian school, sometimes they feel judged. 'Are you saying that I'm not doing enough for my children?' they wonder. And in no way are you trying to say that. You're telling them, 'Hey, I'm just trying to do the best I can for my children in the only way I know how. I'm not looking at what you're doing for your children."

Her husband, Mike, a public-school math teacher who left his career to become a full-time farmer and homeschooler, said that when he started homeschooling nineteen years ago, he was still a classroom teacher, and couldn't understand why so many people he knew were coming at him with hostile reactions.

"I kept feeling like I had to explain it all to them, to justify ourselves, to give them facts and figures," he says. "I've kind of backed off that now, and I'm just now tuning in to the guilt part of it. People feel guilty when they hear you're homeschooling. When I was teaching, I'd have seventh- and eighth-grade kids, when they found out we homeschooled, come up to me and explain why their parents couldn't homeschool. It was strange, but some reason they felt like they had to."

"What will happen to the public schools if good people give up on them?" a liberal friend asked me one night. She was near tears trying to convince me of the moral offensiveness of choosing to homeschool. She said it was un-Christian, and implied that there was something racist about our decision. All I could say was that our first responsibility as parents was to our children's welfare, and we would not put them at risk for the sake of living up to a political or social ideal that we believed, rightly or wrongly, conflicts with what's best for our kids.

It's hard to react to criticism like that without being overly defensive, especially if you're a homeschooling newbie. You'll probably feel really insecure the first year you do it. Homeschooling involves an enormous amount of work. It can become mundane. And if one of your children is having trouble in a subject, you can't self-righteously blame the teacher, because the teacher is you.

And homeschooling is not for everyone. I know homeschoolers who put their kids in public, private, or parochial schools when, for whatever reason, homeschooling was no longer working for them. A friend in St. Louis told me that she grew weary of a harsh spirit of religious separatism that overtook her homeschool group. Some girls in her daughter's group ostracized and bullied her child. For these and other reasons, my friend's family put her kids in public school, and they are satisfied with it. We homeschooling advocates must admit that it is not the best option for everyone.

Still, for those crunchy-con parents who'd like to try it, the only real qualification needed is the will to commit to the mission. The experience of millions of homeschoolers proves that competent, well-informed, and dedicated parents can do this themselves ("Parents are often the best teachers, because they know their child so well," said Frederica). There are extensive curricula available for homeschoolers who desire more direction, and many books offering detailed advice and encouragement to homeschoolers. Additionally, you can find support groups for both religious and secular homeschoolers. In the Dallas area, there is a support group for African-American homeschoolers. Online homeschooling communities offer additional help.

"I think almost anyone can homeschool, but not everyone can do it well," Julia Attaway said. "It's something to take on only because you have a real conviction that this is what is best for your children and your family. A willingness to make genuine and healthy sacrifices is a necessity; martyrdom is not required."

The Attaways live on one income, and not a big one (Andrew is an editor), in one of the most expensive cities in the country. They never eat out, and their entire entertainment budget is spent on museum memberships. Still, said Julia, "I can't imagine any situation other than genuine poverty that would make it *not* worth giving up the extra income. There is nothing I can give my kids that's worth more to them than my time and energy."

It's also crucial to remain open-minded. Things turned out well for Frederica Mathewes-Green's son David, who finished high school at home, but her younger son, Stephen, asked to go back to school, which turned out to be the best thing for him. "Just remember that no decision is irrevocable," advised Frederica. "Take it year by year, and see how well it fits your child's needs."

That goal — tailoring education to fit each child's needs and talents — guided Susan LaBounty, a religious conservative and veteran homeschooler who lives in the high desert of southern Oregon. Her four kids range in age from twenty-two to eighteen, and so far, their homeschooling pasts have led them in different educational directions. The LaBounty kids' homeschooling routine was largely geared toward letting the children follow their own natural interests.

"Some of the things I give highest value to in the education of a child are a wonderful home environment with lots of books and laughter and music, good conversations about all sorts of things as they come up throughout our days, and lots and lots of freedom to play," Susan said. "I think these things make possible the development of wonderful creativity, a unique and special individuality in each child, and an ability to think well and to articulate one's thoughts."

Susan said not to ask her advice if you want to know how to homeschool your kid into Harvard or MIT. When we talked last spring, her oldest child was in a private college earning a dual humanities degree; her third child was planning to attend a state college on full scholarship in the fall. Her youngest was running her own illustration business and trying to decide on colleges. And her second child had dropped out of college after she determined it wasn't for her. That daughter was to marry in June, which made Susan and her husband happy because "we think family life is the ultimate achievement.

"My children are all bright, but they are bent toward the creative side of things — writing, art, music, et cetera — and maybe because of our crunchiness, they don't feel pressured to achieve something that impresses the world," Susan said. "They are more interested in doing something they love, whether or not anyone notices, and whether or not they get rich. I hope they will always put more energy into serving others than into making lots of money or accumulating things for themselves. Of course, it's possible that both may happen, but I hope the money will be a side benefit of doing something they love rather than being a goal in itself."

That sounds like liberation to me — liberation from the cutthroat and corrupting pressure kids today face to succeed on the world's narrow and false terms. Maybe I'm too optimistic, but I think there's a growing army of crunchy-con homeschooled kids, learning not only academics at a higher level than most of their conventionally schooled generational peers, but also how to think — and, moreover, learning how to think independently and counterculturally. This is especially true if their primary teachers — their mothers and fathers — make certain that the core convictions of their faith are the sun around which all the academic learning orbits. When these kids enter mainstream society in large numbers, we could see the beginning of a quiet cultural revolution. And if not, at least the space in which American children can grow up protected from and trained to resist the predatory popular culture and the commercialization of childhood will have been expanded. These kids are going to be rebels with a cause, all because their moms and dads cared more both for tradition and for the spiritual, moral, and intellectual well-being of their children than for social conformity or material gain. That, dear hearts, is the essence of crunchy conservatism.

I hope John Taylor Gatto, a much-honored New York City public-school teacher turned radical education reformer, lives long enough to see it. Gatto calls himself a "lapsed Roman Catholic," but he identifies the Western spiritual tradition — Christianity, which of course incorporates a strong element of traditional Judaism — as the greatest enemy of corporatized mass society, and says that there is no more effective way for the government and big business to impose their will on the American people than by pushing religion to the sidelines of American education.

"Spiritually contented people are dangerous for a variety of reasons," he wrote. "They don't make reliable servants because they won't jump at every command. They test what is requested against a code of moral principle. Those who are spiritually secure can't easily be driven to sacrifice family relations. Corporate and financial capitalism are hardly possible on any massive scale once a population finds its spiritual center."

Now, I don't believe that capitalism is wicked; in fact, I firmly believe it is the most reasonable and morally responsible means to the end of the good society. But it can't be an end in itself, and must be governed by the moral and spiritual energies of the people. Anyway, the world at large has no use for learning about why it should reform its attitudes toward greed, envy, and self-gratification, which are the roaring engines of economic growth. My goal as a crunchy conservative is infinitely modest: to keep the consumerist mind-set from conquering my children. A wholesale commitment to a homeschooling curriculum centered around the values of our religious tradition is the best training my wife and I can give our boys to help them be free men, not target markets.

Wrote Schumacher, "For it takes a good deal of courage to say 'no' to the fashions and fascinations of the age and to question the presupposition of a civilization which appears to be destined to conquer the whole world; the requisite strength can be derived only from deep convictions." And those deep countercultural convictions can best be acquired through home education.

CHAPTER SIX

The Environment

Whether we and our politicians know it or not, Nature is party to all our deals and decisions, and she has more votes, a longer memory, and a sterner sense of justice than we do.

—WENDELL BERRY

I would feel more optimistic about a bright future for man if he spent less time proving that he can outwit Nature and more time tasting her sweetness and respecting her seniority.

—E. B. WHITE

TRUTH? I AM an avid indoorsman, a man who finds it diffi-cult to get all misty about the great outdoors. That's where the snakes live. I am as hopeless about outdoor life as ur-urbanite Woody Allen, but Woody has an excuse: he was born in New York. Me, I grew up in rural southern Louisiana, and spent a lot of time with a shotgun or a fishing pole in my hand. My heart wasn't in it. Many was the morning I spent as a kid in the kitchen at Fancy Point Hunting Camp, on the banks of the Mississippi River, drinking sweet, milky coffee as my dad and the other men planned that morning's deer hunt, secretly wishing I could stay behind in the toasty-warm kitchen to help Preacher, the cook, prepare the meal for after the morning hunt.

Preacher was an old black man who had done prison time for

burying a hatchet in the heads of his wife and her lover when he caught them in bed together. He was a kindly old gent when I knew him, and what he'd done as a young man didn't bother us much. He talked in this gravelly Ray Charles voice, and told the funniest stories. He made us kids jelly cakes on our birthdays. I loved him dearly, and figured my time would be better spent around his radiant stove, helping him roll out biscuits and listening to his crazy stories, than hunting.

But I always went into the swamp, and froze my ya-yas off while waiting for a whitetail buck to run by so I could take a shot at him. As if I cared. One grimly cold morning when I was twelve or thirteen, a big buck finally did run by me, and I pulled the trigger on him. My dad and I found blood on the leaves. We tracked him through the woods, and found him lying on his side atop a ridge, dying. I took another shot, and up the buck went. He didn't get far: he fell dead in the dirt road just before he hit the Mississippi River.

It should have been the proudest day of my life, but I felt sick inside. I'd killed this beautiful animal for no reason but sport (I didn't even like to eat venison), when all I'd really wanted to do was sit in the kitchen talking to and cooking with Preacher. Not long after that morning, I quit going to the swamp with a gun at all, and that was the end of that.

You'd think that would have made a tree hugger and animal lover out of me, but it didn't. Despite the deep sense of spiritual violation I felt at having taken the life of this creature for no good reason, I've never been much of an environmentalist, or interested at all in animal rights. Though I was tenderhearted toward animals, it was plain to me that men like my father and the men of the hunting club cared passionately about wild things and wild places. It sounds paradoxical, but it's true. I've seen it with my own eyes. The respect they had for game, and the rules of the hunt, amounted to a natural kind of piety.

On occasion, someone would bring a rich lawyer or a state politician up to the camp from Baton Rouge, and if one of those city fellows showed bloodthirstiness or any lack of respect for the animals and the unwritten rules of the hunt (e.g., shoot only what you intend to eat), the disgust of those rural men of the club was palpable. Those men — my father and his friends — considered themselves *conservationists;* as far as they were concerned, "environmentalists" were citified liberal pantywaists, uppity sentimentalists who didn't understand a thing about the woods and the creatures who lived there.

To be perfectly honest, for many years I shared their opinion. Every time I heard the word "environmentalist," I'd think of the sanctimonious cultural elitists who seemed to have such worshipful regard for trees and owls, but so little concern for people. The animal-rights people were the worst. When I lived in Brooklyn, every so often this obnoxious crone would set up a table on Saturday mornings along the main street of our neighborhood, and pass out animal-rights literature, stopping to yell abuse at families walking by with children. "Breeders!" she'd scream. "You're crowding out the animals!" And that was the image I had of the animal-rights cause.

What turned me around was reading a remarkable book called *Dominion* a few years ago. Its author, Matthew Scully, and I moved in more or less the same circles. He is a fellow political conservative, and had even worked for a time at *National Review,* where I was then employed. At the time of the book's publication, Matthew, whom I knew somewhat, and admired, was working as a speechwriter for President George W. Bush. I hadn't realized that he was an animal-rights advocate. How did a conservative get hooked up with those kooks? I had to find out, so I bought his book.

It was a revelation — one that didn't make a vegetarian out of me, but one that did make me fundamentally reassess and repent of the cavalier and philistine attitude I had toward both animals and, because nearly every principle Matthew elucidated in their defense also applies to the environment, to the entire natural world.

The first thing I came to understand, simply through the thoughtful, reasoned tone of a fellow conservative, was that I had long been using the image of that crazy animal-rights lady in Brooklyn, and the dye-throwing PETA extremists who always made the papers, in the same way liberals use the shrieking fringe of the pro-life movement: as bogeymen to avoid having to confront difficult moral questions.

One cold afternoon that first winter in Brooklyn, I was sitting in a Starbucks on Court Street and got into a discussion with a young couple about the abortion issue. They were firmly pro-choice, but they were polite about it, and seemed genuinely surprised to find out from me that most pro-lifers do not sympathize with clinic bombers and doctor killers. We had a good talk, and though I didn't win them over, I came away thinking that they were at least willing to give my arguments more consideration than they would have otherwise. I'd violated a stereotype they'd used to justify not thinking about the abortion issue from the pro-life point of view.

In the same way, it took about fifty pages of Matthew's book for me to realize how closed-minded and dishonest I, a conservative, had been about animal rights and the environment. How often had I sneered at environmentalists to hide the fact that I didn't really understand what they were talking about, and, more to the point, didn't want to?

In *Dominion,* Matthew wrote that when we look at an animal (and, he might have said, a forest) and see it only in terms of what practical use it can be to us, we are not seeing what's really there, only an extension of ourselves. Conservatives see quite clearly the danger of sentimentalizing the natural world; hence our dismissive attitude toward those environmental extremists who see no essential difference between a redwood tree, a spotted owl, and a human being. But what we on the right don't see so well is the cost, moral and otherwise, of our hardheaded so-called realism.

Take factory farming. If we only think of farm animals, say, in terms of their ending up on our dinner plates, there's no logical objection to industrialized meat production of the sort that crams thousands of animals into cramped pens, never lets them see daylight, and jacks them up with antibiotics to avoid infection from their unhealthy confinement, and hormones to boost their growth. But people recoil from films and photographs depicting the ugly reality of factory-farming methods, because there is something within us that cannot abide treating creatures this way — even creatures we plan to slaughter for food. Again, this paradox is hard to explain to vegetarians, but responsible hunters and livestock farmers know it instinctively. It's about respect.

"Animals are more than ever a test of our character, of mankind's capacity for empathy and for decent, honorable conduct and faithful stewardship," Matthew wrote. "We are called to treat them with kindness, not because they have rights or power or some claim to equality, but in a sense because they don't; because they all stand unequal and powerless before us."

This is true about the environment as well. Technology and wealth have given mankind dominion over nature unparalleled in human history. Everything in the tradition of conservatism — especially in traditional religious thought — warns against misusing that authority. Yet the conservative movement has become so infatuated with the free market and human potential that we lose sight of what Matthew described as our conservative belief "in man as a fundamentally moral and not merely economic actor, a creature accountable to reason and conscience and not driven by whim or appetite." If we lose our ability to see nature with moral vision, we become less human, and more like beasts.

By his own admission, the *Dominion* author is not a church-going man, but he does understand that Americans (conservatives especially) root our moral reasoning in religion. Perhaps this is why his case for stewardship was so persuasive to me. As a practicing Catholic, I was most struck by the following quote from Pope John Paul II's 1990 encyclical *Centesimus annus:*

> In his desire to have and to enjoy rather than to be and to grow, man consumes the resources of the earth and his own life in an excessive and disordered way. At the root of the senseless destruction of the natural environment lies an anthropological error, which unfortunately is widespread in our day. Man, who discovers his capacity to transform and in a certain sense create the world through his own work, forgets that this is always based on God's prior and original gift of the things that are. Man thinks that he can make arbitrary use of the earth, subjecting it without restraint to his will, as though it did not have its own requisites and a prior God-given purpose, which man can indeed develop but must not betray. Instead of carrying out his role as a cooperator with God in the work of creation, man sets himself up in place of God and thus ends up provoking a rebellion on the part of nature, which is more tyrannized than governed by him.

Well. Many's the time we on the Catholic right were grateful for John Paul's clear and unequivocal statements in defense of the culture of life, of human dignity, and of the sovereignty of truth. But honestly, if we ignore his equally clear teaching about stewardship of the natural world, we are no better than the cafeteria Catholics we disdain as pick-and-choose Christians. And not just Catholics either: John Paul spoke out of an ancient and consistent biblical tradition. No one who claims the Bible as a moral guide can ignore its command to honor creation.

But we do. All the time.

"I don't know how many ministers I've heard say over the years that animals are here for us, and for our use, and so is the entire natural world," Matthew told me when I reached him by phone. "But there's another [Christian] tradition that calls us to respect the dignity of all life, and to be mindful of animals as our fellow creatures. This is the tradition of Saint Francis and many other saints, which recognized above all that a respect for animals is an essential part of living well and living with integrity."

Unlike Matthew, I am a carnivore, and indeed an enthusiastic one. He said that he doesn't think it's necessarily a moral duty to eschew eating meat, but refusing to participate in cruelty is, however, a firm obligation — and that conservatives ought to be the first to point that out.

"Conservatives I respect a great deal are always telling us that man is not just an economic being, but a moral actor," he said. "Well, there are moral costs to efficiency. Most people will tell you that the cruelties of factory farming are intolerable, and they want nothing to do with them. All people have to do, then, is to consult their own standards and live by them."

"That's how I see it too," I replied. "But lots of times, when you point out that this or that way that conservatives live doesn't seem particularly true to conservative principles, boy, does that make right-wingers mad. I don't know about you, but I've found that one of the quickest ways to start a fight with most people in our tribe is to say that factory farming is problematic from a conservative point of view. They get real hot about how if we didn't have these things, where would we get cheap chicken?"

"As if that's the highest good!" Matthew said. "Conservatives have assumed this posture of disdain and even contempt for people concerned about the natural world and animals, but you don't need anything more complicated than a simple standard of animal husbandry."

As Matthew sees it, proper animal "husbandry," which comes from word roots meaning "bound to the house" — that is, the animals were seen as organically connected to the farmer's home — means that man asserts his own legitimate demands on animals, but gives them something in return. You protect them from predators, and you breed them in a way that accentuates their strengths.

"And you let them live their lives as animals," he said, not as biological products mass-produced in a factory farm. This is the same humane philosophy that guides the Hutchinses, the Hales, and the Salatins. And in a way, it is the same philosophy that guides the men with whom I grew up hunting deer: a respect for the natural rhythm and conditions of life, and honor for the animals and their condition.

In a world where efficiency is the highest value, honor comes at too high a price. If you think about it, conservatism today often takes on the characteristics of what conservatives say they hate most of all about liberalism: self-interest above anything else. It is a vision of man as an autonomous being who has only needs to meet and demands to make, no obligations to fulfill.

"At a certain point, they tend to see people more as consumers," Matthew said. "I remember when a particular conservative columnist strolled into my office one day at the White House. We started talking about this issue, and I told him I was finishing writing a chapter in my book about how we needed to get away from factory farming. His response was 'But that's going to cost more money.' Conservatives should be the first to understand that we're not just here to make money, that we have other duties in life."

I admitted to Matthew that for years I had looked at environmentalism, especially animal welfare, as something essentially trivial, something that I could shrug off. I found lots of company on the right.

"My response to that is that you don't get to shrug things off just because they're little things," he said. "Little moral wrongs have a way of growing into much greater moral problems unless you take care of them. And that has happened in the case of industrial farming. All moral values have been subordinated to economic values."

That this fundamentally indifferent or even hostile right-wing attitude to animal welfare also extends to trees, fields, mountains, and rivers hardly needs detailing here. Many conservatives can easily recall having been part of conversations in which fellow conservatives held forth arrogantly about paving over the wetlands, or improving a pasture by putting in a parking lot. Some of this gets said simply for shock value, but it does reflect a fundamental scorn for the natural world, except insofar as money can be made out of it. When I hear conservatives talk like this, I hear the voice of the callow city hunters that I grew up learning to despise — men like the top Louisiana politician who brought his son to the hunting camp one day, and when the kid illegally killed a doe, was shocked when the other hunters refused to laugh it off.

How did the conservative movement become identified with such prideful philistinism? We weren't always like this. In fact, it is an attitude of relatively recent vintage. Readers of Richard Weaver and Russell Kirk, two of the philosophical fathers of modern American conservatism, cannot fail to be impressed with the profound respect those men had for the natural world, and their distress over the way industrial capitalism saw nature merely as a thing to be exploited.

These traditionalists saw an ethic of conservation as entirely consistent with conservative principle, in part because of conservatism's understanding of human nature. If you believe that man is inherently flawed — what religious people call "original sin" (the only Christian dogma, according to English writer and proto–crunchy con G. K. Chesterton, that can be proved by recourse to the daily newspaper) — it follows that man, if left to his own devices, will tend toward ego-driven disharmony. Traditionalist conservatives know that absent the restraining hand of religion, tradition, or the state, there is nothing to prevent human beings from acting in ways contrary to their own best interests, or those of the community.

For a true conservative, that community includes men and women yet to be born, and for whose sake we are morally obliged to be good stewards of the world we have been given. "In America especially, we live beyond our means by consuming the portion of posterity, insatiably devouring minerals and forests and the very soil, lowering the water table, to gratify the appetites of the present tenants of the country," Kirk wrote. He demanded that Americans behave more prudently, to honor "the future partners in our contract with eternal society."

What can that mean to a society and a government putting its children and children's children in hock to foreign creditors to keep the great smoking engines of consumption pumping — and the politicians, including Republicans, who profess conservatism, in power by pandering to voters? Can today's conservatives even understand what Kirk was talking about?

Perhaps the best-known fictional explication of the traditionalist conservative perspective on the right relation of man to the natural world can be found in *The Lord of the Rings*. J. R. R. Tolkien's epic novel was taken to the patchouli-scented bosom of many a sixties counterculturalist, largely for its environmentalist worldview. But Tolkien was a deeply conservative Roman Catholic and a Tory to the marrow. In Tolkien's fictional world, the artisan elves and the agrarian hobbits showed the right way to live in harmony with nature, making use of its bounty while respecting it. In contrast, the wizard Saruman and his wicked master of Mordor represent the all-consuming drive to exploit nature, and eventually destroy it.

You don't have to look to political philosophers and artists of the right to find historical precedent for a conservationist ethic. Perhaps the only true conservationist we've had as our president was Theodore Roosevelt, the Republican who greatly expanded the national parks, and who passionately loved wild things (especially shooting them). He believed that conservation was a moral and a patriotic issue, because America could not be strong if it did not prudently steward its natural resources.

Much less well known is the conservationist streak in Herbert Hoover, also a national parks partisan. He worried that America's material prosperity would turn Americans decadent. His prescription? Go outdoors, get in touch with the wild, and learn something about reality.

Until I talked to Jim DiPeso, I thought the only thing green about Hoover was his love of the greenback. DiPeso, the policy director of Republicans for Environmental Protection, or REP America, is a font of hidden lore about the GOP's conservationist past. One of his heroes is John Saylor, a Republican congressman from Pennsylvania, a die-hard anticommunist who served from 1949 to 1973. In 1956, Saylor stood on the floor of the House and spoke in favor of the Wilderness Act. He said, in part:

> Shall we, exploiting all our resources, reduce every last bit of our wilderness to roadsides of easy access and areas of convenience, and ourselves soften into an easygoing people deteriorating in luxury and ripening for the hardy conquerors of another century? . . .
>
> The stress and strain of our crowded, fast-moving, highly mechanized and raucously noisy civilization create another great need for wilderness — a deep need for areas of solitude and quiet, for areas of wilderness where life has not yet given way to machinery.
>
> . . . [I]n the wilderness, we can get our bearings. We can keep from getting blinded in our great human success to the fact that we are part of the life of this planet, and we would do well to keep our perspectives and keep in touch with some of the basic facts of life.

That last point of Saylor's is his most essentially conservative, because it speaks to the metaphysical truth so many latter-day conservatives have forgotten amid our seemingly boundless prosperity: that we are not the center of creation.

"We wield a certain degree of piety toward creation," DiPeso told me, speaking of his Republican organization. "We don't get into arguing religious faith, but we do feel that the environment is an incredible gift, however it got here. We have a moral obligation to take good care of it, to leave it for our children, and to understand that the other creatures that we share the world with have the right to exist, too, in and of themselves. We don't want to arrogate to ourselves so much power that we don't take care of this incredible gift. It's a matter of humility. Conservatives have got to relearn that the good life and material prosperity are not necessarily the same thing."

When I asked DiPeso how political conservatism came to be seen as the enemy of conservation, he suggested I call William Ruckelshaus, who served as the first head of the Environmental Protection Agency, which was created under Republican president Richard Nixon. I phoned Ruckelshaus at his Seattle office, to which he'd returned not long before from a conference in Tennessee. The conferees were all leaders who had been instrumental in passing the Clean Air Act in 1970, and had gotten together to discuss its legacy.

"It certainly was a very bipartisan effort back in the sixties and seventies, when all this modern environmentalism started," Ruckelshaus told me. "There was also a clear understanding on the part of everyone involved that it was a grand experiment. What we passed was an effort to do the best we could and see how far it took us."

Which most people today agree was quite a long way indeed. The landmark environmental legislation of the 1960s and 1970s is widely credited with choking off the worst sources of industrial pollution. To do that, though, the government established a top-down, centralized enforcement mechanism that when it came to dealing with smaller sources of pollution was like swatting a fly with a sledgehammer.

"Some of the conservative reaction came from the federal government being heavily involved in areas always thought of as either individually dictated or dictated by lower levels of government," Ruckelshaus said. "We tried to address those at the central level, and it caused a strong backlash from conservatives who thought the government was too intrusive, and from economic ideologues who thought government regulation of anything was bad. That has become stronger in Republican administrations."

Tony Dean, a hunter, fisherman, and conservationist well known in his home state of South Dakota through his outdoors-oriented TV and radio productions, is a staunch Republican, but he blames Ronald Reagan for running the spirit of conservation out of the GOP.

"I'm a Teddy Roosevelt Republican—a conservationist who is very conservative on fiscal matters," he said. "I really believe from Reagan on, the Republican Party has left most of us who feel that way. They've become the party of no conservation.

"Today's Republicans—and they're not my Republicans—tend to equate the sportsman's concerns with the gun issue," Dean continued. "I wonder when it became fashionable for conservatives who love the great outdoors to ignore protecting the natural world and focus only on the Second Amendment."

It's true that Reaganism, for all the good it did, also mainstreamed a kind of conservatism that viewed environmentalism with contempt. Scorning environmentalists as tree-hugging kooks became a way of proving one's right-wing bona fides. The role the reactionary liberalism of environmental activists played in empowering conservative ideologues can hardly be overstated. They reacted to every defeat by becoming ever more strident and absolutist in their rhetoric. By the year 2000, a poll by the market research firm Environics found that 41 percent of those surveyed thought of environmentalists as "extremists, not reasonable people."

And yet numerous polls show that support for increased environmental protection is broad, and climbing every year. The problem is that while most Americans are greenish in the abstract, they don't feel passionately about it. Pollster Karlyn Bowman of the American Enterprise Institute told me that "the environment" turns up way down the list of issues factoring into voter choices in national elections. It's much more important in state and local elections, particularly in states like California and Florida.

Conservatives pride themselves on being hardheaded realists, but our lack of serious concern about the environment does not match reality. Despite the presence of ideologically driven junk science, the evidence for global warming caused by human activity is so overwhelming that conservative columnist John Leo likens right-wing deniers to tobacco company executives who claim there's no solid link between smoking and lung cancer. Even if the evidence were inconclusive, given the catastrophic results of a global temperature rise—including fiercer hurricanes, flooding of coastal cities, the loss of vast inhabited and cultivated regions to desertification or frost—would compel the prudent conservative (which used to be a redundant phrase) to act as if the worst was likely. The price of being wrong is incalculable—especially considering the century or more scientists estimate it would take for the earth to rebound from global warming *even if we slashed carbon emissions virtually to the bone tomorrow.*

"Man's power now enormously exceeds natural limits, and we can now do things that were inconceivable only a few generations ago. So it's a new problem, and these are grave new challenges," said Matthew Scully. Global warming is the most serious crisis overtaking mankind as the result of our refusal to live within our means, and to use our immense power wisely, but it is not the only one. In the spring of 2005, a worldwide coalition of 1,360 scientists, under United Nations auspices, issued the Millennium Ecosystem Assessment, a report that its authors called a "stark warning" to the world. Two-thirds of the world's natural resources have already been used up by humans, the report said, and the pressure we are putting on the natural world—the rain forests, the wetlands, the fisheries—is so unrelenting and harmful "that the ability of the planet's ecosystems to sustain future generations can no longer be taken for granted."

The report called out the "dangerous illusions" harbored by the rest of us, who think of nature as something separate from our daily lives, a place we go visit on the weekend or watch on Discovery Channel nature documentaries. In truth, mankind relies on nature to recycle the air we breathe, the water we drink, and much of the food we eat. Man is not an island.

This is something conservatives used to know, before we got puffed up and arrogant. One thinks of a statement attributed to my old *National Review* colleague Jeffrey Hart, a Dartmouth professor: "It is depressing to hear cigar-smoking young conservatives wearing red suspenders take a reductive review of, well, everything. They seem to contemplate with equanimity a world without lions, tigers, elephants, whales. I am appalled at the philistinism that seems to smile at a future consisting of a global Hong Kong."

Except it's worse than that: in the world such conservatives are helping to bring about by their mockery of environmental concern, Hong Kong will capsize under rising oceans.

The problem is that most of us think about global warming, the depletion of fisheries, and the eradication of the rain forests as "environmental" problems. In truth, they are far more than that. They are economic problems. They are national-security problems. They are public-health problems. They are "family-values" problems. They are religious problems. In their iconoclastic 2004 essay "The Death of Environmentalism," liberal environmental activists Michael Shellenberger and Ted Nordhaus leveled this indictment against the leadership of the nation's environmental groups, saying that their near-obsession with the environment as a stand-alone issue is one big reason the environmental movement has lost so much political power in the last twenty years.

This is the kind of thing they were talking about, and which conservatives appreciate: to the paper-mill worker in south Louisiana, "saving the environment" is an abstraction that appeals to elites; he's worried about putting food on the table for his family. It's very easy for business interests to paint environmentalists as the kind of do-gooders who are going to cost him his job by hurting the mill with costly regulation that will force the mill owners to relocate to Mexico. If that's the trade-off, no wonder the mill worker is going to fight environmentalists.

Consider, though, that the same mill worker may be coming home from work most days with nosebleeds from harmful chemicals in the air. (This is not a hypothetical situation; it really happened to a close relative of mine, a staunch Limbaugh-loving Republican.) Consider that the mill's owners threaten the union with moving south of the border, which is a lot easier to do under the North American Free Trade Agreement (NAFTA), if the union pushes for safer working conditions. Consider also how much support environmental crusaders might have gotten from churches and ordinary conservative working folks if they understood the genuine fear these men would have of losing their jobs, but also the natural concern they would have about cancer and other diseases they might acquire from dangerous working conditions, and which would leave their families fatherless. To have made those kinds of connections would have required the environmentalists to rub shoulders with dittoheads like my relative. And it would have required dittoheads to accept that they can have something in common with liberals.

Conservative voters, too, can be such knotheads, and easy picking for industrialists. We have a serious air-pollution problem in North Texas, and the source for much of it is Ellis County, south of Dallas. Ellis County is home to a number of polluting industries, which are protected by Representative Joe Barton, one of the most conservative Republicans in Congress. Barton, an ardent Christian, is as rock-ribbed as they come on social issues, which is one reason why the cultural conservatives in his district keep sending him back to Congress. I wonder why it doesn't occur to these voters — and their pastors — that the fact that their children suffer from asthma and respiratory diseases is a family-values issue.

I live a ways north of Ellis County, but the discharge from its smokestacks follows the wind currents up to Dallas, giving us some of the dirtiest air in the country in the hot months. When I see my asthma-suffering relatives — all of us conservative Republicans — sucking on inhalers and struggling to breathe, I reflect on the fact that this is partly the fault of a pro-life Christian Republican. I am probably the most conservative member of the *Dallas Morning News* editorial board, but for this reason I argued that we endorse Barton's liberal Democratic opponent in the 2004 election season.

Of course, the Democrat got creamed on Election Day, and to be honest, unless Joe Barton gets swept up in an exotic scandal, there's no chance that a liberal Democrat will ever beat him in that district. (Then again, you never know with us Texas Republicans; in 2004, Sam Walls, a stalwart GOP old-timer, almost won a seat in the state legislature in a hard-core Bible Belt district — even after photos of him in a dress and wig became public. Said one supporter, "It's not like he murdered somebody.") Politicians like Barton benefit — and nature loses — from the depressing fact that both parties and the special-interest groups that fund them depend on demonizing each other. Where would the Sierra Club be without Republicans to beat up on, and vice versa?

Bill Ruckelshaus told me that there's no percentage in George W. Bush greening himself, because the environmentalist left gives him absolutely no credit for doing any good. Environmentalists regularly allow the perfect to be the enemy of the good, and in so doing have made themselves captive to the Democratic Party.

"What this does is strengthen the hand of those on the Republican side who say, 'Why bother dealing with those people? You just help the Democrats if you take the environment seriously,'" said Tony Dean, the South Dakota outdoorsman.

"Liberal Democratic environmentalists don't know what to make of us," said Jim DiPeso of REP America. "Usually they

welcome us, but sometimes there is concern by the more partisan of the bunch that 'Hey, this is our issue, go work your side of
the street.' We say there are no Democratic rivers or Republican
mountains. Protecting the environment is everybody's issue."

To be fair, it's hard to blame environmentalists for viewing
conservatives with suspicion, given how badly Republicans have
talked about conservation for the last generation. There are
signs, however, that that might be changing.

In 2005, the *Economist,* not a magazine known for its liberal
sympathies, opined that "the greening of conservatism is a revolution waiting to happen." The magazine pointed out that a
CNN/USA Today/Gallup poll revealed that 49 percent of
Americans approve of President Bush's handling of the environment. What's more, a coalition of Washington defense hawks,
including former CIA director James Woolsey, signed an open
letter to Mr. Bush calling on him to make reducing America's
dependence on foreign oil a priority, citing the country's vulner-
ability to economic shock should Mideast violence severely dis-
rupt our oil supply. The neocon defense strategist Frank Gaffney,
a cofounder of the initiative, told me that he sees action on this
front as "inevitable," given the precariousness of the nation's
Mideast oil supplies.

The most important political development toward the greening of the GOP is a revolution in the thinking of evangelical
Christian leaders, whose movement is the backbone of the
Republican Party, especially in the South. Over the last two
years, key evangelical pastors and lay leaders have embraced
environmental stewardship ("creation care" as some of them call
it) as a biblically sound value, and indeed a divine command.
According to one poll, 52 percent of evangelicals now support
strict environmental regulation. This is not to say that evangelicals have warmed to mainstream environmental activists, some
of whom have semipagan sensibilities that rankle Bible believers.
But in recent years, these same religious folks have worked
closely and fruitfully with feminists to fight pornography and

the international sex trade, so there is every reason to think that once the two sides get comfortable with each other, they will make common cause in political efforts.

Given how serious they are about bringing their basic moral and religious convictions to the public square, the greening of the religious right is the most natural thing in the world. As Wendell Berry, the Christian farmer, poet, and essayist has written, "We are holy creatures living among other holy creatures in a world that is holy. . . . You cannot know that life is holy if you are content to live from economic practices that daily destroy life and diminish its possibility." He teaches that Christians practice, or fail to practice, their faith by how they treat creation, the handiwork of the Lord God.

Berry phoned me one night from his Kentucky farm after chores were done to talk about conservatism and the way we conservatives think about the natural world. Berry is one of the rare writers whose work is prized by folks on the left and the right, though he can irritate both sides for his ornery refusal to fit neatly into the boxes others have prepared for him. In one of his most trenchant essays, "Sex, Economy, Freedom, and Community" (published in a 1993 collection of the same title), Berry chastised both the libertine left and the libertarian right for colluding to destroy community life with their exaltation of individual gratification above all things.

When we spoke, I told him that I found his writing to be prophetic and deeply resonant with my conservative values.

"I call myself a conservative in a way, because I'm interested in conserving things that need to be conserved," he responded. "But I hesitate to call myself a conservative publicly, because I don't think there are too many in the conservative movement today who care about conserving much of anything except money. I have a lot of sympathy for so many conservatives, but when they incorporate themselves politically, nothing seems to account for the way they act."

Berry said the country has become so polarized that you're

either stupid or brave to identify yourself as a conservative or a liberal nowadays. Lately, he's been writing to his liberal friends to tell them that left-wing intellectuals ought to quit demonizing Christian fundamentalists, though he himself practices a more moderate form of the faith. "If they'd just get to know some of them, they'd find they don't all foam at the mouth, and most of them are good people," he said.

But what Berry finds tough to take from so many Christians is their blindness about the environment. "The Bible says that God made the world and approved of it. That means the natural world. One of my favorite texts is in the book of Job, where it says if God gathers to himself his spirit and his breath, all flesh will perish together, and man return again into dust. Now, this is a terrifying idea. It says God is not just transcendent, but immanent in creation, and we and all creatures live by God's spirit, and by breathing His breath.

"How you can get from that to the support that this administration has given, for instance, to mountaintop removal in Virginia and Kentucky is more than I can fathom. These people are destroying the world, and they've fired and mistreated the people who have tried to enforce the law. This has been going on here for forty years, and it's gotten steadily worse. I can't understand why these people claim to be devout worshippers of God, yet have this perfect indifference, even willingness, to this destruction."

I suggested to Berry that the recent news about important evangelical leaders changing their tune on the environment was encouraging, and he agreed, saying that he hoped that the secular left and the religious right can quit anathematizing each other and work together for the sake of the natural world. One important thing the mainstream environmental movement can learn from conservatives, he observed, is respect for human community.

"I've been carrying on kind of a battle with the environmentalists for a long time, because I can't get them interested in the conservation of the working landscapes, the economic land-scapes," he said. "I made a vow that I wasn't going to sign on to any wilderness-protection projects that didn't also try to pre-serve the environment where people made their living. They are assuming that they can preserve the natural world by means of wilderness protection, and I think that's false."

In other words, the dualist view pitting man against nature, one that partisans of the left and right share, is an illusion. To see the two as *inevitably and unavoidably* engaged in a will-to-power death struggle is not only to close off reasonable compro-mise, but also to cause unnecessary and perhaps irremediable harm to either the natural world or the people who live in it. It is poverty that creatures and places that might have been preserved with a substantial measure of dignity should be trampled under so that men may live as they choose. It is also poverty that the livelihoods and legitimate needs of men and their families should be trampled under so that ardent defenders of the natural world can live out their utopian convictions at the expense of people whose names and faces they don't even know.

These are the reasons why environmentalists have made such limited progress with the general public, even as the public's atti-tudes have become greener in recent years: people are pleased to hold the "correct" green attitudes until it costs them something, and they understandably don't want to be preached at by rigidly righteous environmentalists. But the environmentalists, in far too many cases, fail to see how dependent they are on the works of grubby human hands for the things that sustain their own lives. Like it or not, we are all in this together.

What's needed, then, is for both sides to open their minds, to think of ways to cooperate for the sake of a healthier environ-ment—domestic and natural—for all living things. It begins by ceasing to think of man and the natural world as separate and competing entities, destined to be at odds in a zero-sum game. Nothing substantial can be done to find a workable compromise until both sides free themselves from this pointless and destructive dualism. As Berry wrote in a 2002 essay collected in his book *Citizenship Papers*:

> To me, it appears that these two sides are as divided as they are because each is clinging to its own version of a common economic error. How can this be corrected? I don't think it can be, so long as each of the two sides remains closed up in its own conversation. I think the two sides need to enter into *one* conversation. They have got to talk to one another. Conservationists have got to know and deal competently with the methods and economics of land use. Land users have got to recognize the urgency, even the economic urgency, of the requirements of conservation.
>
> Failing this, these two sides will simply concede an easy victory to their common enemy, the third side, the corporate totalitarianism which is rapidly consolidating as "the global economy" and which will utterly dominate both the natural world and its human communities.

Wendell Berry's conservationism is of the sensible kind you would expect from a thoughtful and pious man who lives on and works the land, and who understands the need for harmony, for balance between the nature idolatry practiced by many liberal environmentalists and the blasphemy carried out by many conservatives. As the Bible says, man was given dominion over the things of the earth, but also required to exercise stewardship of the gift. Whether you're a religious believer or not, that is traditional wisdom worth heeding.

And it is wisdom that political conservatives can and should embrace, and translate into public policy. The standard line is that the environment is for Republicans what defense is for Democrats: not an issue that comes naturally to them. Republicans need only familiarize themselves with the teaching of some of modern conservatism's founding fathers, as well as the Holy Scriptures, to find the theoretical basis for a conservative environmentalism.

Here's a brilliant plan, which I'll give to Karl Rove for free: let's brand it "conservation," and act like it was our idea.

Though few people would dare to claim that the GOP is a pro-environment party, there are already solid post-Reagan Republican achievements on environmental protection to build on. George H. W. Bush's "cap-and-trade" policy in the 1990 Clean Air Act was a market-based initiative that substantially cut down on the amount of poisonous sulfur dioxide from coal-fired power plants. The liberal environmental writer Gregg Easterbrook pointed out in the *New Republic* that the current President Bush, demonized by environmentalists and the mainstream media as slayer of the Kyoto greenhouse-gas treaty, shepherded through Congress the world's first international anti-global-warming agreement, a 2004 measure aimed at reducing methane emissions.

Though methane is twenty-three times more potent a contributor to global warming than the carbon dioxide emissions the Kyoto treaty aimed at cutting, and the methane treaty cut just as much of that atmospheric gas as Kyoto promised to cut carbon dioxide in the best-case scenario, the media did not report Bush's extremely significant good green deed. As Easterbrook saw it, "The press corps has relentlessly pretended the Bush anti-methane initiative does not exist in order to avoid inconvenient complications of the Black Hat versus White Hat narrative it has settled into regarding global warming."

Easterbrook said that environmentalists get upset when the methane versus carbon dioxide issue arises because (in his view) the United States is the world's biggest emitter of the latter, while Europe dumps by far more of the former into the atmosphere. Anything that interferes with the story that on environmental issues America Is Bad and Europe Is Good is not to be tolerated. Note well: a well-informed *liberal* said this.

"Maybe it is unrealistic to expect Democrats and enviros to cite Bush's achievement," he wrote. "It would be nice if the press corps would at least report what has happened."

Fair enough, but I have to ask: why haven't Republicans been talking this up? There is no shortage of conservative alternative media outlets through which to spread the good news. Is it because the GOP lacks nerve? Could it be that Republicans are afraid to come across to their own base as pro-environment? REP America's Jim DiPeso says that in general, Republicans simply aren't psychologically comfortable being green.

"Our party has simply got to get over that, and exercise some positive leadership here," he said. "The first thing conservatives can do is to say that we're going to take this issue seriously. We have not understood its importance, and we're going to change that. We really mean it this time.

"Then come forward with serious, market-oriented ways of reducing pollution, improving conservation of wildlife, open space, and farmland to show that economics and the environment don't have to be enemies. It's not either/or, it's both/and. The only way we can successfully deal with that is if people see the tangible benefits to clean air, clean water, and open space. Once liberals see that conservatives are serious about reclaiming our conservation heritage, maybe they'll open themselves up to some of our ideas."

Crunchy cons need to put conservation on the Republican agenda first and foremost by talking about it among our fellow conservatives. Though the idea that to be Republican is to be against environmentalists is considered a bedrock tenet of the mainstream right-wing gospel, it has only been since about 1980 that it was considered disreputable for a conservative to be a conservationist. Both political parties have gotten a lot of mileage out of this rancorous division, but we can't afford to stay dug in to our ideological encampments any longer. All it took for me to reexamine and discard my prejudices was hearing a single articulate and credible conservative voice — Matthew Scully's — making a case for caring for the natural world in terms that made moral sense to me as a conservative. How many more Republicans would be open to the case for conservation if it were put to them not by a flushed and angry liberal, but by one of their own?

We need to hear from people like Paula Graves, an advertising copywriter and graphic designer from Gardendale, Alabama, who wrote to me saying that she has no love for the environmental movement, because it relies on iffy science and agenda-driven illogic. But she thinks the standard conservative response to environmental questions is equally knee-jerk and illogical.

"Responsible hunting and fishing helps to thin the animal and fish populations and helps keep them from approaching a crisis level of overpopulation," she wrote. "Responsible logging helps to clean dangerous overgrowth in forest land that can lead to devastating wildfires. This is the sort of logical conservation that conservatives ought to get behind and cheer, but we're so afraid of actually coming out for environmentalism that we avoid defining these ideas as environmentalism. We've ceded the issue to the environmentalists and let them set the definitions, and therefore the agenda. It's perhaps our biggest mistake."

We need to be hearing from people like Tony Dean, the South Dakota sportsman who says the rod and gun clubs in his state and the environmentalist groups have finally started to trust each other, and have begun to turn their backs on the extremists in their respective parties to work together for the cause of conservation.

"The Sierra Club gained that trust by being very responsible here. They are as deeply concerned as the rod and gun clubs are," Dean said.

"It's true that the environmental movement hasn't been culturally sensitive to us traditional conservationists — you know, the hunters and fishermen — but that's changing," he continued. "Our side is fearful that the environmental side will go after our guns, and that has some validity, but I will say that the thinking sportsman realizes that his views aren't really at odds with the environmental community's. We agree on most things. We all want great habitats and great numbers of wildlife."

"If we could combine our efforts, we could have a powerful voice," Dean concluded. "But we have to get past the bias both sides have against each other. From our side, the NRA likes to keep us divided with scare tactics, because it serves their interests."

We need to hear from people like Greg Yatarola, a consultant in Stamford, Connecticut, and self-described "green conservative." He wrote to say, "For years I have been carping about how the left has cornered the environmentalist market. To me, there are few issues more amenable to the conservative point of view than living wholesome and healthy lives, and being close to the land. G. K. Chesterton wrote that we come from the earth and return to the earth, and that when we forget this, we are lost; but do you think he would be voting for Democrats if he were alive today?"

Yatarola went on to say that he shops at Whole Foods, and gets strange looks in the checkout line when he opens his pack to put away his groceries, and his copy of *National Review* falls out. "I look forward to the day when burly, cursing men and their hordes of rambunctious kids fill the aisles at Whole Foods, and the parking lot is not filled only with Volvos with 'Gore-Lieberman' stickers."

Shopping at Whole Foods (and places like it) as a morally and environmentally responsible act? Don't roll your eyes and think of the bobos (the bourgeois bohemians identified by David Brooks). True, there is some of that, but there is no more powerful force for social change than the consumer dollar, and from a conservative point of view, it is far better to rely on market forces to shepherd society toward beneficial ends than to depend on the government. In fact, Whole Foods founder John Mackey is a committed libertarian and business visionary who believes that just as consumer demand can be destructive of places and human institutions that ought to be preserved, so, too, can it help such things to survive, even thrive.

My wife and I can't afford to buy all our groceries at Whole Foods, but we do purchase meat there, as well as from the organic livestock farmers in our area. Does it cost more? Sure. But we want to be able to trust that the meat is clean, and we feel good about paying a little more to avoid being complicit in the factory-farming system that ruins landscapes and traditional farming communities. Cheap chicken is not worth a compromised conscience.

It all comes back to the hidden costs of consumerism, and its doctrine of efficiency *über alles.* For example, those cheap vegetables we get year-round come to us in part through a national and international transportation system that burns a lot of fuel, befouling the environment. The relatively inexpensive exurban neighborhoods many of us conservatives live in—there are no more reliably Republican precincts than exurban communities—are made possible in part through an attitude toward development that ignores or minimizes environmental impact, particularly regarding their utter dependence on the automobile to sustain life in these areas. One can't help wondering how much good is really accomplished by climbing behind the wheel of a gas-guzzling SUV to make a long haul to the farmers' market downtown.

Still, you have to start somewhere, and conservatives shouldn't let the perfect become an enemy of the good. When we begin to think more holistically—that is, seeing the environment not as something "out there," but as a thing we humans are intimately, inseparably a part of—the desirability of making these kinds of calculated trade-offs comes naturally. To use a theological analogy, it's like trying to explain this or that point of Catholic doctrine. It's difficult to offer a concise justification for something like, say, the Catholic prohibition on artificial contraception. But when you think about the basic principles of Catholic anthropology, which offers a complex but coherent view of human nature and the purpose of life, the logical connection between eschewing the Pill and living according to the Catholic view of reality becomes clear. As Matthew Scully correctly said, little things unattended to can become big problems; along those lines, taking care of little things can become the first steps to creating a big solution.

It's not easy being a green conservative, but if we conservatives want to be true to our principles, we have to move in that direction. It is morally right. It is religiously correct. It is economically prudent. It strengthens national defense. And it makes a better world for our children, and our children's children.

As the most committed indoorsman west of Manhattan, I turned green not because I love to hug trees or bunnies (unless they're baked in mustard sauce). No, I turned green because, as schmaltzy as it sounds, I love to hug my kids.

CHAPTER SEVEN

Religion

For if the trumpet makes an uncertain sound, who will prepare himself for battle?

—I CORINTHIANS 14:8 (NEW KING JAMES VERSION)

SCRATCH THE SURFACE of a crunchy con, and you'll usually find a serious religious believer. That's no coincidence. Philosopher Alasdair MacIntyre has observed that moderns, even those who identify with political conservatism, tend to be liberals in the historic sense, meaning that they accept the Enlightenment's dethroning of religious truth and the resulting privatization of religious conviction. As we have seen, crunchy cons stand apart from mainstream conservatives in several basic ways, but the thread that ties them all together, that gives them focus, is religion.

Why? Because it gives crunchy cons the impetus to orient their lives and their efforts toward an ultimate end: serving God, not the self. By way of contrast, a libertarian conservative sees the point of life as exercising freedom of choice to serve his self-chosen ends, and will support a political arrangement that best serves those principles. Most mainstream American conservatives are to some degree libertarians, as we are all inheritors of the Enlightenment. Our secularist catechism teaches us that the preservation of "life, liberty and the pursuit of happiness" is the goal of our politics. This is a fine thing, to be sure, but it is indifferent as to what happiness is, or how it might best be achieved. All this credo grants us is the freedom to decide for ourselves.

I don't want to diminish the importance of this principle, but its insufficiency is, I'm afraid, all too apparent today. John Adams saw the limit of the American framework in 1798: "We have no government armed with the power capable of contending with human passions unbridled by morality and religion. Avarice, ambition, revenge or gallantry would break the strongest cords of our Constitution as a whale goes through a net. Our Constitution was made only for a moral and religious people. It is wholly inadequate to the government of any other."

In other words, a people lacking in the kind of self-restraint provided by authentic religious belief and binding moral custom are going to find the effects of its private pursuits and passions overwhelming the battlements of constitutional government. The cultural and civic crisis conservatives of all sorts believe that we're now living through bears out the truth of Adams's observation. A straight line runs between that founder's statement in the twilight of the eighteenth century and E. F. Schumacher's insight in the late twentieth century that the only way to renew our culture and set it aright is to regain our metaphysical—that is to say, religious—bearings, which were lost in the nineteenth century.

It needs to be said that even those in the conservative movement who call themselves religious conservatives often do not fully live out the logic of their beliefs. Almost all on the religious right are Christians—and in this broad sense, I am on the religious right—but it's odd how we limit our political concern to sexual issues. Jesus had as much or more to say about greed as he did about lust. But you will not find most American religious conservatives worrying overmuch about greed.

Crunchy conservatism takes a more holistic stance toward the world, one that seeks to be true to the basic teachings not only of classic Christianity, but of Judaism and other great wisdom traditions—what Scholastic philosophy calls the "natural law." As such, the crunchy con cannot separate his essential religious vision from metaphysics. That is, he believes his religion doesn't state an *opinion* about how the world is; he believes it is an accurate guide to *factual* reality.

A statement like that covers a lot of ground, and it's vital not to take it too literally or too specifically. I, for example, believe that the God of the Bible created the world; I do not believe, as some Christians do, that he did it literally in seven days. That is a dispute for another time. The important point here is that for conservative religious believers, the separation of Church and Life is neither desirable nor possible. And this makes, or should make, all the difference in how we choose to live our public and private lives, in what we esteem, and in what we support.

To be traditionally religious, at least in the cultures informed by biblical religion, is to hold in some form a sacramental worldview. As we have seen earlier, a sacramental worldview is an essentially religious way of interpreting reality, even if one isn't formally religious, because it affirms a transcendent order beneath the surface of things. To see the world sacramentally is tosee material things — objects and human actions — as vessels containing or transmitting ideals. To live in a sacramental world is to live in a world pregnant with meaning, a world in which nothing can be taken for granted, and in which no one or no thing is without intrinsic worth. If we live sacramentally, then everything we do and everything we are reflects the things we value.

You don't have to be religious to be sacramentally inclined, but it sure helps. To the religious believer, the world is not a cold, indifferent agglomeration of atoms, but the creation of a loving God who invests it with purpose and meaning. It is the task of the believer, then, to learn how best to live within the divine law.

We Americans are a religious people, but the way most of us live out our religion is fairly superficial. I don't mean that people aren't true believers; rather, I mean that we don't understand the deeper implications of the theology we profess. Church (and synagogue) is something we do on the Sabbath and on religious holidays. Faith is something we add on to our lives, like a hobby. Even many of us religious conservatives who do take our religious commitments more seriously experience it as a mostly devotional thing. Aside from a few obvious ethical areas — our sex lives, say — we don't make deeper connections between what we say we believe and how we live.

I didn't become aware of how deeply my Catholicism had come to inform my politics and my lifestyle until almost a decade after I'd come to the faith. I must say, with considerable chagrin, that this had practically nothing to do with anything I ever heard in mass. If the only contact a typical American Catholic has with Catholic teaching and thought is what he hears at mass, he will remain a self-satisfied ignoramus. It's amazing how hard priests have to work these days to avoid saying anything of consequence from the pulpit. There is an incredibly deep, rich tradition of wisdom in the Catholic Church, almost none of which you can hope to encounter today in ordinary Catholic life. You have to dig for it. American Catholics vote no differently from all other Americans, and do you know why? Because in large part the clergy ceased to teach us, and we became catechized by the culture.

That is not the Catholic Church that drew me in as a searching young man. I was raised as a Methodist in a small Southern town. It was a gentle, nondogmatic form of Christianity, and I have pleasant memories of growing up with it. But like many teenagers, I drifted away from my faith.

Later, as a college freshman, I came to be frightened by the implications of my easygoing agnosticism. In a philosophy class, I began to think through the logic of my beliefs. If there was no God, then there was no right and wrong; ethical conduct became a matter of what I could get away with or rationalize. To live that way was horrifying. And yet I knew how strong my destructive passions were, and how weak my will was in reining them in. When you are a nineteen-year-old American college boy in serious need of restraint, middle-class morality and customs are a fence made of twigs. I could see that, and it not only scared me, it depressed the hell out of me.

But what to do? Become a follower of Jimmy Swaggart? Swaggart was in his heyday at that time, and carried on his ministry across town. The only people I saw on campus at Louisiana State who seemed to take Christianity seriously were his followers, and those who appeared sympathetic to him. I concluded that to become a Christian in any meaningful sense, one had to be a Swaggartarian, which is to say, one had to reject the life of the mind. That I could not do.

And then, one Wednesday afternoon, I went to Free Speech Alley, the weekly forum outside the student union building where anyone could get up and deliver a short address on any topic. It usually attracted a fair share of fundamentalist evangelists, and like many other students, I enjoyed jeering at them. That afternoon, one of the most obnoxious campus preachers was finishing his harangue when up onto the concrete bench leaped Billy, a thin blond kid from my philosophy class. In his left hand he held a copy of *The Portable Nietzsche*. On the edge of its pages he had written in ballpoint pen "THE BIBLE."

"God does not exist!" he thundered. "But if He does — " Billy looked up at the sky, shot out his right arm, and made an obscene gesture.

People laughed nervously. Not me. I left the crowd, unnerved by what I had seen. Either Billy's gesture was merely shocking, or he had just put his immortal soul in danger of hell. When confronted by something like that, the refusal to take sides on the question seemed like a luxury I couldn't afford.

Around this time, I was visiting a friend and picked up from her bookshelf a dog-eared copy of *The Seven Storey Mountain*, Thomas Merton's famous 1940s autobiography, written not long after he'd entered the Trappist monastery. I couldn't put it down. Here was Merton, a fun-loving college student with literary ambitions and a rousing social life — somebody a lot like me —

who found himself falling head over heels for Roman Catholicism. The book really reads more like a romance than a memoir, at least to me. Could this possibly be Catholicism? I thought. The faith Merton encountered was more intellectually profound and aesthetically rich than I ever dreamed. Maybe I could be a Christian after all.

Shortly thereafter, I got around to reading Kierkegaard, and found that he and other serious Christian philosophers and artists had asked deeper questions and given more serious answers than the secular thinkers I so admired. I had to admit to myself that Kierkegaard, Pascal, Dostoevsky, Solzhenitsyn, Aquinas, and the like were company I would not be ashamed to be associated with, no matter what my friends thought.

There was a catch. I may have been becoming an intellectually convinced Christian, but I was not prepared to submit my free will to anyone. I wanted God on my terms—and I knew that that was not part of the bargain in Catholicism. Was there a place where I could have the liturgical beauty I craved, without having to change my beer-swilling college boy sexual ethics? Yes, there was. And so I became an Episcopalian.

It didn't take, of course. No religion that gives you the freedom to make up your own mind about things, particularly matters as powerful as sex, is going to have the power to bind, and to command loyalty. I went to church when I felt like it, and when I didn't, no big deal. Pretty soon, I wasn't going to church at all.

Two years out of college, I had dug myself into a serious hole with my carousing. I knew I couldn't go on like this, but I didn't have the strength to straighten my life out. Out of desperation, I began a thirty-day prayer I'd found to the Virgin Mary, asking her to show me the way to light. If you do, I promised, I'll become a Catholic. I felt slightly ridiculous doing this, but by that point, I was tired of living this way.

One night, after I'd been out partying with my gang, I got a visit from an old friend, who told me bluntly that night that I had to change, and eliminate certain bad influences from my life. He spoke with love, but with authority, and I knew he was right. As we were talking, another friend phoned from out of state to tell me a jaw-dropping story involving a life-after-death experience, the specific details of which spoke uncannily to my own crisis.

I went to my bedroom reeling, and picked up my prayer booklet as I crawled into bed. That was the last night of the prayer. The thirty days were up. And I had just been shown the way out. I considered that a miracle at the time. Still do.

And so, after a few more scrapes, I finally was true to my word and became a Catholic, on Easter Vigil, 1993. Though I couldn't have foreseen it at the outset of this journey, it has been a great gift to learn to live in submission to what I believe is divinely mandated authority, and ordering my life and my priorities according to Catholic truth. Though the Catholic ethos that won Merton's heart and soul is almost impossible to find now, Catholicism nevertheless offers a worldview of great passion, philosophical complexity, and spiritual grandeur. My politics are cultural, and they are wholly tied to my Catholicism. To the extent that I can be called a conservative, it's because I want to conserve the wisdom and humane traditions taught by and celebrated in Catholicism — *even if that puts me at odds with contemporary Republicans.*

I do not think it is possible to be authentically religious without being in some fashion an orthodox traditionalist. I'm in my late thirties; religious believers like me are not supposed to exist. It scandalizes baby-boomer Catholics that Gen Xers would come into the faith and long for the old things they discarded. Nowadays, that sort of thing cuts across denominational lines. Twenty years ago, University of Virginia sociologist James Davison Hunter identified the emergence of a tectonic division in American religious life: the one between the "orthodox" and the "progressives." In Davison's scheme, the orthodox side believes in transcendent, revealed truth to which believers must submit, while the progressives believe that religious and moral truth tends to be relative to personal experience, and that, in Davison's words, it is permissible to "resymbolize historic faiths according to the prevailing assumptions of contemporary life."

This is a fault line without historical precedent, one that runs right down the middle of most churches in America. It's why Catholics like me have more in common with traditionalist Protestants, Orthodox Christians, and even Orthodox Jews than we do with our progressive coreligionists. It's why I'd rather have a staunch self-described "Scotch Calvinist" like Caleb Stegall, whom you'll meet shortly, in my culture-war foxhole than most of the U.S. Conference of Catholic Bishops.

If you ask me, "small-o" orthodox religion is the only kind that makes sense. A god whose commandments conform perfectly to the views and desires of an early twenty-first-century middle-class American is not God at all, and certainly not a god recognizable to contemporary coreligionists living in the slums of Brazil, or on the plains of Africa. It is not a god that will be recognizable to the Americans of the late twenty-first century. And it is not a god who would have been recognizable to previous generations of believers in other times and places.

In short, if one's religion is to mean anything, if it is to last, it has to stand outside of time and place. Its truths have to be transcendent. And though we moderns have to find a way to make the tradition livable in our own situations, we must never forget that we don't judge the religion; the religion judges us. To be blunt, a god that is no bigger than our own desires is not God at all, but a divinized rationalization for self-worship.

Before we examine the way four disparate crunchy cons live out their faith, it's interesting to ask: is religion necessary to crunchy conservatism? If we crunchy cons hope our cultural politics and way of life will in time renew society, does religion play a necessary role? I asked one of the smartest young thinkers I know, New York writer Reihan Salam, with whom I exchange sympathetic e-mails from time to time on crunchy-con topics. If he's not a crunchy con, then he's definitely a fellow traveler. Reihan was raised a Muslim, of Bangladeshi immigrant parents;

even though he now considers himself a secular humanist, he esteems the social role of religion.

When I put the religious question to him, Reihan said it was tough to answer. One of his passions is what his then boss, *New York Times* columnist David Brooks, calls "natalism," or the belief that large families are not a burden, but a blessing, a positive good. Reihan agrees, and believes that the health, and possibly the survival, of our culture depends on fostering a natalist ethic (a very crunchy-con idea, by the way).

Reihan cited a passage from the liberal natalist guru Phillip Longman, who wrote in his book *The Empty Cradle:*

> The number of hours a Brazilian woman spends watching telenovelas, or domestically produced soap operas, strongly predicts how many children she will have. These soaps, though rarely addressing reproductive issues directly, typically depict wealthy individuals living the high life in the big cities. The men are dashing, lustful, power-hungry, and unattached. The women are lithesome, manipulative, independent, and in control of their own bodies. The few who have young children delegate their care to nannies.
>
> The telenovelas, in other words, reinforce the cultural message that is conveyed as well by many Hollywood films and other North American cultural exports: that people with wealth, people with sophistication, people who are free and self-fulfilled, are people who have at most one or two children, and who do not let their roles as mothers or fathers dominate their exciting lives.
>
> Demographers now put much emphasis on the role of imitation in driving fertility trends, since it is otherwise difficult to explain why fertility is falling so rapidly even in underdeveloped regions.

Longman went on to say that barring unforeseen events, the children of the future are going to come from families so alienated from modern culture that they're willing to rebel against the economic and cultural determinism that mandates small families. That's likely to mean religious believers, who will "drive human culture off its current market-driven, individualistic, modernist course, and gradually create an anti-market culture dominated by fundamentalist values."

Longman thinks that secular liberals like himself had better figure out a way to resist consumerist pop culture and to have more children, or they cede the future to religious conservatives. Reihan doesn't share Longman's fear of the faithful — in fact, he wouldn't mind society taking a less individualistic, less "modern" course — but he does wish for a middle way. He's as worried about the corrosive qualities of consumer culture as any crunchy con, but doesn't see that religion is indispensable to building an alternative.

"For me, the idea of an 'ethical culture' has great resonance," he said. "How do we find a better way to live that's in tune with our 'nature' as social animals, oriented toward cooperation and with a basic drive toward successfully propagating the species?"

The early Christians, he pointed out, practiced a way of life that was objectively superior, healthier, and more cooperative than that practiced by the ancient Roman pagans (sociologist Rodney Stark is the one to read on this phenomenon). Reihan observes that the post-Enlightenment attempt to supplant Christianity with secularist orthodoxy as the guiding framework of society has, on evidence of collapsing birthrates, failed to create a social system that can reproduce itself.

Said Reihan, "So I'm looking forward to some kind of moral revival/cultural transformation that will supplant a way of life that's making large numbers of people miserable, and replacing it with another way of life — religiously informed for many, by a secular morality for others — that does not."

Well, me, too, and I sure don't want to live in a theocracy; a society in which one is free to choose one's religion, or no religion at all, is the best of all alternatives, it seems to me. But I don't see how the better society Reihan and I both want to see come into being is going to happen absent a serious spiritual reawakening. It's certainly not that one has to be religious to be moral, but absent an overwhelming spiritual mandate, why would you choose to do the economically foolish thing and have big families, or sacrifice a second income so Mom can stay home and take care of the kids? More fundamentally, without religion, how do you build an ethical system powerful enough to stand up to a mainstream media and commercial culture that propagates itself by exploiting with staggering skill humanity's innate vices of lust, greed, vanity, and egotism? John Adams suggested that you cannot. Alasdair MacIntyre says outright that you cannot, and that the nineteenth and twentieth centuries have proven the Enlightenment philosophers wrong.

However observant one may or may not be, an active religious imagination — an ability to see the material world in spiritual terms — is key to the crunchy-con worldview. But there is more than one way to live out a crunchy-con spirituality.

The Protestant

Caleb Stegall is a thirty-three-year-old lawyer, husband, and father of four who lives on a farm near Lawrence, Kansas. He and his wife, Ann, homeschool their kids, grow as much of their own food as they can, and are working hard to recover the skills of self-sufficiency that were lost in our parents' generation. They are lifelong conservative Presbyterians, as distinct from mainliners. However, Caleb now serves as an elder in a Presbyterian church that's closer to the vast evangelical mainstream than he's comfortable with.

In fact, he said that much of the way he and his family live and think about their faith and its impact on their lives is "strongly countercultural to mainstream Evangelicalism." So why do they identify with Evangelicalism? Because, Caleb explained, with the mainline having largely crossed over to the progressivist side of the great American religious divide, Evangelicalism is just about the only vibrant option left for orthodox Protestants.

From the outside, American Evangelicalism has a cultural vigor that Catholics can only envy. What's not to like? I asked Caleb. For starters, he said, Evangelicalism suffers from an ignorance of Christian history, and does not appreciate the intellectual depth and spiritual rigor in the church's tradition.

"And there's a tendency to be taken in by the latest and the greatest thing," he said. "Evangelicals have a great deal of energy and zeal, and that's a good thing. It's borne great fruit in some ways. But it's tempered hardly at all by depth and rootedness. That's the dynamic you see at work with a lot of zealous movements and so on that don't put roots down very deep. One year it'll be *The Passion of the Christ,* and the next year it's Rick Warren and *The Purpose Driven Life.* There's a lot of susceptibility in Evangelicalism to cultural shifts."

That's why you can see the self-help sentimentality of middle-class American culture playing itself out in sometimes embarrassing ways among evangelicals. Evangelical friends of mine who have been to the annual Christian Booksellers Association convention come back aghast, as if they'd beheld kitsch-mad moneychangers in the temple. For Caleb, this hunger for *Chicken Soup for the Soul* therapeutic religion is not just an evangelical problem.

"It's a cultural issue," he said. "There's not much preparation in our lives today for deferred gratification, and the validity and value of working harder for something. Getting to the depth of the church's history and teachings is hard work. We want to feel better, and feel better now."

More fundamentally, Caleb believes, the evangelical church has to grapple with the central cultural role of the family, and especially the "necessity of children." He's talking about having more than the requisite 2.1 children per couple. You find that a surprising number of crunchy cons have larger than normal families, despite the financial hardships.

"Birth control is a real issue for evangelicals," he said, startling my Catholic ears. "My own view is that how a community approaches that issue is going to be very telling with respect to any other issue that comes up. There's an unlegislatable mandate to communities to be faithful to future generations, which means replacing yourself, or exceeding the replacement rate. When a community's healthy, it will do that, and it will only do that when people essentially love the community more than they love themselves."

Caleb is a founder and editor of a smart, edgy webzine called the *New Pantagruel*, which published some eye-opening criticism of the GOP during the 2004 campaign. I asked him how he felt about the popular perception that the evangelical church is merely the Republican Party at prayer.

"I think it's awful," he said. "Which is not to say good things aren't being done as the evangelical church works to gain influence in the Republican Party. But if that's the sum and substance of what the church is, then it's completely abdicated its true role, which ought to be higher and deeper and broader and wider than that."

Caleb is a Republican, and has always voted GOP. Yet he sees the party as having more in common with the Democrats than with his kind of conservatism. Why? Because Republicans view the individual as sovereign, and freedom of individual choice as the highest good. The midcentury conservative theorists who advanced a more family-oriented, communitarian politics — Caleb cites men like T. S. Eliot, Russell Kirk, Eric Voegelin, the Southern Agrarians — have been given little or no voice in the contemporary Republican party.

"Their natural home is in the church, and to the extent that the church speaks the language of Republican politics, it loses that older, deeper, truly conservative political philosophy, which advocates rootedness, continuity over time, order, and fidelity to a higher good," he said. "And that higher good is expressed religiously in the transcendent, and in our lives in terms of our connection to family, community, and the land."

Do you ever get the feeling that conservative Christians are in some ways fighting the wrong culture war? I asked him. Absolutely, he said; the culture war is beside the point of what's really important to religious believers. Too many Christians busy themselves trying to figure out how to change the political culture, but they're not noticing how the culture is changing them, and the church.

"The question is not what do we do with this culture, but what do I do with myself? It's not about lifestyle. It's about figuring out the difficult complexities of our own lives, and how to resist the disordering pressures of our age," he said. "It's exceedingly difficult, and calls for a lot of sacrifice and probably false choices. That to me is far more important than any political action point that people may rally around."

We talked for a bit about how dismaying it is to live in places that are as Christian and conservative as any in America—Dallas, Texas, and Lawrence, Kansas—and yet see traditional Christian values making so little apparent difference in the lives many conservative believers lead. A lot of people don't know it, but northeastern Kansas, where the Stegalls live, is one of the most prosperous areas of the country. Like North Texas, where I live, there are a lot of country-club Republicans around, Caleb said, and you see materialism play itself out in conservative church life.

"That's disturbing, and ought to be disturbing, but people don't feel comfortable saying it. If you say that progress and unhindered free markets are not unmitigated goods, and that we conservatives ought to be thinking of this, the kind of Republicanism we have now calls you a liberal or a traitor to conservatism," he said. "We need that critique now on the right, and if it's not going to come from the church, I don't know where it's going to come from."

When asked about the future of Evangelicalism in America, Caleb says it can only survive in a meaningful sense in material culture if it reconnects with the depth of its sixteenth-century Reformed tradition — and beyond. There has to be a renewed openness to Roman Catholicism, and the insights to be found in pre-Reformation Christianity. Otherwise, in time, Catholicism will be the "only game in town," meaning the only expression of Christianity with the depth and awareness to challenge the wider culture.

"There is a strong understanding of the sacramentality of all of life, the sacramental nature of all things, in the Protestant tradition, but evangelicals have a very stunted understanding of what that means. There's very little sense of that in the way most evangelicals live their lives," he said. (It's true for Catholics, too.)

"George Santayana is one of my intellectual mentors," he continues. "He wrote a brilliant essay on the American sensibility, and he described American materialism as a moral materialism. That's how I've come to think of evangelicals. It's the underlying material view of life, which essentially says this is just stuff all around us, stuff to be manipulated however we want, without regard for the transcendent order. Overlaying that is a moral goodness, this sense that there should be a strong work ethic — you know, the thrifty good American. That's the picture.

"But for Ann and me, the decisions we've made have been out of trying to recapture some of that, that sense of all of life being sacred, getting close to the land, growing as much of our own food as we can, even homeschooling."

In fact, on the night we spoke, Caleb was preparing to quit his fast-track job in a prestigious law firm to open his own office — for the sake of his family.

"I hope it won't put me in the poorhouse. But even that is connected to what we're talking about — this desire to move closer to home, to develop more of a home economy and be more connected to community," he explained. "As I've talked to people about my decision to leave, their jaws hit the floor. Giving up a potential partnership in the state's largest law firm to be closer to my family doesn't compute to a lot of people."

Meanwhile, he's going to continue working on the *New Pantagruel,* which he and his colleagues are committed to making into a prophetic conservative voice shot through with Rabelaisian wit. Caleb said, "We stake out our position as being called to a renewal of the kinds of cultural order that people like Russell Kirk and Eric Voegelin talked about, and a call to church renewal at all levels. We're finding out that conservatives are very open to hearing what we're saying."

Before we ended our conversation, I asked him why he was determined to stick it out in evangelical Protestantism, even though he was such a strong critic of it. Because, he said, that's where his roots are. He and his family are committed to that tradition, as many generations before them have been, and to their particular church. Even if there are disagreements with others in that faith community, and things they would like to see done differently, the Stegalls believe in sticking.

"The modern answer to everything is to just move down the street," said Caleb. "I refuse to do that."

The Catholic

As a frequent peruser of Catholic blogs, I kept tripping over the comments by a guy named Maclin Horton, and finding myself agreeing with most everything he said. I thought that this guy had to be some sort of crunchy con. One day I was Googling for information about a cherished but defunct Catholic magazine called *Caelum et Terra,* which in its heyday (1991–1996) was the closest thing crunchy-con Catholics ever had to their own journal. Turns out that Maclin Horton was one of its founders! I had to find out more about him.

« »

Mac is a fifty-six-year-old Catholic convert living on Mobile Bay in Alabama, and working at an area college. He and his wife, Karen, have three grown children and a high schooler still at home. When I contact him, I ask Mac about *Caelum et Terra* (Latin for "heaven and earth"), why he helped start it, and why it failed.

Mac explained that it was a journal for Catholics who were dissatisfied with the standard left-right polemics both within the church and in society.

"It was by and for people who treasure and venerate the Catholic tradition and the culture of the West, which was rooted in Catholicism, and who see both the mainstream right and the mainstream left as being hostile, albeit in different ways, to that tradition," Mac recalled. "Maybe in the most fundamental sense it was for Catholics who seek contact with the *real* on a direct physical and cultural as well as a metaphysical level."

After five years of exhausting labor, the magazine finally folded. There weren't enough subscribers, and very few patrons among the Catholic establishment. More recently, *C&T* writers and partisans have resurrected it, at least in spirit, on a blog, where Mac and others keep a daily journal of their thoughts and observations.

His journey into Catholicism was much like my own (an intensely religious child, he was raised a Methodist, lost his faith, became an Episcopalian, and ended up a Catholic). But he is a generation older than I am; while I was still in my crib, Mac was a devout counterculturalist—until he came to see that the anti-establishment stance was a pose that masked a predatory and self-destructive hedonism.

Yet when he turned his back on the left-wing counterculture, he didn't return to the establishment. Instead, he embraced Catholicism as a more sane and truthful response to the emptiness against which he first rebelled. I asked Mac if he still believed that mainstream American culture is worth fighting against.

"Well, in a sense I have accepted it, in that I have entirely lost the mind-set of the revolutionary who wants to see a radical over-throw and restarting of society," he replied. "I have a much more reasonable conception of how much or little can be expected of life in this world. But since my early, incoherent, and spasmodic rebellion, I've spent a big part of my life trying to figure out exactly why I thought there was something seriously amiss in American society and whether I was correct in thinking so."

He believes now as much as he did when he embraced the six-ties counterculture that man's spiritual life matters most of all, and that our society has discarded this essential truth to a dangerous degree. Despite the rise of the religious right as a political force, Mac believes that if anything, the decline in authentic spirituality has gotten steeper in the past couple of decades. Rebelling against popular culture is "a matter of life and death," he said — and yet, one feels almost powerless to resist.

"In the mid-twentieth century two books were written that laid out opposing visions of a plausible coming dystopia. One was *1984* and the other was *Brave New World,*" he said. "The threat described in the former was clear and distinctive and something we could fight, physically and politically and intel-lectually — and it was defeated, at least for the time being. But the threat described in the latter is greater than ever. *Brave New World* in fact represents precisely the society toward which much of our so-called progress is directed, quite often explicitly so."

The 1932 Aldous Huxley novel describes a future world in which multinational corporations rule humanity through several means. Genetic engineering, control of reproduction, social pro-gramming, entertainment, the promotion of promiscuity, and copious doses of a feel-good drug called "soma" — all these pro-duce a thoroughly contented, thoroughly exploited population. It is a mass society in which self-absorbed humanity is alienated from its true nature, and prefers to live in contentment rather than truth.

"I think there is now a very large number of people who simply would not understand *Brave New World* at all," says Mac. "They might balk at the stratification of the population by intelligence level, but otherwise would not see anything wrong with this vision of a scientifically controlled hedonistic paradise. I'll die fighting that in whatever way I can."

Mac cautions that he dearly loves America, and doesn't believe that it's intrinsically bad to lessen life's hardships. The problem arises when maximizing pleasure and minimizing pain become ultimate goals. "The question before us is, at bottom, the old one of whether a people can live in luxury without destroying themselves," he said. "The indications at present are not all that favorable."

I asked Mac to explain why he thinks that industrial capitalism and conventional left-wing bohemianism are two sides of the same coin. He brings up Woodstock, the baby boomer counterculture's Bastille Day. There was nothing about it objectionable to hardheaded businessmen.

"It was the very acme of consumerism," he said. "You had several hundred thousand people willingly reducing themselves to a condition of infantile dependence and passivity in the expectation that competent adults would take care of their physical needs. It was that, more than the doping and fornicating, that was really most disgusting and even frightening about it. I think of the Eloi and Morlocks in H. G. Wells's *The Time Machine* — the Eloi are these pretty, sweet, stupid creatures who frolic on the surface, while the Morlocks live underground and do all the work necessary to feed and clothe the Eloi. The catch is, the Eloi are also the Morlocks' food supply."

In short, Mac said, practical capitalism and conventional left-wing bohemianism agree that the purpose of life is to maximize pleasure and minimize pain. The bohemian wants his desires satisfied; the capitalist wants to make money by satisfying these desires; it's a perfect match. Hence the difficulty in solving our cultural crisis.

From his sixties counterculture days, Mac remembered that

many of his friends had been like him: quite religious as children, but proudly atheist as teenagers. Does growing up with a strong religious sense prepare one to be a countercultural adult, whether from the secular left or the religious right?

"The human longing for God can't be killed. But the American genius is pragmatic and worldly — think of Benjamin Franklin — and although we are willing to let a thousand religious flowers bloom, we tend to want to keep them in the greenhouse," Mac said.

"A young person who feels this longing for God with particular intensity is likely to be equally affected by his or her sense that on the official and public level this longing — which, to him, puts everything else in a far lesser light — is, in practice, denied. If he manages to stay on the God track, or to get back on it if he gets off, he'll inevitably cast a cold eye on the culture and thus be at least somewhat ready to stand against it if necessary. God only knows how many people who go far astray in pursuit of a drug or sex paradise are really driven by a misdirected religious impulse."

It's interesting, I mention, that both 1960s counterculturalists and right-wing Catholics love *The Lord of the Rings* passionately. J. R. R. Tolkien, a Tory Catholic, is a crunchy-con saint.

"I had an office mate back in the 1980s who was a more or less unreconstructed hippie," said Mac. "He was a huge *Lord of the Rings* fan, even a fanatic, and it was in the context of discussing it that he used a phrase that has stuck with me: 'the magic truth.' He was contrasting this with material truth, like the laws of physics, and he thought it was to be found, or at least glimpsed, in the book. That's certainly the way I felt when I first read it: as if Tolkien's fantasy world was somehow more real than the one we see around us.

"And the people who react this way don't mean it's simply a *nicer* world, or a more interesting one — they mean that somehow this is what life really is, this adventure, with its infinitely high stakes for good and ill. A Catholic recognizes the truths of his faith in this and recognizes the sense of being called as coming from God. A hippie may not know exactly what's going on, but he still feels the call. If a higher percentage of hippies than of the general population responded this way, then maybe that's a bit of evidence that there really was a spiritual component in the hippie rebellion."

Are crunchy cons really right-wing hippies? Now there's a thought. It will be news to many people, I suggested to him, that there are people like me and thee who believe that being truly Catholic in this time and place is to be truly countercultural. That you will find the real radicals not on Sproul Plaza at Berkeley, but with their eight kids in a Latin Mass at a forgotten inner-city parish in Baton Rouge. Why is this? Essentially, said Mac, because those who are most serious about defending the primacy of the spiritual against our materialistic, hedonistic consumer culture are those most committed to the life of the spirit.

That does not mean simply being in church on Sunday and holy days of obligation. In nearly every Catholic parish I've been in, comfortable accommodation with bourgeois American life seems to be the order of the day. How can Catholicism really be countercultural when the actual experience of American Catholicism seems never to challenge prevailing cultural norms, no matter what the pope says?

Mac said that the hierarchy bears a lot of the responsibility for this. Since the 1960s, they've been afraid to challenge their flocks, and now, even though they've got plenty of pew-warmers, most Catholics don't agree with core church teachings — if they even know what those teachings are. If the bishops and their priests had had the courage merely to proclaim Catholic doctrine, Mac postulated, they probably would have been surprised by how many Catholics would have followed them.

"A couple of years ago Karen and I were assisting with RCIA

in our parish," he says, referring to the Rite of Christian Initiation for Adults, the process through which adult converts to Catholicism join the church. "We were humbled and occasionally surprised by the spiritual insight and hunger we saw in some of these seemingly very conventional people, both the catechumens and their sponsors: a guy who sold boats for a living, a teacher who'd been a lapsed Baptist for many years. It may not have occurred to them that they really need to challenge the culture, but that's at least partly because nobody has pointed it out to them.

"People long for God, and more of them than we might think are willing to accept the idea that getting close to him might be painful. The church needs to worry less about coddling our superficial tastes and impulses and more about giving us the whole truth."

For many decades in America, Catholics were solidly identified with the Democratic Party. Now, they vote in precisely the same percentages as the American mainstream. I know Mac is a conservative, but I had to ask him if he was also a Republican.

"I am not now and never have been a member of the Republican Party. I almost always vote Republican, but it's a tactical alliance," he said. "The Republican Party is at least somewhat hospitable to religious traditionalists, while the Democratic Party is hostile, or at a minimum has made itself unable to oppose those who are hostile. It's the difference between an unreliable ally and an enemy."

He considers himself an anti-ideological political conservative, and said he most strongly dissents from GOP orthodoxy over "the Republican assumption that whatever business wants is probably right."

"I am a passionate believer in economic liberty and widespread property ownership. It's precisely *because* of that belief that I think the dominance of economic life by large corporations is a bad thing. You don't ensure economic liberty for all by eliminating restraints on the accumulation of capital and market share any more than you ensure physical liberty by eliminating the police and the courts and turning everyone loose to sort out the pecking order on their own."

Mac believes in the general set of ideas that G. K. Chesterton and his circle taught under the label "distributism." Broadly speaking, distributism holds that the best society is one in which the widest number of people are property owners. Distributists idealize small businesspeople, family farms, and local economies. To Mac, distributism is much more compatible with Catholic social teaching than an economic regime in which most people are passive workers for large, far-off corporations.

"I don't understand why the social-justice people don't drop their attachment to socialism and embrace the ideal of widely distributed property," he said. "I don't understand why patriotic conservatives don't seem to care that soulless corporations are destroying the old weird America — a phrase coined, I think, by left-wing rock critic Greil Marcus. This is the rich, vital, genuinely diverse, eccentric America that conservatives love, or claim to love."

I had noted in some of Mac's postings on various Catholic blogs a certain sense of despair over what has become of Catholicism in America. This resonated deeply with me. I was attracted to the Catholic faith for the same reasons he was, but I am finding it intensely difficult to hold on as a Catholic in this time of trial. It's not just the sex scandals with the clergy, but the vacuous homilies, the bare, ruined liturgies, the purposelessness and overall loss of grandeur. In most ways, this is not the church I thought I was joining, though there is absolutely no reason why it should not be, and could not be again. I confessed to Mac that my chief emotions when I think about the Catholic Church these days are anger and disappointment.

Said Mac, "I suppose I was somewhat ready for disappointment, because, aside from the fact that I'm a natural pessimist, from the moment I set foot in what ended up being our first

Catholic parish church, which happened to be in a prefab steel building, and picked up my first tacky newsprint missalette, I knew I was going to be giving up a lot."

The music was horrible, the priest was kind but daffy and was later murdered in a love-triangle killing. But the strength of Mac's intellectual commitment to the faith sustained him. But as time went on, the necessity of constant struggle against progressivist crusades took its toll. His belief in the efficacy of the sacraments sustained him, even though his normal state of mind after leaving mass became one of oppression and dryness.

As his children grew and began to drift away from Catholicism, Mac began to nurse a sense of bitterness that the church didn't offer more to hold them.

"I can remember any number of Sundays when we would come back from mass and the children would pile out of the car and Karen and I would just sit there morosely for fifteen minutes, trying to articulate exactly what it was about the liturgy that left us feeling this way afterward. I should add that I was and am equally bitter toward the surrounding culture that makes it so very, very hard to raise children these days."

So why do you hold on? I asked.

"It's really quite simple: there isn't anything else," he said. "It's Catholicism or nihilism for me. In the last couple of years my gloom has lifted somewhat. Maybe this is just age. It helps that the liturgy at our parish is now at least dignified and respectful, even if it's stuck with those banal translations and all the rest of it."

Before our conversation ended, I said to Mac that I don't believe that crunchy conservatism can be practiced sustainably without some sort of serious religious commitment. It's just too hard to resist the spirit of the age, and the siren song of consumerism, absent a deep and abiding faith in spiritual ideals, and the conviction that the choices we make now matter for all eternity.

"I agree, mainly because such a sensibility will cease to be itself if it does not involve some amount of submission to that which is more than itself, that which poses an obstacle to the attempt to force the cosmos to conform to one's own immediate preferences," he said. "Without that humility, it can't be a traditionalist sensibility; one becomes a consumer of a different sort, as we see in New Age religion and its alliance with environmentalism. And it's hard to see how that humility can be genuine and lasting if its object is merely chosen—that is, if it doesn't stem from some sense of obligation to a real power.

"In retrospect," he concluded, "I think one of the underlying psychological shifts that eventually led me to the church was the realization that I could not simply be 'spiritual' in any serious way by browsing various religions and selecting what pleased me. It would be necessary to *submit* on some fundamental level."

The Eastern Orthodox

Because they're committed to nurturing roots, both Caleb and Mac are sticking with their separate religious traditions, despite the shortcomings of those traditions as they are practiced in contemporary America. After taking the spiritual grand tour, Hugh O'Beirne, a thirty-three-year-old Atlanta attorney, husband, and father of two, put down roots in exotic *terroir* for a young American: in Eastern Orthodoxy, the third great historical expression of Christianity.

It is not an exotic choice by any means outside of the United States. There are hundreds of millions of Orthodox believers, mostly in Russia, eastern Europe, and the eastern Mediterranean. But in this country, only about 1 percent of the popultion is Orthodox, which is to say, roughly speaking, that there are about as many Orthodox in America as there are Jews and Muslims. Yet their numbers are fast increasing through the conversion of other Christians, especially evangelicals, who want the historical continuity — like Catholicism, Orthodoxy claims an unbroken line of priestly succession, dating back to the apostles — with the early Christian church, as well as the lavish liturgy and intense sacramentality, without buying into Roman Catholic doctrine and ecclesiology.

Hugh's wife, Addie, came to Orthodoxy from an evangelical background. But he was Catholic. His mother, a Boston nun and missionary, left the sisterhood to marry, but she has always been a staunch Catholic.

The liturgical and doctrinal insanity of 1970s Catholicism made Hugh an atheist at age thirteen. He started reading Nietzsche, who despised Christianity as a weak, feminized religion. That struck adolescent Hugh as an apt description of disco-era Catholicism.

"The church was emasculate, and it loved it," he said. "It was linen and velvet banners, and guitars and hugging. When you hit puberty, you just dislike that stuff. And I think like many people in my generation, when I was young, I had a strong aversion to all that hippieness."

In his late teens, Hugh flirted with Eastern religions, but halfway through college returned to his strident atheism. But sharing quarters in grad school with a devout Southern Baptist, and being friends with an Orthodox Christian, gradually led him to accept the existence of God, and finally go back to his Catholic roots.

He became deeply traditionalist, and engaged in apologetics, persuasive argumentation for the faith. He met Addie during his last year of law school at Vanderbilt, and he loved to argue theology, in a friendly way, with her Texas parents, who are Protestant fundamentalists. Yet even as he deftly deployed syllogisms in defense of the Catholic faith, the actual practice of that faith in contemporary American life left him increasingly uneasy.

"I liked Catholic doctrine, but was deeply dismayed with Catholic practice," Hugh recalled. "The liturgy seemed abysmal, and at odds with these wonderful pronouncements, and what I was reading about the fathers of the church. It made no sense."

He drifted into Orthodox liturgies, but didn't feel the need to convert because he was enamored of the logical case for Catholicism. Plus, he didn't want to get mixed up with what is in the American cultural context a politically marginal Christian sect, one whose followers all too often sideline themselves with arguments over ethnic identity. Addie wanted to go Orthodox, but Hugh resisted.

"In the meantime, I was debating her father on the merits of Catholicism versus Protestantism. One night, after having thoroughly done away with his arguments against purgatory, or so I thought, it hit me that I was playing a big logic game, that I was enamored of a God who was more like the God of the philosophers than the Lord. It was at that point I realized that I can't keep doing this, I've got to become Orthodox."

Within one year, the O'Beirnes were received into the Orthodox Church. That was in 2000. Since then, they've found their religious burden increased in some ways, but lightened in more important ones.

"We have a lot more fasting that we're called to do. We have much longer liturgies. It's a busier religious experience in the sense of practice, but it's much more joyful, and more peaceful," he said. "I used to fight the intra-church battles in the Catholic church as much as I'd fight against Protestants. But there's no war footing within Orthodoxy. You can go that way, and I've seen it happen, but it's not there in the same way as it is in Catholicism. Our lives have become more spiritually attuned."

I mentioned the growing exodus of converts out of liberal Christianity, and into the more traditional, morally rigorous forms of the faith. Orthodoxy owes its new birth in this country to that awakening. Why is this happening? I asked.

"I think it's because traditional churches to varying degrees maintain the embodied tradition of Christianity that was handed down by Christ and preserved by the apostles. The church is a living entity, shared among its people; it can't be just a solipsistic experience. It includes us all and is greater than us all. The traditional expressions just maintain what was the original truth of Christianity."

Besides, Hugh adds, religious orthodoxy is "really the only game in town. Modernity has reached an irresolvable crisis, because it has spawned only postmodernism, which doesn't itself propose anything. We've seen the great icons of high modernism falling. Marxism, Darwinism, Freudianism—all these things that were inspired by the Enlightenment, and carried the Enlightenment to its logical end, have suffered serious blows. The only thing that explains life and how to live it in any way that makes sense is traditional religion."

As Hugh sees it, traditional religion—in his case, Orthodoxy—provides a reasonable and truthful interpretive lens through which to judge the world. It is not simply a set of opinions; it is a metaphysics, an entire way to conceive reality.

"If you are an orthodox religious believer, you tend to make political choices that would further what I guess you would call the conversion of the world. And that doesn't mean a theocracy at all; those have been tried, and they've ended in disaster. It has to mean a balanced position that allows for people to freely communicate," he said. "A theocracy, and any kind of comprehensive identification of individuals with an ideology, is de facto not Christian. Christianity cannot be coercive like that. It doesn't come up with a legal system, like Islam."

Is it possible to be a traditionalist Christian and vote for liberal Democrats? I asked. Not really, he said. He is sympathetic to the Democratic concerns about the environment and the just distribution of wealth. He is especially eager to reverse the industrialization of agriculture. But overall, Hugh believes the Democrats, particularly on issues related to abortion, biotechnology, and sexual morality, are irredeemably hostile to traditionalist Christians.

As for the GOP, "they're not above corruption, but at least

they tend more often than not to champion an agenda that is more beneficial to the nation as a whole — economically, internationally, and regarding the ethical requirements of politics."

What most engages Hugh's political imagination, however, is what he called the "consumerist ideology" that has co-opted both the Republican and Democratic parties, and the American political and moral character.

"You sit back and look at the current situation and say, 'Gee, there's got to be an end to resources somewhere. There's only so much you can build.' I don't know where we fit as people who are traditionalists, who are more motivated by what could be called social concerns than by strictly economic concerns. I like the idea of subsidiarity" — a key principle of Catholic social teaching that says decisions should always be made at the most local level possible — "and I like the idea of solidarity. We don't have either in this country at the present time."

That, said Hugh, is the crunchy-con dilemma. You cannot take seriously the individual's responsibility to the community, and the community's responsibility to the individual, and go along with an economy and a society that exist on boundless production and boundless consumption. Something's got to give.

"And the first casualty of that kind of consumer society is going to be beauty," Hugh said. "We as crunchy cons see beauty as an irreducible facet of the world, and something that we have to take care of. We have a responsibility for upholding it and caring for it. But consumerism gone mad, that's got nothing to do with traditionalism, that's modernism. Adam Smith and Karl Marx are two sides of the same coin: they define man as primarily economic man. We traditionalist Christians believe man is called to be something far greater. If you are producing and consuming ad nauseam, you are destroying beauty. That is an affront to Creation, and it is the fruit of an ideology gone wrong. And we've got to resist that."

Theologically, Orthodoxy is much more mystically oriented than Catholicism and Protestantism. In fact, a centuries-old

Orthodox critique of Western Christianity is that it is too logical, too cerebral, and doesn't take seriously enough the reality of mystical illumination, and the transformation of matter by the spirit of God. It's easy to see why the ancient traditions of Orthodoxy, which are aesthetically ravishing, morally strict, and have been liturgically and doctrinally unchanged for over a thousand years, captivate the crunchy-con imagination.

"I've often noted that Orthodoxy attracts a tremendous number of what you might call 'alternative-lifestyle' people," Hugh says. "We see a lot of former hippies. You go to our churches, you see a lot of people in Birkenstocks. We get a lot of people who reject the overlay of contemporary consumerist values on the church. So we don't put an emphasis on that, but at the same time you see gold and icons everywhere."

How do you explain that to someone who says the sacramental churches are the worst materialists? I asked.

"See, we're not against material things, except as an end. The created world is fundamentally good, it just has to be rightly ordered. We understand where the beauty needs to be. It's the proper ordering of life that Orthodoxy requires us to embrace and to strive for that really gets us going," Hugh says. "It calls these kinds of people because there is something about the beauty of the church that is at odds with beauty right now as determined by the consumerist culture. We attract people who get that, and when they find it in the Orthodox Church, they run with it."

He said that among the serious Orthodox believers and the new converts, you find lots of people into Slow Food, organic gardening, and more natural, sustainable ways of building. Hugh said, "In Orthodoxy, it all seems to go together. Don't ask me how; it's just part of the mystery of this old, old church, which asks us to reorient our lives."

That's the common link among the various religious orthodoxies: they demand that the individual submit to the demands of the tradition, rather than expect, in the modern fashion, the tradition to conform to the individual's expectations. It's incorrect to say that tradition is frozen in time; all tradition, if it is to be a living thing and not something for a museum of antiquity, has to be incarnated in a meaningful sense into the lives of individuals and communities. The general rule, though, is that authoritative traditions have a right to expect individuals to yield to the collective wisdom and experience they embody. Chesterton called tradition "the democracy of the dead." If we wish to keep faith with our fathers (and mothers), we will honor and exalt tradition, not as an end in itself, but as the most trustworthy path to God, if only because so many saints have walked it before us.

The Jew

It is hard, though, to explain to people outside traditional religion how and why it can be so liberating, especially to those of us raised in a less rigorous, more modern faith or style of worship. I didn't myself foresee it, how yielding to the discipline of Roman Catholicism made me more free and joyful than I could have imagined. Tikva Crolius knows how it goes. She is a forty-four-year-old Orthodox Jew, a convert who says following the 613 commandments required of all Jews is, paradoxically, a yoke that brings liberty.

I found Tikva through Rabbi Chaim Adelman, the Chabad-Lubavitch leader in Amherst, Massachusetts. Chabad is a traditionalist, charismatic, dynamic Jewish movement often referred to in the media as "ultraorthodox." In New York City, you can usually recognize Chabadniks by their distinct black garb, of the sort their ancestors wore in eastern Europe.

I'd called Rabbi Adelman because several years ago he helped found a kosher organic farm in Massachusetts. How crunchy con is that! Moreover, I knew that Chabad and other Orthodox sects like it attracted numbers of young Jews who were raised without religion, or in one of the more modern forms of Judaism

(Conservative, Reform, Reconstructionist, etc.). He told me that when Jewish people grow weary of the moral relativism of secular society, they find themselves drawn to traditional Judaism, which offers them "real goals in life, truth grounded in God's word, instead of being after money, possessions, whatever.

"The young come to Chabad because it's vibrant, it's alive," he continued. "It's ancient, but we're worldly in the sense that we know what's going on. We're interested in world events. For a young person, we talk their language. We're actually living a holy lifestyle in the modern world."

The idea for the farm was to live out biblical ideals in an agrarian setting. In our telephone conversation, I told Rabbi Adelman about the Hutchinses and the Hales, the fundamentalist Christian farm families in rural East Texas, and how they believed they were obeying God and playing a part in redeeming creation by their farming. All of this resonated with him — especially the part about the sacramental mentality.

"Everything's in the world for a reason," Rabbi Adelman said. "If we're given these items and they come into our possession and space, we are commanded to imbue them with holiness. Anything can be utilized if it's kosher. If you use it for good intent, you bring holiness down to the world. Who you are, what you eat, where you live, everything has a purpose."

As we have seen, if you believe that, if you *really* believe that, you cannot live like everybody else in American culture. Your attitude toward the world and your place in it undergoes revolutionary change. You might even do something like move to rural Massachusetts to raise organic crops and wait for the Messiah to come. Eight Chabad families did just that.

Turns out the farm hadn't worked out because of financing and organizational difficulties, but all the families who had been part of it remained in the Amherst area, were gardening organically in their own backyards, and were trying to figure out a communal arrangement they could sustain. I was sorry to hear that the experiment had failed, but was still inspired by the religious vision that would cause modern Jews, nearly all of them raised either without religion or as Reform Jews, to embrace Jewish Orthodoxy, and leave the world, in a sense, to commit themselves to a traditional agrarian way of life.

"You need to talk to Tikva," he said, then gave me her number.

And so, late at night on the eve of the beginning of Passover, I spoke by phone to Tikva Crolius, who was making the final preparations for the holiday. She was baking brownies when I reached her in the home she shares with her son, Ezra. Tikva is a divorced single mom, a writer, and a former newspaper journalist who has lived in Amherst since 1988.

She is not formally part of the Chabad movement, but she prays with them, and participated in the farming project. When the community lost the land, she and another woman put their heads together and figured out how to continue the organic farming ideal. They now drive weekly over the Vermont border to get kosher milk, which they culture into yogurt.

As it happens, she knew something of crunchy conservatism, having read my original *National Review* story excerpted in what was then called *Utne Reader,* the *Reader's Digest* of the crunchy left. She told me straightaway that she was "all over the map politically," and was conservative on social issues, but in other ways not so much to the right. Not to worry, I told her; crunchy conservatism is primarily about cultural traditionalism and the way you live, not the way you vote.

Tikva—whose given name is Ali—was born a Gentile, and raised Unitarian Universalist. Her spiritual life has been a tour of non-Christian religions. In college, she majored in comparative religion; later she spent time in Native American sweat lodges, and practiced Zen Buddhism. "I've done it all," she says, laughing.

One day when she was an undergraduate, her boyfriend, a rabbi's son, wrote out the Hebrew letters for her. "And I just had this chill. It wasn't that 'This guy is my destiny.' It was this alphabet, that it was going to be significant. And it was!"

The guy did play a pretty important role: she married him, and converted to Judaism in her twenties, later formally converting to Orthodox Judaism at age twenty-seven. They had a son together, but later divorced. Tikva thought she didn't want to be Jewish anymore, but a rabbi told her she couldn't renounce her conversion. So she quit being observant for a few years. She tried going back to the Unitarian faith, but it didn't move her spiritually. Besides, her ex-husband objected to their raising Ezra in two religions, so she shrugged and decided she may as well start practicing Judaism again.

Over the years, Tikva slowly grew into a traditional Orthodox Jew, though one whose sensibility she matter-of-factly describes as "hippie-dippy." She's now dressing modestly, in the typical style of the Orthodox—a practice she attributes as much to a reaction against sloppy, slatternly female fashions as the dictates of her faith.

"At some point I looked around and saw these [Jewish] women who were observant, and they always looked really put together," she said. "They had to cover their legs below their knees—usually it went much farther down—and their arms to the elbows. And yet they looked very stylish. Because western Massachusetts is very bohemian and Amherst is a college town, it's much, much more relaxed. It's not a hippie dress or anything. It's just very simple and nice. It's such a nice, relieving contrast to the Britney Spears look that's so prevalent."

To follow a truly Orthodox Jewish life is exceedingly demanding. Tikva had just finished having her kitchen koshered—meaning ritually cleansed—which meant, among other things, that she would have to follow an intricate set of procedures when cooking and serving food, to stay in line with Jewish dietary laws. I mentioned to her that I had stayed away from religion for years because I was afraid not only of what I would have to give up, but what kind of duties I would have to take on.

"Yeah, I was so afraid of being left behind, missing out on something in society," Tikva said. She also feared having to change her diet, and worried that her feminist ideals would be compromised.

As it turned out, though, the prohibition against women reading from the Torah in the synagogue service hadn't bothered her, and she found the divider between men and women inside the synagogue to be an aid to prayer, saying that she doesn't want to worry about looking good for men when she's trying to pray.

"I married Orthodox, I converted to Orthodoxy, that's what I've known. It took leaving temporarily and deciding to go back to make it authentic for me," Tikva said. "At this point, I don't care what the world thinks. It's so proven itself to me as a satisfying way of life that I'm willing to explain it to anyone who will listen. I no longer worry that it's inscrutable to other people. So many people I know, Jewish or not, are floundering. They're very interested, in a respectful way, about Orthodox life."

And why not? There's a great deal to be said for the confidence, the contentment, even the joy shown by people in our culture who believe in truth, and who are unafraid to show the truth of their convictions by the way they live their lives.

Of course, everything depends on the particular understanding of the truth to which one is committed. Some traditionalists believe in strict separation from the outside world. Not Tikva, who believes observant Jews should be in the world, but not of it ("I don't get into the Amish thing"). Other religious conservatives take an aggressively hostile, even violent, stance toward outsiders — a problem that Islam is now struggling with, a fight into which the rest of the world has been drawn against its will.

Still, in a world that is too hostile or timid to admit that truth exists, and is knowable, those who do — *as have most people throughout history* — live in a state of freedom that can be quite attractive to those wearied by the off-the-rack soft nihilism that is the way of the modern Western world.

"I liked it when the pope, Benedict XVI, condemned the

'dictatorship of relativism,'" Tikva said. "To me, that's the truth. It's really the truth. I felt so empty when everything could be true, because the flip side of that is nothing is true."

As James Davison Hunter first identified, the "dictatorship of relativism" decried by Benedict exists not only in the secular world, but within Judaism and Christianity. Catholicism may be a dogmatic, revealed religion that looks solid from the outside, but it is filled with believers who assert their right to decide independently of tradition and authority which parts of the faith are true and which aren't. Many of those who do this are priests. I told Tikva that I don't get these people at all. If I wanted to worship the Zeitgeist rather than the Holy Ghost, I would have stayed agnostic.

Tikva feels the same way about non-Orthodox forms of Judaism. She told a story about how the question of gay marriage had been discussed and decided in her local Jewish community when the State of Massachusetts legalized the practice in 2003. Tikva didn't want to accept without question the anti-gay-marriage party line at Chabad House, where her friends were. Then the rabbi at the Amherst Conservative temple announced that his congregation was going to spend the entire summer discussing the issue, and were going to vote as a congregation at the season's end about whether or not to perform same-sex weddings in their synagogue. Tikva decided to go to these meetings and events to hear the issues debated.

"I thought it was fascinating that the congregation decided it would make up its mind on its own," she said. "Right up front they decided that *they* would decide by popular vote, rather than decide if Jewish law, the *halacha*, would be the authority." Not good.

Tikva's heart was, and is, torn. She has lots of gay friends, and wants them to be happy if they find someone to love. As a divorcée who would like to marry again, she yearns for the same thing. But she would not be able to go to a gay marriage ceremony, because it violates her deeply held religious principles. I could hear pain in her voice as she talked about this dilemma.

At the end of the summer, the synagogue held an open debate among rabbis from the Conservative, Reform, and Orthodox traditions. All made good cases, recalled Tikva, but the weight of tradition and authority settled the question in her mind. "In the end, I'd really rather have my decision be the one that hews closest to the traditional interpretation of the Torah. The other interpretations were twisted around what human beings want."

There is a famous passage in the Gospel in which a wealthy young man approaches Jesus, asking what he has to do to have eternal life. Jesus tells him to sell all his goods and follow him. The wealthy young man goes away unhappy, because he is not willing to part with the things he loves, period. This story is the story of modern religion: trying to give people real communion with the eternal God while telling them they don't have to give up anything to have it. And yet, I told Tikva, religious traditions that make the way easy are dying out; it is a paradox of religious sociology that those religions that make the most demands on people are the ones that are now thriving.

"If you really put yourself in a relationship with God, where you really sincerely are trying to conform to the wisdom of his plan, you have to be open to the fact that you might get answers about your lifestyle that you might not want to hear," she mused.

"It's really hard to keep kosher, but I do it because I honestly want to do what God wants, not what I want. I think the genesis of all this for me is growing up in the seventies and eighties and seeing that all the man-made devices for freeing ourselves as individuals in society haven't worked. They've all backfired. So if you just open your eyes, you can't miss the utter failure of relativism, of humanism, of things that really seemed like great ideas. I definitely was aware of the new society they were trying to create in the sixties and seventies. I went to San Francisco. I tried drugs. I tried the free-love thing. Now I look back and see that none of that satisfies."

It fascinates me that the "small-o" orthodox believers most enthusiastic for the old ways are often converts. I don't know about you, I said to Tikva, but it amazes me how so many people who were born into my own religion, Catholicism, ignore or disdain this incredible tradition they've been given. It's like they're spoiled, self-absorbed teenagers who don't know the value of what was preserved for them, and don't care if it falls to pieces on their watch, leaving them with nothing to hand on to their children.

"I'm often really saddened by the way that a lot of Jewish faith has been replaced by this reviled and stereotypical materialism," she replied. "I'm always shocked when the people hauled in for scandals are Jewish. I mean, why bother being Jewish if you're not going to follow it? It's such a treasure trove of ancient wisdom, and anybody who denies themselves the opportunity of studying Torah and partaking of the life — they're losing out on something totally satisfying, and a whole and complete system affecting everything from your approach to the workweek and the way you raise your children to, well, everything."

The enormity of that terrifies people. I get that. I *lived* that. For a handful of years, I tried in vain to make a deal with God, agreeing that I would submit to him in every area of my life except my sex life. And like the young fool I was, I was surprised when the bargain proved meaningless. It was only when I reached the point of such spiritual despair that I said I'd rather live chastely with God than unchastely without him that faith took on real power in my life. A religion in which you can set your own terms amounts to self-worship. It has no power to restrain, and little power to inspire or console in times of great suffering. No matter what religion you follow, unless you die to yourself — meaning submit to an authority greater than yourself — it will come to nothing.

"It's like you either see it or you don't," Tikva said. "Everybody comes to faith in their own way. I didn't have a eureka moment, but I let the normal status quo convince me that as glorious as Western civilization has been, it has brought us to a point where it will destroy us if we give in to it. When you see that the world as presented by pop culture can't add up to anything worthwhile, the logical next step is to look into the wealth of a religious or spiritual tradition. And you know what? It might as well be a real one."

It might as well be a real one. Crunchy cons are big ones for authenticity. In a world filled with the cheap, the flashy, the plastic, and the immediate, we hunger deeply for things that endure. We are the kind of people who long for the Permanent Things; it makes sense that when we search for the most Permanent Thing of all — the immortal and unchanging God — we would approach the journey with great humility and utmost seriousness. We will be satisfied with nothing less than the Truth.

This is why we "small-o" orthodox believers — Protestant, Catholic, Eastern Orthodox, or Jewish — have more in common with each other than with the more lax believers within our own communions. This is not an ecumenism of indifference. Either Jesus was the Messiah, or he wasn't. Either the pope is the final religious authority, or the bishops teaching in legitimate council are. Either the Bible alone is a sufficient guide to religious truth, or the authoritative tradition of the institutional church — Eastern or Western — is. We cannot all be right, but what unites us is a fundamental conviction that the ultimate truth or falsity of these concerns is knowable, and matters more than anything else.

Who God is and what he wants from us is what gives us the basis of our metaphysics; that is, it teaches us what reality is, and how we should deal with it. As Tikva put it, "Once you put God at the center of your thinking, everything else falls into order around that new idea." Or to look at it from a different angle: all of us — even atheists — worship some kind of god, meaning some source of ultimate authority, even if it is the Self, that teaches us what to value and how to live. Can anything be more important than this?

Over and over again, in the course of talking to people as I was writing this book, I discovered that the single most important and common factor in determining how crunchy cons developed their lifestyle and cultural politics was their bedrock commitment to religious faith. And not only the *content* of that faith, but the degree to which they took it seriously.

Unlike in past eras, when the faithful persecuted each other over religious differences, contemporary America is forging new bonds of fellowship among Catholics, Protestants, Eastern Orthodox, Jews, and sometimes even Muslims — all of whom, however they answer the God question, agree on the objective nature of Truth. It is a postmodern paradox that those of us who cannot agree on what is true agree that truth matters. As such, we are all comrades in the conservative counterculture.

This is why I can have a wonderful conversation with an observant Orthodox Jew on the eve of Passover, in which she generously praises the countercultural witness of two Roman popes, John Paul II and Benedict XVI, precisely because they believe in God, in truth, and in the unassailable dignity of humanity — and aren't afraid to say so. An evangelical friend dropped me an e-mail the other day in which he said the very same thing, adding, "I love this Benedict. I feel that he's my pope too." These are indeed interesting times.

"For if the trumpet makes an uncertain sound, who will prepare himself for battle?" In Saint Paul's question to the Corinthians, we see why orthodoxy — and by extension in our pluralistic society, orthodox ecumenism — matters. We Americans who share a commitment to traditional forms of faith understand the seriousness of the cultural battle in which we and our families are engaged, and how vital it is to embrace and live by traditions that stand outside this time and this culture, and to fight the dictatorship of relativism, the tyranny of the everlasting now.

CHAPTER EIGHT

Waiting for Benedict

The great obstacle is simply this: the conviction that we cannot change because we are dependent on what is wrong. But that is the addict's excuse and we know that it will not do. . . . We can ally ourselves with those things that are worthy: light, air, water, earth; plants and animals; human families and communities; the traditions of decent life, good work, and responsible thought; the religious traditions; the essential stories and songs.

—WENDELL BERRY

Why do you spend money for what is not bread, and your wages for what does not satisfy?

—ISAIAH, 55:2 (NEW KING JAMES VERSION)

I AM SITTING in my neighborhood hangout, a wine store and bar next to an Irish pub. It is a warm spring afternoon, and I am relaxing over a book, with an open bottle of tart California white at my elbow. There are worse ways to spend a Saturday afternoon. The owner, John, a youngish man who buys and sells companies for a living (wine is his hobby), is telling me about his friend the psychiatrist, who said to him the other day that in all his years of practice, he has never seen more unhappy people than he does today.

"People work and they work and they work, but they're miserable," John says. "I remember growing up in a small town in Oklahoma, how great that was, how everybody made time for each other. We don't have that today. People go from their office to their house in the suburbs, and they don't have time for their friends, or for their families, really. There's such an emptiness. I thought it was just me noticing it, but then when the shrink told me no, it's real, I thought, Damn, we're in trouble."

I reach into my satchel and pull out a copy of the *New York Times,* dated March 12, 2005. "Here, look at this," I say, and hand the merchant a story about a book called *American Mania: When More Is Not Enough,* by Dr. Peter C. Whybrow. Dr. Whybrow — what a name! — is a prominent neuroscientist. He contends that contemporary Americans are driven by the brain's pleasure centers to seek greater power and more possessions, even at the expense of the only thing that grants any of us true happiness: human relationships.

According to Dr. Whybrow, we are hardwired to consume. The act of consumption causes the neurotransmitter fireplugs in our brains to unleash floods of dopamine, giving us the same feeling of euphoria provided by drugs like cocaine. In the past, the pursuit of this pleasure rush was checked by social conventions; those days are long past. There are virtually no restraints — social, religious, or otherwise — on America's appetite for consumption. Dr. Whybrow quoted U.S. government statistics to the *Times,* revealing that 30 percent of the population reports being anxious, double the number of a decade ago. Depression is on the rise, too.

And I think, Yep, I'm part of this. I'm working ten-hour days, trying my best not to get caught up in the rat race, and not really succeeding. When I take my little boy Matthew to school in the morning, we pray. Lately, he's been saying, "Dear God, please help Daddy come home earlier and be with us." And I feel like — well, I feel like a jerk, and I keep telling him it's going to get better, don't you worry, but I'm thinking, So when do you tell him the "cat's in the cradle" part?

I love my job, but I don't like this, and I can't see how it's sustainable. Maybe you live like this, too. Maybe you're sick and tired of it. I bet your kids are. Here I am, knowing the right thing to do, certain of my ideals, and yet I'm still struggling to live up to them. I read once that a good society is one that makes it easy to do the right thing. By that measure, American society has a lot to answer for.

Consider one case in point. Collin County, Texas—the north Dallas suburbs—is the richest county in Texas, one of the wealthiest in the United States, and one of the most churchgoing and solidly Republican anywhere in this country. Yet a 2005 analysis by the *Dallas Morning News* found that a startling number of its residents are spending themselves into ruin pursuing a materialist lifestyle. Local residents and experts interviewed said that the relentless social pressure to acquire symbols of one's upwardly mobile status drives a spending frenzy that leads to bankruptcy, foreclosure, divorce—and, in the end, a generation of children corrupted by false values. This might be what it means to live in somebody's idea of a Republican paradise, but what on earth is conservative about any of it? Are the kids being raised this way going to find it easier or harder to do the right thing?

We live in what should be the golden age for conservatives. The Republican Party controls the presidency. It controls the Senate. It controls the House of Representatives. Liberalism is on the ropes. So why do I, a conservative, feel so anxious about the present and depressed about the future?

It's because I fail to see just what American conservatism has conserved. We live in a time when the family is falling apart. Conservatives are divorcing at the same rate as liberals. The free market extolled by conservatives as the holy of holies is destroying communities, and turning us all into slaves of the economy. The freewheeling media culture pumps 24-7 a message of liberation through unfettered sexual expression and consumption. A few years ago, there was a popular stage play in London—you'll have to pardon me, but I'm quoting accurately — titled *Shopping and F***ing*. That's an apt description of the passions of our era, the goals most of us, liberal and conservative, aspire to. Democrats are the Party of Lust, Republicans the Party of Greed — both are individualist and materialist to the core.

THE TRUTH IS, liberalism — if liberalism is understood as the setting free of people from all limits — has triumphed. Most of us do not believe in restraining our appetites; our politics merely concern which appetites ought to be restrained. Most conservatives believe that sexual appetites should be held in check, but on evidence, they don't really believe it, and our side is virtually silent on the matter of our desires to get rich (except for a certain strain of religious conservative, for whom prosperity is next to godliness). Liberals believe that consumer desire and the ardor for wealth should be reined in, but it's hard to see that they take their own rhetoric seriously. And they are silent about the social and personal destruction wrought by the institutionalization of the sexual revolution.

Bottom line: both sides posture, but they are fundamentally content with the way things are.

Let it not be said that crunchy conservatism is the Party of No Fun. Sex and material goods are not intrinsically bad things; in fact, we are meant to enjoy them. The trick, though, is to rightly order their use, to live artfully, keeping our spiritual and material needs in equipoise.

Our political and social life in America today is badly out of balance. The United States, under Republican leadership, is spending itself into oblivion (the Democrats are no better, but they are not my responsibility). My children and grandchildren will be in hock to China and other foreign holders of our debt so that the generations now in adulthood may live as we like. Tax cuts? Oh, we're all for them. Government benefits? Don't even think about cutting them. The Something-for-Nothing regime is popular on the left and the right.

But Republicans rule in large part because our side is also nationalist to a degree that the Democrats cannot match. We love America, and we conflate patriotism with nationalism, so that we allow ourselves to be convinced that the worldwide triumph of American power is a victory for patriotism. We are American; we have a divine mandate to rule the world, and the favor of heaven rests on our shoulders. An evangelical friend who is worried about the environment tells me that whenever he brings up his concerns to the people in his church, they tell him not to worry, that God will provide.

How on earth did such presumption, such unmitigated arrogance, come to understand itself as conservative? Have we lost our right-wing minds?

Elect a Democrat, elect a Republican. It matters less than either party would like us to think. Show of hands: how many conservatives really believe that if the Democrats had run Congress over the last decade, the budget deficit would be much worse than it is today? How many of you, when considering this or that failure of Republican government to implement truly conservative policies, console yourselves by saying, "But if the Democrats had been in power, it would have been so much worse"? Are you satisfied with that?

Can we be honest for a second? Look back over the past few decades and ask yourself, has America been a force for conservative values in the world? No one can deny, of course, that America has on many occasions been a force for good relative to the alternative. But that is not the same as being a force for upholding or restoring traditional values of faith, family, and community. Is there a major Republican politician alive today who has the guts to stand up against business when its demands threaten families and communities? Where are the conservatives bold enough to stand against the crusading nationalism of the GOP? When as devout a right-winger as Peggy Noonan criticized President Bush for the evangelical utopianism of his second inaugural address, in which the president vowed to spread democracy worldwide, grassroots conservatives pounced on her as an apostate.

Conservatives today have gotten to be as politically correct as the liberals we sneer at. American politics has come to resemble the First World War, when powerful armies clashed endlessly and fruitlessly, with neither side gaining much ground, both having forgotten what they were fighting for, remembering only who they were fighting against.

So I'm sitting there in the bar on that spring day mulling these things over when three women and a man, all middle-aged, take the seats across the table from me. One of the women recognizes me from my picture in the paper, and compliments something I'd written. I thank her, and we all start to talk about life in Dallas. At some point, we start talking about politics, and it emerges that these nice people are liberals. No problem there. And then somehow we get to talking about what brought us all to Dallas — none of us is a native — and I said that one thing that's nice about living here versus New York City is that you don't worry about terrorist attacks, even though there's a serious problem in North Texas with Islamic extremism.

"Given the sort of things these Baptist fundamentalists around here say, I wouldn't blame Muslims for being provoked," said the man.

"Wait a minute," I said. "I'm not a fundamentalist, but I don't worry that Baptists are going to blow up buildings to make a theological point. You can't compare the two."

"Well, maybe not," said the man. "But these Baptist types are so horrible. You can see how they would provoke Muslims into an attack."

The man's wife then said she wouldn't mind a bomb going off in a well-known suburban Baptist megachurch here. She laughs. They all laugh.

And I realize I am talking to imbeciles. These people are so bent by hatred of the right that they blame conservative Christians for Islamic terrorism — and can even joke about terrorists detonating a bomb in a church. I smile and tell them that I really need to get back to my book. We exchange pleasantries, they finish their wine, and they go. But I can't read any further. I am so upset by what they said that I pay my bill and leave. I drive home and think all the way there about what I saw on September 11, and all the death and destruction and grief. I pull into my driveway and sit in my car and cry like a big baby.

Trying to pull it together, I think how much I hate those nice people in that bar. Stupid goddamned liberals. Hell, yeah, I'm a Republican!

And then I think, *This is how it happens.*

That is, this is why we conservatives put up with just about anything the Republican Party does. Our hatred of liberals is what holds us together, just as the liberals' hatred of us holds them together.

Fear and hatred, the conservative historian John Lukacs has written, are the primary emotions motivating modern democratic politics. I remember the run-up to the Iraq War, listening to some conservatives arguing that there was no real evidence that Iraq threatened us, and besides, it's an arrogant fool's errand to set out to install democracy in a country that has never known it. They made solid arguments from conservative principle, but I didn't want to listen. I hated the Islamic terrorists who killed so many of our people on 9/11, and I hated the liberals who hated the war. *USA! USA! Let's roll!*

I am ashamed of how easily I let my emotions get the best of me in that time, allowing myself to be manipulated into supporting the war. Understand: I'm not trying to start an argument over whether the Iraq War was right or wrong. Honorable people have taken both sides of that question. I am, however, trying to make a point about how emotions substitute for thought in what passes for political deliberation these days. We are all guilty of it to some extent, especially in this time of terrorist-driven high anxiety. Most all of us, left and right alike, are on more intimate terms with what we fear and what we loathe than what we embrace and what we love.

It is time for conservatives who believe we are called, *as conservatives,* to live more responsibly and more humanely, to stand up within the broader conservative movement, and speak out for our principles.

To restate the most important principles of the Crunchy-Con Manifesto:

• We believe that culture is more important than politics, and that neither America's wealth nor our liberties will long survive a culture that no longer lives by what Russell Kirk identified as "the Permanent Things" — those eternal moral norms necessary to civilized life, and which are taught by all the world's great wisdom traditions.

• A conservatism that does not recognize the need for restraint, for limits, and for humility is neither helpful to individuals and society, nor, ultimately, conservative. This is particularly true with respect to the natural world.

Politics and economics will not save us. If we are to be saved at all, it will be through living faithfully by the Permanent Things, preserving these ancient truths in the choices we make in everyday life. In this sense, to conserve is to create anew. Crunchy conservatism is not something brand-new; it's simply reminding conservatives what we already knew, but forgot.

We conservatives have to do this because the plain fact is that nearly all the important philosophical and ideological debates in American life are now taking place on the right. Last year, Professor Lukacs published an important book called *Democracy and Populism.* In it, he prophesied the following:

It may be that in the future the true divisions will be not between Right and Left but between two kinds of Right; between people on the Right whose binding belief is their contempt for Leftists, who hate liberals more than they love liberty, and others who love liberty more than they fear liberals; between nationalists and patriots; between those who believe that America's destiny is to rule the world and others who do not believe that; between those who trust technology and machines and others who trust tradition and old human decencies; between those who support "development" and others who wish to protect the conservation of land—in sum, between those who do not question Progress and others who do.

If crunchy conservatism stands for anything, it's the questioning of Progress and thoughtful but radical dissent from an ideology that believes the material universe is ours to manipulate to suit our ends. This is what the theologians call the Gnostic heresy, and it's almost as old as Christianity. Yet it is the ideology that rules the modern world, the spirit of the age. There are no traditions, no ideals, no spiritual truths that cannot be violated to serve man's wants. Modernity conceives of man as an autonomous being who owes homage to nothing and no one save his Almighty Self.

This is an ideology that serves industrial capitalists and sexual liberationists, mainstream Republicans and mainstream Democrats, equally well. It is, however, the death of families and communities. And it may be the death of our civilization if not challenged and refuted.

You think I'm exaggerating? Look at Europe, shambling toward senescence, literally expiring for lack of spiritual vision and ideals. Since the 1960s, the Europeans have built materialist paradises that have consciously excluded God or any mention of spiritual ideals from their public thinking. Indeed, a couple of years back we were treated to the asinine spectacle of the European constitution writers deliberately excluding reference to

Europe's Christian heritage from the document — as if the continent had made a giant 1,200-year leap from classical culture to the Enlightenment.

The Europeans have their reasons for denying the spiritual heritage that, for all its terrible failures, built the most free, most humane, and most advanced civilization humankind has ever known. Now they live wholly for their material desires, and have done so for two generations. The results are in: the European family is collapsing.

Studies show that a majority of children in Scandinavia are now born out of wedlock. Marriage in Sweden is now at its lowest rate in recorded history; across northern Europe (which is typically the leading edge of social changes throughout Europe and the West), marriage is quietly disappearing, as more and more couples are choosing to cohabit (and breaking up at two and three times the rate of marrieds).

And the bottom has dropped out of European birthrates, with the continental average a dismal 1.5 children born for every 2 adults that die. (The replacement rate — that is, the birthrate that would guarantee a stable population — is 2.1.) According to Phillip Longman, writing in *The Empty Cradle,* if the birthrate doesn't rise by 2020, there will be a projected 88 million fewer Europeans at century's end.

Meanwhile, a rapidly aging continent will have to have someone around to do the work. Enter Islamic immigrants, who are pouring into Europe at the present moment, and will continue to do so at a higher rate because of the demand for their labor. Though the birthrate in Islamic countries is also dropping, Muslims still have significantly more children than Europeans. Princeton University's Bernard Lewis, one of the West's leading authorities on Islam, predicts that by the year 2100, barring some unforeseen event, Europe will be predominantly Islamic.

The point here is not that Europe needs to return to Christianity, though an argument can easily be made for that. The point rather is that human beings cannot sustain their communities over time without a commanding spiritual vision of some sort. Demographically, we Americans are not far behind Europe, and secular Blue America comprises the most childless regions of the country. Like it or not, we've got to put the cult back in culture. As George Weigel, author of *The Cube and the Cathedral*, put it to me, "Europe is experimenting to see whether it is possible for a civilization to survive luxury. So far, the results are not promising."

Lukacs posits a future in which political debates will arise chiefly between those who believe in Progress, and those who do not. Kentucky farmer and poet (and, if you ask me, prophet) Wendell Berry puts a slightly different spin on it, foreseeing a future divided between "people who wish to live as creatures and people who wish to live as machines." Berry's formulation precisely identifies the great and fundamental problem of our time: whether man is a creature possessed of an essential nature, one that can only be fully expressed and satisfied living purposefully, under certain conditions; or whether man has no essential nature, only a panoply of individual desires, the fulfillment of which is the secret to happiness and our reason for being.

In other, older words, the great political and social question of our time is, *can man live by bread alone?*

If the latter vision is true, then the purpose of the state and society is to provide the greatest material happiness for the greatest number of people. If it's the former, then progress is to be measured by the quality of our individual and communal lives as judged mainly by the strength and integrity of our relationships to each other and to the land.

Crunchy conservatives know on which side we take our stand.

The first idol crunchy cons have to smash is efficiency, the guiding principle of free markets, but an unreliable guide to building institutions that serve human nature and human community. We have to start living by our ideals, judging things not by what works most efficiently, but by what's good, what's true, what's beautiful — in other words, what's right.

What does that mean in practical terms?

It could mean dropping out of the mainstream, moving to the country, and living as a farmer. That's what the Hutchinses and the Hales of Greenville, Texas, did, and you won't find more peaceable, joyful people at home in the world anywhere. The Stegalls of rural Kansas have found a way to live the farm life while the family breadwinner, Caleb, maintains a law practice in the city.

But that can't and won't be the solution for most of us. I pity the cow that depends on the likes of me to milk her. I was once at a men's gathering near Dallas, listening to a wise teacher from Oklahoma talk about the philosophy of the late John Senior, a scholar who believed that Catholics should return to the land, and live agrarian lives more in tune with the natural rhythms of the earth. That's great if you feel called to it, but I grew up in the country, and unlike my sister (who remains there), the rural ideal holds no appeal for me. And even if it did, I couldn't move my family to the countryside without abandoning journalism, which I deeply believe is not merely my job but my vocation.

There are many other ways in which we can live more conservatively no matter where we are. The most important thing we can do is toss out the television or commit ourselves to drastically curtailing its use. Putting ourselves and our families on a strict mass-media diet is vital; how can we ever hope to think on the Permanent Things if we fill our minds with nothing but ephemerality?

We can divest ourselves of stuff we don't need, and begin to train ourselves and our families to live simply. Remember William Morris's dictum: "Have nothing in your houses that you do not know to be useful, or believe to be beautiful." That's an ideal that those of us with small children will scarcely be able to reach, but it's not a bad way to mount a disciplined approach to household management.

Why not consider some form of homeschooling — even if it means Mom quitting her job, and the family having to lower its material standards? Given the state of the schools and of teenage culture, the question for serious conservatives may not be "Can we afford to do it?" but "Can we afford not to?" There are states where it is much easier to homeschool than others, and in some cases it may be so much less expensive to live there that if family and communal roots don't make a greater claim on your family, it makes sense to relocate.

Having Mom at home (or Dad, if you prefer) pays other benefits too, such as establishing a home economy in the kitchen and in the garden. Julie works with Matthew on his lessons, and he helps her with her cooking, shopping, and gardening—opportunities for Julie to teach him practical biology and chemistry, as well as help him learn how a family works organically to support its life together.

If you homeschool, you are not bound to choose your home by school district. It becomes possible to move into graceful old neighborhoods, and rehab houses long abandoned by the middle class in its flight to the exurbs. My job requires me to spend long hours at the office; unlike some colleagues who work equally lengthy stretches, I'm home with Julie and the boys while they're still on the road to the suburbs. Besides, our little bungalow is big enough for us; it's good to live without McMansion envy.

We can choose the goods we consume mindful of whence they come. Julie and I don't mind paying significantly more for meat raised locally, without antibiotics and hormones. Not only do we trust that it's clean, but we like being able to use the fruits of our labor to support the local economy, and specifically to make it possible for families like the Hutchinses and the Hales to live close to the land and raise their children the old-fashioned way. We prefer to buy our vegetables from local farmers, if possible, for much the same reason. It helps build a web of mutual care and obligation in our economic relations, teaching us that we are humans, not machines, training us to cherish the places we're from and the people who live there, helping us learn, in Edmund Burke's phrase, "to love the little platoon we belong to in society."

This costs more, of course, but as I've tried to show in this book, you can save money by living more frugally in other ways. More important, the social cost of making all one's lifestyle decisions according to the economic bottom line is intolerable.

With religion, we might quit thinking of faith in consumerist terms, evaluating it on the basis of whether or not it "works for us." Rather than picking and choosing a church based on personal preferences, we should be asking whether we should conform ourselves to a particular religious tradition. How liberating it is to quit the self-help shallowness of contemporary religion and return to the joyful rigors of traditional faith, which plumb the depths of existence more studiously, and embrace more fully the mystery and beauty of God.

We should also labor to reclaim leisure — leisure in the philosophical sense, which is time consecrated to pursuits that nurture the soul and build culture. The rarest thing in the world today is time to rest, and silence in which to contemplate, and to enjoy our lives together. Of all people, conservatives should understand that life is tragic, that suffering is inescapable, and that the only lasting meaning available to any of us is in sharing our suffering and our joys with each other in the beloved community.

You may have noticed that in outlining a practical approach to crunchy conservatism, I haven't yet said a word about politics. Why not? Because crunchy conservatism is a cultural sensibility, not an ideology.

You're not going to find a set of crunchy-con policy prescriptions. Crunchy cons are, for the time being, on the margins of the Republican and Democratic parties. Most of us vote Republican as the lesser of two evils, particularly because we perceive the Democrats as hostile to traditional religion and to our convictions on "life issues" — cloning, abortion, euthanasia, genetic manipulation, and the like. But we're realistic about the effect we can have on the mainstream GOP. People who are making financial sacrifices to homeschool, or who favor frugal living in other ways, are never going to have a lot of money to give to politicians, and certainly never enough to compete with the corporations whose interests run counter to our own. Anyway, aside from a few exceptions, most of the crunchy cons I know are skeptical of mainstream politics. When it comes to addressing social problems, they know that politics is necessary, but not remotely sufficient.

At the risk of oversimplifying, Americans think of the government's purpose today as chiefly to maximize economic prosperity and personal liberty. Crunchy cons, by way of contrast, are primarily concerned with virtue, both personal and social, and the common good as determined by the degree to which our politics embodies a particular and transcendent vision of what it means to live as fully human. To the crunchy conservative, statecraft is, in one sense, soulcraft. "Not that the soul of the citizen is the direct concern of the State," wrote Dominican priest Aidan Nichols, "but what does concern the State is the virtuous quality of the conduct of the civil life at large. [N]o State can afford to be emptied of all meaning save the material satisfaction of its clients."

A crunchy-con political agenda might look like this:

• Abolish or greatly restrict abortion and the death penalty.

• Ban cloning, strictly limit human genetic research, and closely regulate the biotech industry.

• Pass laws making it easier to homeschool, create alternative schools, or otherwise opt out of public education.

• Make commonsense environmental protection a legislative priority.

• Reform the agricultural, health, and commercial regulations to permit and encourage the flourishing of small farms and producers of local foodstuffs, and in turn repopulate rural America.

• Shape zoning restrictions to favor the preservation of old buildings of historic value, require new development to conform to high aesthetic standards, and provide more public spaces for human interaction.

- Adopt an attitude toward business laws that favors small businesses over large corporations.
- Strengthen legal prohibitions against pornography, and appoint judges who believe in the rights of communities to set their own standards.
- Use government, within limits, to look after the poor and the weak without creating a culture of dependency.
- Reform the tax code to offer extra support to married couples who choose to have larger families.
- Orient government toward encouraging an expansion of the role of civil-society institutions — religious, fraternal, and service organizations — particularly at the local level.
- Discourage "one-size-fits-all" national standards in education and other areas. Devolve control from Washington to states and localities.
- Impose an energy policy designed to sharply reduce our dependence on foreign oil, and to develop alternative sources of energy.

Those are my ideas; you no doubt have your own, and certainly libertarian crunchy cons will tend to oppose most restrictions on abortion, property rights, and pornography. That's fine; crunchy conservatism is a sensibility, not a rigid ideology. As a traditionalist, I would support all of the above positions in most instances, and would with great pleasure reach across political lines to work with liberals of goodwill when they share the same goals.

But I've got to tell you, pursuing any or all of these things as a policy matter doesn't strike me as the most pressing task at hand — which is why I've left them rather vague. And in any case, it is not politically possible without a broad movement in America away from a culture of individualism and immediate self-gratification, and toward a culture of limits and self-discipline.

Cultural change through persuasion and leading by example is preferable to a top-down agenda coming from Washington. This is something on which both libertarian crunchy cons and traditionalist crunchy cons can agree. There will be times when government has to step in, of course, but crunchy conservatism has a much better chance of creating conditions for lasting and sustainable cultural improvements if it is seen as *proposing* solutions rather than *imposing* them.

Thought experiment: imagine that we had a president who, taking stock of the troubling energy situation today and the general crisis of overextension—military and economic—that America finds itself in, took to the national airwaves, and said:

Look, folks, we've got a problem with energy consumption in this country; the price of gas is going way up, and our dependence on Mideast oil means we're going to have to be militarily involved with that part of the world for a long, long time. Our addiction to foreign oil is only a symptom of a deeper problem. The truth is, we Americans have lost our way. We used to believe in hard work, in family, in our communities, and in sacrificing, when necessary, for the greater good of all. We believed in being good stewards of our resources.

But our power and prosperity have made us spoiled and self-indulgent, and we have given ourselves over to the idea that we can find our greatest happiness in unbridled consumption. It's a dead end, one that starts with fragmentation and self-interest, but ends in chaos and immobility. We can turn things around, and restore our common purpose, and become more self-reliant, if we wish—but there is simply no way to avoid sacrifice. If we are truly patriotic, we will turn back to the old ways, regain our self-discipline, rebuild our families and our communities, and keep America free from foreign military entanglements. Regaining our liberty and independence is going to cost us in the short run, but we are fools to continue on this path. The choice is ours.

Can you imagine a U.S. president leveling in that fashion with the American people? What courage it would take to offer such visionary leadership! What a stark and inspiriting contrast a White House speech like that would have been immediately after 9/11!

You don't have to imagine it: it happened in July 1979, when Jimmy Carter went on national TV and delivered what came to be called his "malaise" speech. Surprised? I was. I was twelve years old at the time of the Iranian hostage crisis, and all I remember was how hotly everybody I knew despised Carter as a depressive wimp. All these years as an adult conservative, I had lived with the Myth of the Malaise Speech as the key to the failure of the Carter presidency, yet had no idea what the president actually said in that speech . . . until conservative historian and military strategist Andrew Bacevich, in his 2005 book *The New American Militarism*, cited it as a turning point in American history.

Why? When President Carter delivered that speech (phrases of which I wove into the imagined address above), he was roundly mocked and rejected for it. He learned a bitter lesson: telling the American people that they should learn to restrain their appetites is political suicide. Bacevich wrote that in January 1980, facing a tough reelection fight, Carter "had come to realize that what Americans demanded from their government was freedom, defined as more choice, more opportunity, and, above all, greater abundance, measured in material terms. That abundance depended on assured access to cheap oil — and lots of it."

The president then promulgated the Carter Doctrine, defined in his own words thus: "An attempt by any outside force to gain control of the Persian Gulf region will be regarded as an assault on the vital interests of the United States of America, and such an assault will be repelled by any means necessary, including military force." Though Carter lost office humiliatingly to Ronald Reagan, who had not an ounce of malaise or doubt in him, his policy shift has guided every president of the last quarter-century.

To put it bluntly, America is prepared to shed blood — its own and that of others — to protect access to cheap oil, which is to say, to protect the American way of life. Bacevich — who, again, is no liberal, but a respected conservative — said that we are already in World War IV (the Cold War was the third), and it's a fight over control of Mideast oil. We Americans couch our ambition in lofty democratic rhetoric, but let's not kid ourselves over what this war is really about. American troops are going to be in the Mideast for a very long time, and, warned Bacevich, unless we Americans fundamentally change our priorities, our nation may be doomed "to fight perpetual wars in a vain effort to satisfy our craving for limitless freedom."

This is why I say that it won't be enough to tinker around the political and policy margins to effect a restoration of American strength and purpose and moral clarity. The American way of life is now synonymous with the idea of endless material abundance, at low cost. It is an intoxicating vision, but that's not how the world works. This fundamental worldview is at odds with what humankind knows from tradition — but the laws of metaphysics cannot be repealed in the U.S. Congress.

President Carter was the wrong messenger, but he had pretty much the right message — and I regret that ideology and historical ignorance blinded me for so long to the commonsense prescriptions he offered. Don't get me wrong, I am grateful to Ronald Reagan for restoring optimism, confidence, and vigor to America. But think of how much better off we'd be today if the Great Communicator had further strengthened the nation by helping us to value living within our means, financially and otherwise. How is it that we call ourselves conservatives, yet so many of us see nothing wrong with an America that lives like a spoiled child who believes he's been granted a hall pass by history? Do we think we can get away with it forever?

I don't. You don't either. There is another way.

Crunchy conservatism is a way of life that calls for a change of culture. It's about returning to tradition, in the face of a rampant and energetic consumerism, to reclaim a way of life that's richer,

more satisfying, more grounded, more sustainable, more meaningful and, in the end, more authentically joyful than what mainstream American life offers. Given the fragility of our present
social arrangements, it also happens to make a lot of sense.

People don't like to think about it, but we are all living on the
skin of a bubble. All it would take to burst it is a severe economic
crisis brought on by a catastrophic terrorist attack, a deadly pan-
demic, a sustained energy shortage, climatic eruptions, or some
other disaster. Here's what died for me on 9/11, right in front of
my eyes: the illusion that the kind of Big Nasty Thing That Happens to Poor Suffering Bastards in Third World Countries can't
happen here.

Most Americans don't appreciate how quickly things could
collapse. Consider four possible scenarios:

1. Stephen Flynn, the former U.S. Coast Guard officer who is
one of the nation's leading experts on port security, told me that
if terrorists set off a small nuclear device in an American port, the
government would have to shut down every port in the country
immediately until radiation detection devices could be installed.
To cut the global supply lines for that short a period would be
enough, said Flynn, to bring down the American economy, and
with it the world's.

2. As of this writing, epidemiologists are terrified that a
vicious strain of bird influenza in southern Asia will leap into the
general human population. Some humans have been diagnosed
with it in the region, and what scientists have seen staggers them.
Laurie Garrett, an international disease specialist at the Council
on Foreign Relations, estimates that if avian flu reaches America,
a city like Dallas could lose between 20 and 30 percent of its population before the epidemic played itself out.

3. Experts say that the world will have reached its historic
peak in oil production by 2011 (some say it already happened in
2005). Meanwhile, the fast-rising industrial economies of India
and China will be fiercely competing with the United States for

access to the diminishing resource. When the demand for oil far exceeds the supply, the cost of the stuff will shoot through the stratosphere. The entire American economy and suburban way of life depends on affordable petroleum — which, barring a technological miracle, will soon cease to exist. Imagine that you can't afford to buy broccoli from California, because the cost of shipping it is astronomical. Imagine that cost factor overlaying an entire economy.

4. In 2004, a little-noticed blue-ribbon panel reported to Congress that the danger of an attack on the United States from an electromagnetic pulse (EMP) weapon was high. All it would take is a conventional nuclear bomb launched atop a Scud or other missile type, and detonated high in the atmosphere over the U.S. mainland. The gamma rays from the explosion would interact with atmospheric molecules to produce a powerful electromagnetic pulse that could take down the nation's electrical grid in moments. Defense expert Frank Gaffney told me that the successful detonation of a single EMP weapon could "take the United States from a twenty-first-century society to an eighteenth-century society instantaneously."

None of these are Chicken Little melodramas. They are all clear and present dangers. In any of these cases, society would have to pull together and work cooperatively in order to survive the hardships. Folks would have to learn to do more for themselves and for each other. Economies would of harsh necessity become a lot more localized. It doesn't take a genius to see that the people who will thrive under such conditions are those who have preserved, or relearned, tradition.

Think about Hurricane Katrina and its aftermath. As I write this, New Orleans remains 60 percent underwater from the storm, which struck just over one week ago. No terrorist detonated a bomb, yet a major American city has been partially annihilated with hundreds killed and the surviving population sent into diaspora. The city, state, and federal governments upon which the people relied to get them to safety and deliver them relief failed catastrophically, and shocking anarchy was loosed on the weakest and poorest of the survivors. All week long after the storm hit, a stunned and sobered nation could not believe that this was happening in America, that the veneer of civilization was so thin, and that all the might of the most powerful government since Rome of the Caesars could do nothing for destitute American citizens fighting for their lives.

You don't need a weatherman to tell you that politicians, especially the ruling Republicans, will eventually reap the political whirlwind from their deadly incompetence. But at this moment, there is immediate concern that the loss of Gulf Coast refineries and offshore oil rigs in a tight world market could push the price of gasoline and home heating oil into the stratosphere, threatening to plunge the global economy into a deep recession. If it does, American life will have to be fundamentally reinvented along the lines I have suggested to account for our greatly reduced circumstances. And if it doesn't, no American can feel secure that our good luck will last forever.

Given the swift breakdown in civil society and the pathetic governmental response in Katrina's wake, no American can indulge himself in the fantasy that the state can be relied on to protect, defend, and relieve him and his family in a time of maximal crisis. We are all likely to be on our own, us and our little platoons, and the virtues, customs, and habits of the heart by which we have been living when disaster strikes will largely determine whether we will swim to safety or sink while waiting for help that might never come.

As a child growing up in south Louisiana, I always heard the legend that one day, a big, bad hurricane was going to score a direct hit on New Orleans and wipe it out. Everybody did. Everybody knew this was coming. But nobody wanted to believe it, because to have done so would have meant changing personal and public priorities, and preparing for the future instead of living for the moment. Any one of the scenarios I've listed above could be the next Big One, or any number of major and minor apocalypses forming undetected over the horizon. We had better change our priorities while there is still time, and build the networks, social and economic, that will help us prevail over or at least withstand what terrible things might be coming.

Even if none of this were to happen, we're still left with the unhappy fact that the American way of life is too often rich in everything but meaning and purpose. When you get tired of living to shop, have sex, and be entertained — and more to the point, when you realize you don't want your kids' character to be formed by a culture in which those pursuits are priorities — you'll want something better for yourself and your family.

That's what crunchy conservatism is for. This book has been filled with the thoughts and stories of American conservatives who aren't sitting around waiting for the Next Big Idea to renew our culture, or expecting that if we just elect more Republicans to office, that the world will begin anew. The Republican Party, and indeed political conservatism, is not offering an affirmative view of culture. It seems only capable of saying what it's against, not what it's for, except in the vaguest terms. "However you define family, that's what we mean by family values," said former First Lady Barbara Bush, speaking before the 1992 GOP convention. I'm sure she meant well, but that's about as deeply as most political conservatives have thought about family and culture.

This won't do, won't do at all. We're living in a time of rapid cultural fragmentation, and the right hasn't figured out a viable alternative to the radical individualism that is balkanizing America. The center is not holding. I do not think the pessimism with which Alasdair MacIntyre ended *After Virtue*, his 1981 masterpiece of moral philosophy, is unwarranted:

> It is always dangerous to draw too precise parallels between one historical period and another; and among the most misleading of such parallels are those which have been drawn between our own age in Europe and North America and the

epoch in which the Roman empire declined into the Dark Ages. Nonetheless certain parallels there are. A crucial turning point in that earlier history occurred when men and women of good will turned aside from the task of shoring up the Roman *imperium* and ceased to identify the continuation of civility and moral community with the maintenance of that *imperium*. What they set themselves to achieve instead — often not recognizing fully what they were doing — was the construction of new forms of community within which the moral life could be sustained so that both morality and civility might survive the coming ages of barbarism and darkness. If my account of our moral condition is correct, we ought also to conclude that for some time now we too have reached that turning point. What matters at this stage is the construction of local forms of community within which civility and the intellectual and moral life can be sustained through the new dark ages which are already upon us. And if the tradition of the virtues was able to survive the horrors of the last dark ages, we are not entirely without grounds for hope. This time, however, the barbarians are not waiting beyond the frontiers; they have been governing us for quite some time. And it is our lack of consciousness of this that constitutes part of our predicament. We are waiting not for a Godot, but for another — doubtless very different — St. Benedict.

This is radical stuff. Saint Benedict, you'll recall, inspired men and women of goodwill to leave the collapsing cities of the late Roman Empire and establish monasteries in the countryside. As MacIntyre notes, the monks kept alive the light of knowledge, of faith, of virtue, through centuries of chaos and despair, and gathered around them communities they helped support, spiritually and otherwise. The key thing to notice here is that the original Benedictines understood that the process of civilizational decay was, in the short run, irreversible, and that therefore the only reasonable thing to do was to make a strategic retreat behind defensible borders. Clearly, MacIntyre believes we are living in such a time today, and that those who want to preserve the old ways and traditional wisdom had better figure out how to be monastic in the first century of the third millennium.

Crunchy conservatives are already doing this in a variety of ways. Some, like the Hutchinses and the Hales, have literally decamped to the countryside, where they have taken up the agrarian life. Most others, though, are like Julie and me: living in cities and suburbs, getting on with life, raising up, as Russell Kirk prescribed, new generations of friends of the Permanent Things. And we know that the only way to do this successfully is to be consciously and intentionally countercultural. That's what it means to raise the monastery walls today.

It means to leave behind what the famed twentieth-century Trappist Thomas Merton called "a certain set of servitudes that I could no longer accept — servitudes to certain standards of value which to me were idiotic and repugnant and still are." It means not only saying no to those things, but saying yes to other men and women in the community of virtue, and supporting each other in our attempts to live counterculturally. It can be something as simple as buying meat and vegetables from your local farmers. It need be no more complicated than joining a home-school collective, or choosing to live and raise children without mass media, in a more contemplative atmosphere.

Or it could be something as serious as what my friends Phil and Leila Lawler did a few years back. Serious Catholics, the Lawlers relocated their large family from Boston to rural central Massachusetts, and settled around an abbey, which they knew they could make the center of their family's spiritual life. Seven or eight other orthodox Catholic families, all involved in the same schooling method, joined them. Their little community celebrates holidays together, and supports each other through the ups and downs of daily life. Leila told me that if you don't find some kind of community to be a part of, being a countercultural family is almost impossible.

While many, perhaps most, of us find it neither possible nor desirable to relocate to the countryside, it's exciting to think about how that is becoming ever more possible, thanks to the Internet. With broadband connections, many people can do their urban and suburban jobs from home offices. Online shopping means you can have almost anything you want delivered to your door. Want independent or foreign films? Try Netflix.com. Need a copy of the new Alan Furst spy novel? Amazon.com can have it in your hands in days. Crunchy conservatism is not about rejecting technology, only about making it work to support the family and conservative ends. The Internet is opening up new ways for crunchy cons to form virtual monastic communities.

Now, as Wendell Berry has warned, and every homeschooling conservative knows, "Any group that takes itself, its culture, and its values seriously enough to try to separate, or to remain separate, from the industrial line of march will be, to say the least, unwelcome" in the mainstream. That's just the way it is. But if we are right about what matters in life, and if we successfully live out our convictions intelligently and with joy, people sick and tired of the empty materialism of mainstream culture will join us.

Wherever and however we erect our monastery walls, there's one thing we should definitely keep out: the nasty spirit of intolerance and incivility that dominates American political and cultural debate today. Life is too precious, and too important, to waste taking seriously people like the liberals who laughed at the prospect of bombing a Baptist church, or conservatives who talk of liberals not as if they were human beings but enemies to be destroyed. The challenges facing us as individuals, as families, and as a society are grave, and the knee-jerk, party-line viciousness that drives our politics today gets us nowhere. I know too many liberals with whom I disagree on some pretty fundamental ideas, but who are also thoughtful and kind people who could even be my allies in public disputes over things important to both of us.

It's happening on my own streets. When it comes to conserving the old houses in my neighborhood from the developers who now threaten it, I will stand with my liberal neighbors on the common ground we share, and fight the fat-cat Republican homebuilders, absentee landlords who turn up on the TV news at night saying that the free market must be the only principle guiding development. If those of us on opposite sides of the political divide on most questions lose sight of each other's humanity, we won't be able to stand with each other to protect things we all cherish.

The monastery metaphor may be off-putting to some. It calls to mind an ascetic, gloomy, otherworldly cloister, when in my experience, crunchy-con families are warm and open and full of flesh-and-blood joy. It's just that crunchy cons know what they believe in, and understand that if those beliefs mean anything, and are to be passed on to their children, certain walls must be built, and the family must live with a certain intentionality that will unavoidably come across as separatism.

Moreover, while the idea of the "domestic monastery" may appeal to settled families, it offers little to inspire the most idealistic conservatives of all: the young. The truth is, just as the medieval church needed both its monastics and its worldly orders, crunchy conservatism needs families and young single people working together toward cultural renewal, or at least self-protection. Crunchy cons need to be active in the political world, if only to carve out for us a safe place to exist, to raise our kids, and to live out our values.

In 1991, several years before he died, Russell Kirk, the paterfamilias of all crunchy cons, addressed a gathering of young conservatives at the Heritage Foundation in Washington, counseling them against despair, and attempting to inspire them to "redeem the time." "You will not need to be rich or famous to take your part in redeeming the time: what you need for that task is moral imagination joined to right reason," Kirk said. "It is not by wealth or fame that you will be rewarded, probably, but by eternal moments: those moments of one's existence in which, as T. S. Eliot put it, time and the timeless intersect. In such moments, you may discover the answer to that immemorial question which now and again enters the head of any reflective man or woman: 'What is all this? What is this world that surrounds us, and why are we here?'"

Kirk counseled that being true to the Permanent Things won't necessarily win one "any of the glittering prizes of modern society," but that ours is still a world "sun-lit despite its vices," a world of wonders where men and women of virtue and conviction need not yield to the dull vulgar grind of the modern age, but can choose their role in the great human drama of hope and restoration. There is a reason these truths have endured: because they have offered men and women across the borders of culture and time the secret to the richest, the most purposeful, and even the happiest life. And no civilization that forgets the Permanent Things will ever be wealthy enough to guarantee its permanence.

More than two decades ago, the philosopher discerned that the world was waiting for a new Benedict to forge a compelling cultural vision, one that leads people out of the ruins of a culture that no longer sustains life, and shows them how to form a life-giving counterculture. We still are. If you ask me, it's time that we became our own Benedicts. Why not? We have nothing to lose, and everything to gain, including nothing less than (in Robert Hutchins's phrase) the hearts of our children, and as much as custody of a civilization that is fading, but which may one day return if we live well and hold fast.

Do not be surprised if many, probably most, contemporary conservatives sneer at this vision as idealistic silliness, as romantic daydreaming. *Be realistic,* they will say.

We shall answer this counsel of discouragement with the final paragraph of Schumacher's *Small Is Beautiful:*

> The type of realism which behaves as if the good, the true, and the beautiful were too vague and subjective to be adopted as the highest aims of social or individual life, or were the automatic spin-off of the successful pursuit of wealth and

power, has been aptly called "crackpot-realism." Everywhere people ask: "What can I actually do?" The answer is as simple as it is disconcerting: we can, each of us, work to put our own inner house in order. The guidance we need for this work cannot be found in science or technology, the value of which utterly depends on the ends they serve; but it can still be found in the traditional wisdom of mankind.

Hope is memory plus desire. Given how things are these days, it's hard to be optimistic about the future. But if we are to find our way to a future worth having, we will have to return to the wisdom of the past. If we conservatives dare to rediscover and reclaim our authentic traditions, and seek with cheerful hearts and generous spirits to make the old ways live anew in our everyday lives, well then we have every reason — *every reason!* — to hope.

Acknowledgments

O VER AND OVER in this book, I've talked about the central importance of the family to our lives, political and otherwise, and the first thing that needs saying here is that *Crunchy Cons* would not exist were it not for my own. First, of course, is my wife, Julie, whose generosity in supporting her husband's vocation in every way—from constant encouragement and inspiration, to proofreading, to taking the kids out of the house for the afternoon so Daddy can get something done on his book, for heaven's sake—is the sine qua non of my life as a writer. I owe a debt of gratitude too to my sons, Matthew and Lucas, who displayed more patience with me and this project than any dad has a right to expect. I also wish to thank my father and mother, Ray and Dorothy Dreher, for teaching me by example to make devotion to family the measure of a man's character. And Nora Marsh, who first taught me the virtues and pleasures of cheerful nonconformity, shared the most wonderful of all houses with me, encouraged me to cherish the written word, and most important of all, noticed a kid drowning and saved him.

This book wouldn't be here without the opportunities given to me by Rich Lowry, Kathryn Jean Lopez, and the gang at *National Review* and National Review Online, in the pages of which *Crunchy Cons* was born and where I spent one of the most gratifying years of my professional life. Nor would it have been more than a passing fancy were it not for the labors of my agent, Gary Morris, and my publisher, Annik LaFarge, both of whom believed I was onto something with this crunchy-con business—and both of whom, Annik in particular, displayed heroic patience in the time it took to draw this book out of me. Thanks as well to the folks who were kind enough to give me their time in interviews, especially Mr. Wendell Berry, a great American. I also owe more than I can say to the hundreds of *National Review* readers who wrote to me after reading my crunchy-con essays, and who shared their own thoughts and stories. I wish I could have given each of you remarkable people a voice in these pages. I hope that in some way, I have.

Index

About the Author

ROD DREHER is a writer and editor at the *Dallas Morning News,* and a conservative journalist who has worked for *National Review,* the *New York Post,* and the *Washington Times.* He is a Southerner, a convert to Roman Catholicism, a devoted amateur cook, and an avid indoorsman who lives with his wife in a small cottage filled with books, icons, and two rambunctious little boys. He bought his first pair of Birkenstocks in 2000 and never looked back. He and his family live in Dallas, Texas.